Walter Theob
311B Outer M
Potsdam NY 1

3/10

MW01285479

A PIECE ⚬⁄⚬ KANSAS SOIL

JIM COSSAART

To WALT-
Best wishes,
hope you enjoy
my story -
Thanks,
Jim Cossaart

INFUSIONMEDIA
Lincoln, Nebraska

© 2015, 2016 Jim Cossaart. All rights reserved.

No part of this publication may be reproduced, distributed, or transmitted in any form or by any means, including photocopying, recording, digital scanning, or other electronic or mechanical methods, without the prior written permission of the copyright holder, except in the case of brief quotations embodied in critical reviews and certain other noncommercial uses permitted by copyright law.

Infusionmedia
140 North 8th Street #214
Lincoln, NE 68508-1353
www.infusion.media

Cover art and title page illustration of big bluestem grass by Tom Meyers

ISBN: 978-0-9964283-1-6

LCCN: 2015956213

10 9 8 7 6 5 4 3 2 1
First Edition

TABLE OF CONTENTS

Where I Am From

"I see the agricultural degree from Kansas State." My patient pointed to the diploma on the wall of my dental operatory. He was an attorney in our small Vermont town and after several appointments had finally given in to his curiosity. The top two certificates, framed in nine-by-eleven glass and in plain sight of the dental chair, were my state dental license and diploma from University of Nebraska College of Dentistry. Directly below them was my KSU ag diploma, and next to it and for comic relief, a certificate proving I was a Stihl factory-trained two-cycle engine mechanic.

"I heard you were a farmer from out there somewhere. In one of those big states in the middle with the straight lines for borders."

I smiled. "Yes, I was," I said, turning my attention from the X-ray of his upper right first molar. Decay two millimeters from the tooth pulp. No root canal required. This guy will get out of here without too much damage.

"Then let me ask you this," he prefaced, curious and a bit afraid to hear the answer. "How in the world does a person go from farming to dentistry?"

After a decade and a half and thousands of people in my chair, I have answered the question often. I try to keep my chairside manner personal. It's one of the reasons the job will never be done by a machine. When someone wants to know something about the man who is about to administer anesthesia and drill a small hole in their tooth, I try to give them something personal.

"Yup," I began in High Plains vernacular, "did it fer twenty years. Goin' back to school was my version of a mid-life crisis, without the convertible and the blonde. Probably cost about the same, though."

My patient's eyes widened. "Twenty years!" he exclaimed, probably calculating years and numbers in his head.

I continued talking as I swung the stainless-steel tray of instruments toward me. "I was the oldest guy in the class. But not the only farmer; there was another fella from North Dakota. Yup, dental school in my early forties was quite an adventure."

I thought back to the first day of dental school, when I was one of forty-three eager and frightened sets of eyes focused on the upper-middle-aged professor at the front of the class, leaning slightly on the podium while his naturally stern face tried hard to be welcoming. He spoke slowly, authoritatively. "How many of you students have really looked closely at the inside of the oral cavity?" I looked around and knew that several of the students likely had fathers that were dentists; others probably had some medical background. The air was tense and the entering freshman class was sufficiently intimidated, as the medical education model called for. It's a long tradition in the pursuit of any medical degree: The faculty beats the academic hell out of you because the same was done to them when they were in school. I sat in the shared silence and thought back to the practice of "mouthing cows," a method to check the age and general health of a beef animal as it is restrained in the holding chute. I raised my hand, not resisting the chance to lighten things up a bit. I was too old to spank, certainly. The professor pointed to me with a smile.

"Yes, mister, uh ... Co-..." I interrupted him and provided the correct pronunciation of my last name. Cuzz-art.

"Thank you, yes. Give me numbers. Could you give me a rough idea of how many you have seen?"

"Probably, oh, eight hundred."

His eyebrow rose a bit, and he asked, "Eight hundred?"

"Cows," I flatly answered. My group of new classmates, bright-eyed young strangers, all turned to me and burst into laughter.

Pulled from the Earth, 1993

———————————

Nobody understood it. Nobody. My love for a piece of Kansas soil was only shared by those who were long buried in it. My father had been raised in the big two-story farmhouse I was standing in, but when he grew up, he chose not to be a farmer. From the time I was fourteen I had spent my summers here in the semi-arid plains of north-central Kansas, and when, by default, the farm came upon me, I eagerly embraced it. Twenty-three years later, I was the last Cossaart farmer left. My chosen lifestyle of rural poverty could not be justified to anyone living.

I stood staring out the second-story bedroom window of my farmhouse, rocking my baby boy in my arms. My son and I had this daily nap ritual and I cherished every opportunity to rock David to sleep. I found it easy to postpone or forsake farm tasks or part-time work. For all his eighteen months, his sleeping pattern had been wonderfully predictable. He had that heavenly clean baby scent and silently snored in my arms. He was an easy baby.

Beyond the bedroom window lay the hundred-acre pasture that I always referred to as my "backyard." It was a waist-high sea of native prairie grasses comprised of what Great Plains ecologists call "The Big Five": big bluestem, little bluestem, switchgrass, Indian grass, and sideoats grama. These make up an ecosystem that, since the origin of the prairie soil, has adapted and thrived. The incredible entanglement of root systems, often reaching depths of ten feet, can sequester enough carbon per acre to compete with the Amazon rainforest.

This piece of land was part of a vanishing acreage, the other 97 percent of it plowed up three generations ago to make the vast tilled lands of the Midwestern Corn Belt. The pasture I looked upon rolled across the broad and low treeless hills toward the unbroken northern horizon. Tiny occasional streams were carved into the black soil and thick, tangled sod with outcrops of limestone strata. In the ditched valleys, small islands of willows and cottonwoods interrupted the ocean of waving grass.

From the second story I was high enough to look out over the tops of the dense shelterbelt of cedar trees, an L-shaped row fifty yards out from the house. It had been planted by my grandfather and uncle thirty years prior to protect the house from the vicious northwest winds. The grassy main pasture of my family's sixth-generation farm undulated like mile-long sheets blowing on a clothesline.

The air of the baby-blue room felt warmed with a reassurance from the past. My father and his younger brother, Alvin, had shared this room as young boys. My uncle Alvin, who never married, slept nearly every night of his entire life in this room. I had repainted the smooth plaster walls and ceiling prior to the

baby arriving. In this clean and quiet room I could be alone with my son and escape, briefly, from my life in poverty, from a once prosperous and rewarding farming career in a tailspin, and from a marital relationship that had become too awful to deal with. The floor creaked quietly under my feet as I slowly paced back and forth and felt David's tiny breaths blowing through the sleeve of my worn T-shirt.

When all other aspects of my life would not work, being a dad was a job I was damn good at, and there were many mornings when that role was the only reason to get out of bed. During some prolonged periods of depression, it may have been my only reason to live. When we were together, both of us were happy. Our daily afternoon dance to sleep consisted of a deliberate and fluid rock, my hips swaying as I walked back and forth. Ordinarily I moved with a stereotypical Midwest-farmer tight-assed motion, my leg muscles hammered into stiffness from overuse and accidents, and the knees and hips pounded inflexible from years of day-long tractor driving. I found any sort of social dance awkward and made halting, stilted movements; but when I rocked my baby, man, I had soul.

The floor on which we paced was made of rich brown slats of oak, each two-inch-wide board snug against the next. Around 1972, when my grandmother was in her early eighties, she began laboriously refinishing the oak trim and all the doors of the entire house, complete with sludgy chemicals and a lot of scraping, in her "spare time." In 1991, a year before David's birth, I finished her job and power sanded and refinished all oak floors on both stories.

There have been three dwellings on this farm since the time of the pioneers. First was a "soddy," a dugout constructed of sod walls. My grandmother never lived in the sod house but as a young girl knew of plenty of women that had such homes. She described the living conditions as filled with bugs, snakes, and stinky seeps of water penetrating the walls. "It was hard to tell where the dirt stopped and the house began," she told me.

The second house, a crude clapboard structure, was built close to the small creek and housed my grandparents as newlyweds. Three children were born, all in the kitchen with the help of the local doctor, Doc Wall: Aunt Ruby, then my father, Raleigh,

The farmhouse. David's room, upper right window.

and finally the youngest son, Alvin. When my father was seven years old, a new house was built.

In 1929, over the course of an entire calendar year and with no power tools, my grandfather and two other men built my farmhouse. It was boldly erected in the face of the national financial collapse, and Grandpa faced the direct criticism of his relatives and peers in the community for spending so much money in the dawning hard times of the "Dirty Thirties." Little did they know it wouldn't get any better for another decade and a half. The structure represented my grandfather's largest tangible life accomplishment. When ferocious thunderstorm winds blasted through the country in the spring, this house stood like a rock and never so much as creaked. They used the best of materials, right down to the southern pine lumber, which had enough natural turpentine in it to prevent termites. It was also fully wired, in anticipation of rural electrification soon to come. While some men strove for bigger farms and a larger net worth, my grandpa sowed, tilled, sweated, and handed the money to Grandma to be saved. "Daddy has always been *so* good to me," she would say with a broad smile.

The one-hundred-acre rolling pasture supported countless generations of cows and calves that had helped provide a living for my ancestors, me, and now my son. As often as possible David and I would take hikes out to check on "the girls." From infancy on, and when the weather permitted, little David was a keen observer as he would look over my shoulders, securely bundled in a backpack carrier, quiet and content, with his face nearly hidden behind the little hood drawn tight around his cheeks. The cows were a sedate group as a rule, and David would coo and giggle as we trod through the green grass among fifty resting reddish-brown bovines.

I recalled sharing my optimism with my grandmother only ten years earlier, when she and I would happily talk about cows and wheat acreages. I had become a very good farmer and cowman, but my determination was no match for the great economic shakeout in American Midwest agriculture through the 1980s. Multigeneration farms were failing all around me, and although I knew how to work like hell, I could feel the previous four generations of Cossaarts looking at me with disappointment.

It was unseasonably warm for an early spring afternoon, and after gently closing David's door, I silently crept down the oaken staircase, mumbled to David's mother that he was asleep, and went for one of my walks out into the pasture. It was my refuge, where I sat alone and thought and listened to the meadowlarks' song carried away on the wind gusts. My racing mind and its continuous list of farm tasks never let me stay too long; before ten minutes went by, I always snapped back to duty and searched for the next chore on the list. But on that day I could not focus. The wind, too brisk to allow a hat to remain, died as I disappeared from the world and sank down into my tall grass sanctuary; the previous years' dried growth was chest-deep and dense enough to hide in. The silence, that precious commodity found in abundance here, was therapeutic as always. No cars, no voices, no sign of any other humans on the earth.

I knew the silence well. When I was seven years old, I gathered enough courage to walk out into the pasture alone. I was exhilarated and fearful of the vastness of it all as I plodded through the tall grasses that stretched forever in all directions. As I scanned the panorama of treeless horizons, I became viscerally aware of my solitude. I pretended that I was the only person in the world, and all that I could see was mine to enjoy.

Back to reality: There had been more than enough conflict during the day, both with my wife and with myself. The first five years' accumulation of profits in my farming career had been wiped out by the last five, first from drought and then flood. The barn, the corncrib, the garage, and the house all had a shabby look due to the peeling paint and the occasional missing board. My tractors and other implements were showing the strains of their age. It was the apex of "The Farm Crisis," when a fifteen-year stretch of dirt-cheap agricultural commodity prices eviscerated the population of the Great Plains. Countless neighbors and myself were living hand-to-mouth and rapidly chewing up our equity by more borrowing. To survive, I had mortgaged this farm that was passed to me from my grandmother, and now the debt was insurmountable, and that cold fact enraged my father when he surveyed his boyhood farmstead and reflected upon his own son's life. My baby was dependent on WIC vouchers. Outside jobs to supplement what little the farm would produce were hard to find and even harder to show up for.

There had been little if any communication with my parents for almost a year; an argument about my stagnant career and financial woes on a very cold Thanksgiving eve the year previous had been fought out largely between my always-combative spouse and my lovingly exasperated father. My wife was in a constant state of rage toward me and the very environment in which we lived. Everything I had worked for over the previous two decades added up to nothing that could be spent or measured. Through the years I had steadily increased the potency of medications needed to function with a profound state of depression. At this point my body felt like a walking toxic balloon, since I was taking Prozac, Lithium, and Xanax on a daily basis. I could look back and recall the good times, but they were merely stories to anyone else. I sat in my little grass nest for a very long time trying to rid myself of the last fleeting hopes. As far as I could see, hope had led me down this miserable path I was on.

When I rose to my knees, the stiff wind tore the tears away from my face and the death of a dream whispered from my throat. I sat down and curled into a ball and slowly slipped into a numbed calmness. Nothing could be heard but the wind currents buffeting the long mixture of thick prairie grasses around me. Other than my baby boy, the solitude was the only thing I had felt grateful for since I woke up. I needed the peace to recharge and get through another tough day.

Without warning, the silence was broken by a piercing voice from another dimension exploding over my left shoulder; it jerked my attention like an escaped calf caught in a lariat and slammed to the dirt. Michelle had walked out from the house, a good eighth of a mile, to my little safe spot. Her dirty blonde ponytail was whipping in the wind around a face full of extreme irritation, and her open hands jutted toward the earth. "What are you doing!?" she shouted. There was initially an echo of concern in her words, quickly overshadowed by boiling frustration. I had been sulking around, sullen and quiet, for months. Together, sometimes with a baby boy yelling his disapproval and terror above our shouting, we had endured one continuous argument about our future and the need to do something. Neither of us could picture any solution.

I fiercely clutched a wad of dry stems in each hand and screamed so hard it made my lungs burn. *"I have to leave this place! Goddamn it! Don't you understand what that means to me?"*

Her posture of frustration relaxed momentarily, and she looked stunned by my screaming. I briefly felt a little sorry for her. This smart young woman, city born and raised, was at one time naively eager to live in a remote rural expanse and break away from a life weary of crime and traffic. However, she was unprepared for the stark hardships and social isolation that came with living on a Kansas farm. When I first invited her to move to my place, I tried to warn her, but I knew she would never understand until she lived the life. I was mindful of the amount of adjustment required; I just hoped that with time she would develop a love for the life and the land, if through nothing else but the influence of my love for it. But deep in my gut, I am ashamed to say that I knew she would not last on this place very long. Michelle had, at first, tried to be encouraging as the finances spiraled downward. But the dirt wasn't in her veins, and to her, moving off the farm would be as easy as it was to move onto it.

"Oh, for God's sake, Jim! Get *over* it!" She just didn't get it. I had grown weary of explaining how the land and I were one. She never would understand it as long as she lived. She didn't *want* to understand. She thought this deep love I had for the land was ridiculous. She had no idea of who I was and she never would. My wall went up permanently from that point forward.

I watched her walk away and get several hundred yards ahead of me. I rose to my feet and dragged my body against the south wind toward the farm buildings and the house. I walked up to the barnyard and began assessing the broken disc harrow. It was parked out in front of the large and brightly lit repair shop; six years prior, my hired hand and I had gutted the old corncrib and built one darn good shop to work out of. My worn boots kicked up little clouds of dust as I studied the broken farm implement and prepared it for welding. I paused before striking the welding arc to the iron. I glanced over at the garden, where I had dug potatoes for Grandma twenty years before.

Jumping into the air and landing with both of my work boots onto the lip of a spade shovel, I would dutifully turn the earth in the precise spot where Grandma pointed, until the black soil revealed handfuls of small spuds with tender red skins covering the white cores. She told me how strong I was and how it made the work so much easier to have me around; wise words to motivate a teenage boy. "You can do that so much better than Grandma can..." I laughed out loud as I tried to picture her in her early eighties with her bent back and spindly frame, trying to jump on a garden spade. There was nothing more delicious than those little red potatoes, sliced thin and fried in a cast-iron skillet to a light brown, soft crunch. The key was the dab of bacon grease, spooned out of a solidified opaque form from a small coffee cup kept on the back of Grandma's stove.

I stared down at the soil as my usual dissociated numbness returned. It felt as if the dirt and I *were* each other. You are what you eat, and this soil contributed to the cellular composition of me, my father, and three generations prior to him. When planting my crops, the mud penetrated under my fingernails. Even after a scrub brush and a bath, I still had dirt in the cracks of my skin. While I herded cattle or drove a tractor through the field, the soil particles were inhaled, driven into my eyes, and crunched between my teeth as I clenched my jaws.

The looming prospect of leaving this soil, perhaps forever, spun me off into a daydream. I pictured myself as one of my grain sorghum plants in the field, and I felt a giant hand grasping the entire plant and violently ripping it out of the dry July soil. The searing southerly wind blew on the blood dripping from my mangled roots, leaving me to wither and die of exposure, long before I had the chance to bloom.

My entire adult life was in this thing, and the formative years of my childhood were as well. I hated my dead grandparents and uncle for leaving me as the last man standing, and hated everyone else beyond the reaches of Republic County for not possessing my appreciation of this little far-away corner of the earth. I hated the rest of the citizens of this country; grain farmers and ranchers had become expendable in a radically transitioning farm economy. When this farming dream began, I knew it would be an uphill task and had told myself that I would give it my best into middle age. At thirty-seven years of age I found myself perilously close to bankruptcy. My baby's shoulders were too tender to carry the tradition of the past five generations. My son may never hear the glorious, unspoiled silence. David would not be able to bask in the kaleidoscopic sunsets or save the life of a newborn calf, nor would he have the burden of living in social isolation and poverty. But how would I survive if I were forced from the soil?

Grandma

"Would you like Grandma to fix you some oatmeal?" Those are the first words I can remember my Grandma saying, when I was four years old. The year was 1960, and I had curiously ambled down the chilly, cavernous, and echoing oak staircase, shuffling along on the slightly dusty floor in my flannel PJs with the feet in them and into the kitchen of the old farmhouse. "Oh, my stars. You *are* an early riser." My grandmother and I were the only ones yet awake. I stared up at her in wonder. There seemed to be a thousand things clamoring for my attention: the rich smells of frying bacon and rising biscuits, the funny little repetitive print on my pajamas, warm air rushing up through the copper furnace vent against the wall. An old aluminum pan was waiting by the door for the dog, a bit dirty and full of broken, stale bread scraps bobbing in discolored milk. Strange geometric designs were embedded in the worn linoleum floor. The kitchen stove seemed to be the center of activity, with bubbling and sizzles and gentle pops that came from several pots and pans simultaneously. It was cozy and warm in the room, and

I could feel the heat radiating from the blue gas flames under each pot.

This was a strange house to me; I had been born in the industrial town of Sharon, Pennsylvania, and then we moved to a more suburban setting and a new house in Indiana before my fifth birthday. The farm was where my father would take my mother and sisters and me to visit, once a year. If we were lucky, twice. My sisters and I looked forward to the long drives from Indiana to Kansas because the farm was full of adventure and an abundance of love from Grandma, Grandpa, and Uncle Alvin.

There were small but noticeable fissures in the beige plaster walls of the kitchen, and for a boy who had been raised in a home built with perfectly smooth drywall, the cracks concerned me about the possibility of collapse, like I had seen in a few cartoons. Small amounts of dirt were drifted in the corners of the floor. The wooden cabinet doors were darkened and worn with stains and indentations near the handles. The bright morning sun was peering over the horizon and through the east windows several feet over my head. It cast a warm orange glow upon the opposite wall and the cook stove.

"Or maybe you would like some bacon? Would Grandma's boy like some bacon?" She quizzed me gently while vigorously rolling out a measure of dough as the flour poofed up in a small cloud over the counter. She had a full, thick head of curly gray hair with small specks of black. I could not break my attention from her eyes, as they wavered back and forth behind her eyeglasses, studying me intently as if she knew me well. It felt like thunderclaps could spring from her slate-gray eyes at any

My parents, sisters, and me visiting the farm.

moment, just a little scary, as I sensed something powerful inside of her. Still, that room felt as warm and fuzzy as the blanket I had just crawled out of.

I had never heard such a soft and beautiful voice. "Now you just climb up here and let Grandma find you something to eat." The round wooden spools were loose, and my squirms made the wobbly stool creak and flex. The worn and bare wood had a shallow scoop to the seat that cradled my little bottom perfectly. It was parked away from the stove and out of Grandma's path, and my little legs dangled as I watched from my new perch. The familiar stranger darted back and forth between boiling pots, the refrigerator, and the cutting board that was pulled out from the cabinet. She seemed to be managing a hundred things at once, all the while fully engaged, facing me in conversation and exploration.

My grandmother's full name was Ruth (Davenport) Cossaart. She had been given no middle name; it was an efficiency that fit her well. Grandma was a good student in her youth.

Her father, in wisdom apparently rare to his character, encouraged her to attend training after high school to become a teacher, so as not to be dependent upon any young man vulnerable to the draft of World War I. Ruth taught in a one-room schoolhouse for several years before meeting my grandfather, and at the time of their marriage she was twenty-one and he was thirty. As I grew up, upon my urging, Grandpa would tell stories of his life as a respectable young single man in the 1910s. One time I interrupted him and asked where Grandma was at the time. He puffed on his pipe with a quiet chuckle, looked off into the distance, and softly uttered, "I was waitin' for her to grow up."

Grandma's father, John Davenport, was part American Indian, but in that era this was only discussed in hushed tones. The exact tribal origin was likely Pawnee or Otoe. My great-grandfather had an explosive and unpredictable nature, and Grandma's more outspoken brother in adulthood referred to their father as "that crazy Indian." He could be harsh to his six boys but was far kinder to his two girls. Admitting he was wrong was apparently impossible; one afternoon in the heat of the summer he

Reuben and Ruth Cossaart, May 1918.

burst into his own house and demanded to know where his ax was. He had unwisely driven his tractor into an entanglement of thorny Osage-orange trees, which were commonly planted in dense rows as living fences throughout the Plains. With no reverse gear, the machine was hopelessly stuck. When asked why in the world he would need an ax in such heat, he roared out, "We need a proper supply of firewood."

Once in a while Grandpa Davenport became incensed if a Chevrolet passed him and would not let the insult go unanswered. He drove ferociously on gravel and dirt roads until he repassed the offending car. As a ten-year-old boy my father remembered his own small hands hanging on for dear life in the back seat as his grandfather lost control and crashed into a field after overtaking one more Chevrolet. My grandma summed up her father with tempered amusement: "I don't know how Mother endured it all."

In my grandparent's courting days, shortly after the arrival of the Ford Model T, my future Grandpa Reuben drove his father's car to pick up future Grandma Ruth, who at the time was a pretty twenty-year-old and who lived two miles directly north of where they would eventually set up housekeeping together. She lived with her brothers and sister in a crowded farmhouse at the base of one of the steepest hills in the area, on one of the poorest places to farm. Young Reuben Cossaart was never comfortable with the modern automobile and much preferred the handling of a horse, but the Model T made for a better impression and more comfortable ride. He dressed in his finest clothes with a smart black derby hat and arrived at her home with a quiet announcement and proper deference to his future father-in-law, who greeted him with a stern glare. The couple climbed into the car and proceeded up the steep hill, but, halfway to the top, Reuben missed a gear. "I wasn't paying attention to my driving," he admitted to me. Unable to locate the brakes in a moment of panic, the driver miraculously guided the car at increasing speed, backwards, down the hill and over a narrow wooden bridge. Amazed at his own skill/luck, Reuben finally braked the automobile to a halt in the middle of the road.

Reuben and Ruth Cossaart, fiftieth wedding anniversary.

Pausing from the excitement momentarily, the young couple recovered their composure and proceeded back up the hill with their date. "And she went out with you again?" I quizzed my grandfather as he related his tale. "Yes, she *did*," he replied, facing me with a very satisfied smile.

Playing in the yard one day as a six-year-old, I watched Grandma enter the chicken house, and to satisfy my curiosity, I ambled over and peered in the doorway. She had not noticed my presence. Grandma always moved fast and had a definite purpose in her day as she went from chore to chore. On this particular morning, her purpose was to stew a pair of chickens for our supper, as a large meal was needed for her, Grandpa, Uncle Alvin, and the five of us visitors. As Grandma stepped into the dusty henhouse, she was intent on gathering up one of the older hens who had reached the end of its egg-laying days to stew the bird for an evening meal of chicken and noodles.

I was unaware of how lightning fast a grandma could move. In a flash of dusty confusion, deafening squawks, and feathers flying, the wiry little woman seized a chicken by the legs and swatted it to the dirty concrete floor. The demonic-looking bird was thrashing about and pecking furiously at Grandma's arm. She immediately stepped on the struggling bird's neck with her boot and separated its head from the flailing body with a forceful yank skyward, violently ripping the chicken's body by its feet toward the low and straw-laden wire mesh ceiling. The hen flopped about momentarily in Grandma's right hand, and she laid it down on the concrete floor. I could see the chicken's head, still underneath Grandma's bloody boot, and watched in amazement as its eye slowly closed. Until that single, terrifying moment, I had never seen anything more frightening than that frantic chicken. But my grandma vanquished it.

Her sweetness, her sharp mind, and sometimes her temper earned respect from everyone. She certainly deserved it. As I grew into adulthood, there remained this tiny corner of me that was always just a little afraid of Grandma. Yet I loved her like no one else on earth.

The major focus of Grandma's days was the preparation of large meals to feed herself, two hungry farmers, and any visiting grandchildren. As a teenage boy, I stopped my fieldwork a half hour before my uncle quit and drove the pickup truck back to the house to help her. Her eyes sparkled as I entered the kitchen, full of mouthwatering smells from the fried chicken and homemade rolls. As I mashed the potatoes and set the table, she and I bonded in a way few people of such different generations and backgrounds could. "He confides in me," Grandma once said to my mother. "And he doesn't think I'm an old fuddy-duddy." To my parents, I could act like any other lazy teenage boy. But when Grandma smiled, I hopped to whatever menial task she asked me to do.

Sunday mornings on the farm could hardly have been more different from my city experience. As I was growing up in the city, every Sunday morning I reluctantly attended my parent's large and affluent church in Muncie, Indiana, complete with a virtuoso playing a thundering pipe organ and a dynamic elder minister. The expansive marble-and-brick sanctuary contrasted to the tiny rural church in Mahaska. I wasn't any more enthused about going to Grandma's church. Grandpa was somehow excused from attending. "I don't think he hears well enough to enjoy it," Grandma said. I just thought he didn't want to go, and he conducted his own private worship of the Lord by puttering around with little tasks in a quiet barnyard on Sunday mornings. Alvin was, for some reason, exempt from attending as well. And in Grandma's eyes, Alvin could do no wrong.

I drove Grandma to the Mahaska church even before I could legally do so and sat with her in one of the creaking wooden pews. The organ was hopelessly out of tune, the elderly and sometimes tone-deaf singing was sadly comical, and the sermon was only good if Reverend Tom was speaking at this church in his rotation between three others in the county. Nevertheless, Grandma shone like the sun, dressed in her finest dress and clip-on earrings, accented by a delicate broach that Grandpa had bought her for their fiftieth wedding anniversary. We sat together and soaked up the affirming smiles from the other parishioners. Grandma looked at me like I was really something special.

One summer afternoon workday I came home early from the field and found the house eerily quiet. Grandpa was the only one home and relayed that my uncle Alvin had taken Grandma to the hospital in Fairbury to get her hand stitched up. She was in a hurry, as usual, vacuuming the living room floor and already had her mind on the evening meal yet to be prepared. She had reached to move the old Emerson electric fan while it was still running and absentmindedly stuck her fingers in the open cage, slicing her fingertips and splattering blood in a faint red ring circling the room from floor to wall, across the ceiling, and down the other wall.

The in-office surgery was uneventful, and the only report from Grandma was the kind manner and handsome face of the young doctor that sewed her two fingers up. Over the next week her church lady friends supplied us with a constant sampling of new and delicious dishes that only farm women of their age could cook. Grandma loved to repeat to her friends what I had said, as she and I gazed upon the small collection of cakes and pies on the kitchen counter. "Maybe you ought to leave those bandages on for a few more days, Grandma."

The stamina and effort she put forth, trying to keep her house and laundry done for three farmers, was amazing. She sometimes wearily described the big two-story farmhouse as a "woman killer." Every Monday was laundry day. If the sun was out, and that seemed to be always the case in the scorching Kansas summers, she hung wet clothes out on the line to dry after bringing them up from the basement where the washing machine was. After the sheets and overalls dried in the sun, she unsnapped the hinged clothespins with crisp movements of her fingers, folded the clothing and bedding into a basket, and carried it up to the second-story bedrooms.

On an August afternoon a year after her fan incident, she took a tumble down the stairs and lay unconscious on the concrete basement floor for perhaps twenty minutes or so. She awoke, gathered up all the spilled wet clothing into the basket, and climbed back up the stairs to pin all the shirts and towels onto the clothesline. She walked back to the house, cleaned up her bloody face, and went back outdoors to search for Grandpa out in the barn. She declined another trip to the hospital. The next day she was back to cooking and finishing the laundry, albeit at a slower, more labored pace, and a few days later she seemed to be back up to her whirlwind speed.

Grandpa

God, I hated thistles. Musk thistles are nasty-looking invasive noxious weeds with cactus-like dark green leaves and a pretty tuft of pink for a flower. They will take over and destroy a good pasture in a few years if not controlled. Chopping thistles was my first task in the adult world of work on the farm, and at fourteen years old I felt I was being tortured. Grandpa and I trudged through the steep little ravines in the pasture, areas where the tractor and sprayer could not reach, and it made me wish the rolling grassland was entirely flat so Alvin could spray it all with the tractor and herbicide sprayer. Thistles are easily killed with a quick stab of a narrow spade shovel, and eradication needs to be done in a three- to four-week time period after the last spring frost but before they bloom and scatter their thousands of seeds into the wind.

Grandpa loved the job. In his early eighties, he no longer drove any tractors and was uncomfortable driving the newer pickup truck, so he enjoyed filling his days with an ambling walk through the pasture in the hot sun. He never seemed to tire. As my legs grew weary in the long afternoons, I became convinced in short order that he was going to outlive me. Up-town the men heard my uncle tell amusing tales of his nephew groaning about the work. Up to then, mowing a small suburban lawn was the toughest thing I had ever done. My uncle's buddies teased me as I waited at the counter of the tiny Mahaska grocery store and carried cardboard boxes full of groceries for Grandma. "Jimmy, I hear you're goin' to college someday to be a thistle specialist..."

Modestly disguised behind Grandpa Reuben's perpetually easy mood was a clear-minded intelligence and quick wit. I learned to drive the pickup and struggled with a clutch and four-on-floor shifting, mostly with my uncle Alvin as the instructor but often with Grandpa as the supervising passenger. No sooner would I pick up some decent speed, and his reminder would come forth, "Slow down, boy, this is not a time machine..." As we rolled to a stop next to the sheet-metal mailbox at the end of the long gravel driveway, I leaned out the window and eagerly opened it to find no contents; this was before the advent of junk mail. "Empty!" I spoke in disappointment. Grandpa cocked his head in a mock display of studious observation of the mailbox. "It's full," he proclaimed flatly. "Of emptiness." Occasionally he would spontaneously break into song, or better described as talk, in precise and exaggerated proper diction: "Rise-and-shine-and-pay-your-fine, when-you-are-riding-on-the-dummy, on-the-dummy-dummy-line."

One day as Grandpa and I chopped thistles and paused to wipe our brows, he motioned to a depression, about one hundred feet round, in the pasture that was not within any line of drainage.

Grandpa and Jim on the Farmall "H" tractor.

He told me the little swamp was nearly always wet, which is unusual in the semiarid environment of northern Kansas. In the spring it teemed with the sounds of croaking bullfrogs and insect life dancing in the air above the mossy-green water. This was a small quarry, one of many down the line that supplied the track bed for the Rock Island Railroad when built around 1884. Limestone rock was dug out from this site and hauled by horse team and wagon a half mile to the south.

Two parallel and faint gullies can be seen heading from my home farmstead in a northeasterly direction toward the original farm of Charles Cossaart, where Grandpa's brother Leslie lived most of his long life. In my father's time it was used as a driveway between the two cooperating farms. This was a part of the original "Y Road" that branched off toward the towns of Reynolds and Hubbell, Nebraska, both of which were established on the banks of Rose Creek. Both villages had stream-powered flour mills and lumberyards that supplied the sodbusters. Decades later, grid-pattern dirt and gravel roads dissected the land into mile squares.

Half a mile northward into the pasture is a low and flat area, dead center of Section 1-1-1. In this valley once stood a large stockyard where my great-grandfather would gather up his cattle crop for the year, sort out the marketable head, and then drive the herd to Mahaska. There they were re-penned and loaded on a train. Dad told me that in the prosperous times following World War I, Great-Grandpa shipped freight car loads of cattle to Omaha or Kansas City each fall, sending one of his sons along to garner the proceeds and return the next day with the check. Soon thereafter, another farm would be purchased to be eventually deeded over to one of his children.

In all the time I knew him, I never heard my grandpa refer to himself as an old man, even when I was sixteen and he was in his mid-eighties. Although he viewed himself as poorly educated, he amazed me by adding columns of two- and three-figure numbers out loud without paper and pencil. He parceled out his soft words sparingly to answer my queries as he sat on the cast-iron cistern lid covering the underground holding tank of water located in the front yard. On rainy afternoons I found him in the basement furnace room, smoking a cigar and drying his muddy overboots next to the small propane heater.

Grandpa was naturally thin, even slight, yet he ate huge meals. He methodically plowed through the main courses of meat, potatoes, and vegetables and then had a big piece of pie or cake, followed by a helping of canned fruit. As a growing and working boy, I consumed large amounts of milk during the meals, and we bought it by the gallon from the store in Mahaska, as the gallon plastic jugs had just hit the market. "Where's the hose for that?" he asked, pointing at the jug, which weighed enough to sag the leaf of the big oak table a little. Then with a grin and a wink: "I was weaned some time ago, myself."

Grandpa knew that I had more than a casual interest in the teenage granddaughter of our nearest neighbor, Russ Long. I looked for her as we drove past their farm, occasionally seeing her sunbathing. When I showed up at the table with a large rip in my blue jeans, Grandpa nearly spit out his spoonful of tapioca pudding and choked out, "I didn't know the Long's had a dog!" Red-faced, I playfully tossed my dinner roll at him. Grandma's soft voice broke into an abrupt and harsh shout. Her eyes burst into flames. "*Here* now, you two! We will act proper at this table!"

Grandma described Grandpa as she and I watched him from a distance. "He never worries. And he is the steadiest guy I ever saw. I remember looking out the kitchen window and seeing your grandpa scooping ear corn out there in the corncrib," she pointed toward the building with the wooden slats for walls, fifty yards out into the barnyard. "After a time, he disappeared behind a ten-foot-high pile of corn. I couldn't believe anyone could scoop for two hours straight." She smiled warmly while speaking of his nature. "He has one speed, you know."

In 1973, as Grandpa passed his eighty-fifth birthday, he seemed to take a cue from me. When I was on the farm in the summers, I brought along a bit of suburban lawn care standards, using the rickety lawn mower to keep many of the grassy areas around the house and barn trimmed. Grandpa began a bimonthly ritual of chopping the tall bromegrass edges next to the wooden siding of the barn, where the mower couldn't get. It was a line of tough and stemmed grass, about fifty feet long, and Grandpa got down on his hands and knees and methodically swung his sharp corn knife, an eighteen-inch-long straight machete with a wooden handle. He wore cheap cotton work gloves over his long-sleeved denim shirt that he kept tucked under his overalls as he labored in the hot summer sun. "Better go tell your grandpa that dinner is ready," Grandma would instruct me to notify him of the noon meal. "Grandpa, dinner time," I announced. He looked up from his hands-and-knees posture, sweat dripping off his nose, and faced me with a smile. "Well, I've got an awful big job to do here. But if the rest of you are going to sit down and eat, I guess I better get it while it's on the table." We both laughed. There are not many jobs left for an eighty-five-year-old workingman. He just looked like he was having fun.

Grandpa and I chopped thistles at his pace during the next several summers. Each year it became easier. Now, as a mature adult, I often find myself in methodical, almost meditative motion in my physical tasks. There is a peacefulness that settles in as I work. I'll bet the expression on my face looks like Grandpa's used to. I still have his corn knife in my workshop.

The Sixth Principal Meridian

Around 1870, land was plentiful in the Kansas-Nebraska territory, and the farther west one wished to venture, the cheaper it was. The Great Plains lay stretched out in an enormous table-top-flat sea of incredibly rich black soil, of Cenozoic windblown origin and piled up to twenty feet deep under the dense protective membrane of sod. Beginning at the Missouri River and stretching westward, the elevation imperceptibly rose 1,500 feet on the endless stretch to Denver, a major new outpost six hundred miles to the west, where the Plains bumped abruptly into the front range of the Rocky Mountains, rose into the atmosphere, and created a rain shadow five hundred miles eastward across the Plains.

Rainfall on our farm averages about twenty-seven inches annually, punctuated with an occasional year or two of drought. Unbeknownst to my ancestors, our farm misses the Ogallala Aquifer by six miles; therefore, without irrigation, grain farming is still profitable but often marginally so. Fifty miles to the west, the rainfall thins out and only the hardiest winter wheat and sunflowers are worth growing. Fifty miles east, however, it

THE SIXTH PRINCIPAL MERIDIAN

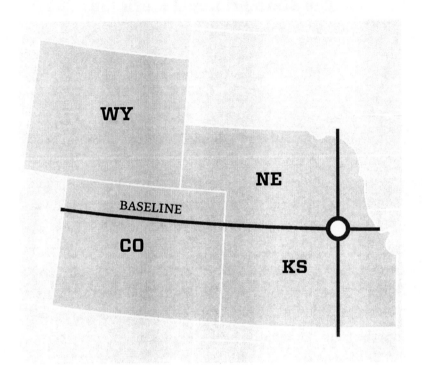

THE INITIAL POINT OF THE
PUBLIC LAND SURVEYS OF THE
SIXTH PRINCIPAL MERIDIAN

The Kansas-Nebraska Act of May 30, 1854
created the territories of Nebraska and Kansas,
which had to be surveyed before settlement
of the prairies could proceed. On May 8, 1855
Charles A. Manners set a cast iron monument
on the bluff west of the Missouri River at
40° north latitude.

In 1855-56 Manners surveyed westward from
the cast iron monument 108 miles establishing
the base line, the boundary between Kansas
and Nebraska and the Initial Point of the Sixth
Principal Meridian. This Initial Point, a red
sandstone which lies under the manhole cover
behind you, controls the system of sections,
townships and ranges of the public land surveys
in Nebraska, Kansas, and parts of Colorado,
Wyoming and South Dakota. This Initial Point
is referenced in all ownership records throughout the system.

On June 11, 1987 the Professional Surveyors
of the 6th P.M. dedicated the memorial on your
left. The memorial is made of Colorado red
granite with Wyoming and Nebraska rubble
stone. Each side of the cap contains a state
name, date of statehood and the logo of each
state's professional surveying association.

Professional Surveyors of the 6th P. M.

is noticeably wetter, and so the Cossaart land marks the western end of the North American Corn Belt.

The railroads, owning vast tracts of unsettled land, were eager to make a quick sale of their land holdings to fill their hungry coffers with capital to continue their expansion of infrastructure. Opportunities were limitless in the Kansas-Nebraska territories; the tales of making the big trip to California sounded tempting, but new livelihoods arose in the small settlements—that were rapidly evolving into thriving little communities. The new town of Hubbell, Nebraska, was where Reuben Griggs Cossaart chose to settle.

Reuben Griggs came from the Finger Lakes region in upstate New York and served in a New York regiment during the Civil War. Reuben, his wife, and Charles David, his sole-surviving son of twenty years, moved to Locport, Illinois, for two years before taking a train out to establish a life in Nebraska. Reuben wed for the third time after his first two marriages ended with the death of both spouses, and one infant, during successive childbirths. He established himself as Hubbell's town undertaker and furniture maker.

Charles and his dad bought 560 acres of unbroken Kansas prairie; 80 acres shy of a full 640-acre, one-square-mile section, and hugging the Kansas-Nebraska border. Son Charles developed and worked the new farm on the Kansas side of the border while father Reuben tended to business in Hubbell. The purchased Kansas land is located at the intersection of the fortieth parallel (the Kansas-Nebraska border) and the sixth principal meridian. It was the initial base point for the surveying and

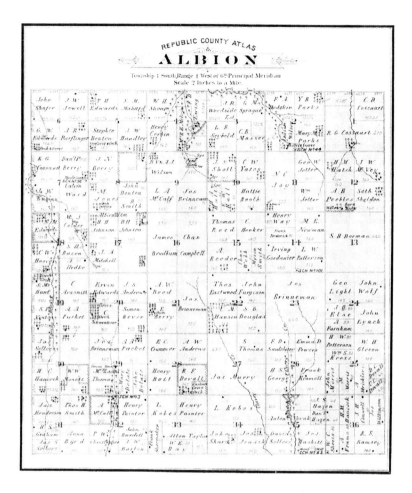

Albion Township, Republic County, Kansas. Section 1-1-1 is in the top right.

subsequent distribution of lands in the new American territory and a result of the signing of the Land-Grant Act by Abraham Lincoln.

A government-sponsored survey was conducted by a small party on horseback in 1856, measuring with transits and lengths of chain and originating from an established base point on a bluff overlooking the Missouri River. A party of four men measured 250 miles due west into the frontier and placed a survey marker at the intersection of the sixth principal meridian and the fortieth parallel. From this point, the giant grid of surveyed lands in precise square-mile sections emanated. All the lands of Kansas, Nebraska, North and South Dakota, and the flatlands of Colorado and Wyoming were plotted from this origin. A "section" of land, or 640 acres, is one square mile, and each parcel was numbered with three coordinates per section, indicating their exact position on the grid. The initial survey marker is located on the northeast corner of our section; hence, my family farm is legally described as Section 1-1-1, Albion Township, Republic County, Kansas. Standing on the manhole cover in the center of two dirt roads puts one in two states and four counties at the same time. One-fourth of that section, or 160 acres, was the most common land size purchased or granted in the settler days. It was the intent of US government policy to encourage settlement to establish vast areas of agricultural production for the growing nation.

Beneath the sod, the soil was virgin and productive beyond belief. The steel moldboard plow, a recent invention, sliced through the web of roots, and the bare soil was exposed and smoothed into seedbeds. With the ample rains, huge crops of corn and wheat burst from the fresh black dirt, leading pioneer farmers to believe they had been delivered into the land of milk and honey. Fortunes were quickly made, and Charles David was no exception. Although later years would reveal the cruelty of drought and dust, the first few years after settlement were blessed with good moisture and produced bumper crops. If one was bold enough to borrow, often the land could be completely paid for from the first year of corn or wheat.

In early post-settler years a one-room country schoolhouse was located two miles due east of Narka, Kansas. It was argued by some in our area, mainly my family, that the school should be relocated in a more convenient place, say, two miles farther north, in the center of the Cossaart/Joy farmsteads. On a Halloween night, when nineteenth-century pranks consisted of stolen garden gates and overturned outhouses, the perfect opportunity arose. In the darkness, my great-grandfather Charles David Cossaart, single and twenty-three years of age, joined with a handful of other young farmers in jacking the schoolhouse up and supporting it upon four wooden farm wagons. Two double teams of horses pulled the school building on a two-mile journey through the October moonlight. A bank of clouds rolled in from the western horizon, and the rain turned into a deluge. The mud swallowed up the narrow wooden wheels of the wagons, and the entire rig became firmly mired in a field of corn stubble. The pranksters had no choice but to abandon their efforts and flee with their horses for the shelter of their stables and homes.

The rains ended before sunrise, and my great-grandfather's future father-in-law, Aden Joy, rolled open his barn door for his morning chores and was astounded by the sight parked toward the eastern horizon: a small white schoolhouse, minus a foundation, balanced upon four wooden wagons sitting helplessly in his soggy cornfield. Apparently a decision was made to complete the intended relocation, and the one-room East Star School was where my grandfather and later my father were educated through the eighth grade. It sat exactly a mile west of our driveway.

Nora Comfort Joy and Charles David Cossaart married in 1890 and established a busy farmstead on Section 1-1-1. They built a small frame house, a half-dozen farm buildings, and soon a larger and more ornate home with indoor plumbing and gaslights. The growing farm economy provided steadily increasing prosperity as the crops were good and the local population multiplied. The railroad soon came through and provided even better markets, and commodity prices spiked with the beginning of World War I.

The couple had nine children, eight of whom survived to adulthood; the last baby girl died in infancy. The first born was a son named Reuben Comfort Cossaart. Sixty-eight years later, the younger Reuben became my grandpa.

By the time Charles Cossaart was fifty years old he had purchased six separate quarter-section farms, providing a ready-made, working farm for six of his adult children and a cash equivalent paid to the other two. Nora's inheritance added more wealth. When the Mahaska State Bank suffered embezzlement during the Great Depression, Great-Grandma Nora and the town doctor's wife, Mrs. Wall, were the bank's two major shareholders. Together they made good on all the lost deposits out of their personal pocketbooks.

Charles and Nora retired from farming and moved to a home in Mahaska. Sweet and plump Nora died in her late sixties from complications of diabetes; the vigorous and slender Charles lived to age ninety-four. I recall seeing black-and-white snapshots of Great-Grandpa at around ninety years old: big white mustache blown back by the wind and fire still in his eyes, chin up and shoulders squared, Nora absent.

Charles spent his retirement days socially active and involving himself in his offspring's farming interests, and then getting in their way as his wits became duller in extreme old age. There is a spot of pasture a few miles north across the Nebraska line, at one time a tilled field, where my dad watched his grandfather pulling a drag harrow back and forth across a small field with his Hudson "Super 6" automobile. His grown children had hidden the keys to the tractor, so he used his tank-like automobile, known for its power, on one of his last attempts to be productive.

Great-Grandpa Charles' final two years were spent under the care of my grandparents in the farmhouse. Grandma relayed that old Charles was somewhat out of his mind in the last year or two; she said he "got that way after a real bad fever." But he was fairly easy to care for and a joy to have around in many respects, fully ambulatory and usually in a good mood. As his ability to converse evaporated, he would softly sing church hymns as he walked about. He was a proud and independent old man but at times could be as stubborn as the mules he once walked behind in the fields. My uncle Alvin, at the time a strong young man, was assigned the task of forcing the old man to take a weekly bath, whether he agreed to it or not. Before Great-Grandpa's burial in the Narka cemetery, his body was prepared by the family, and his casket lay for three days in the small sunroom on the first floor of my house as the guests and relatives filed through to pay their respects.

Alvin and the Blacksmith

It was the first week of August, 1971, and I was a month shy of fifteen years old. The unforgiving Kansas sun had made the inside of the light-blue pickup truck an oven, and both sets of door hinges groaned as my uncle Alvin and I slid into our seats. The heated gray vinyl burned through my blue jeans, and I jumped up in the air a little, tentatively dropping my backside a few times until I absorbed some of the heat. The truck doors slammed in close unison, and Alvin piloted the pickup up the long gravel driveway. On the farm, when something breaks, you must drive somewhere to buy a new part or get it welded. Just another day of wheat farming, another long and hot day.

"There's no use in me trying to weld that thing," Alvin said, as he gave a worried glance to the broken chisel shank that lay between us on the seat. "That guy over at Hubbell is pretty good. You got to talk to him nice, though. Those old-time blacksmiths are awful cantankerous." The iron piece was about two feet long, an inch thick, and was curved like a big letter C, with the granulated metal surface at the break sparkling in the sun, an eye-catching contrast to the dull polished face of the long shank. Pulled through the soil at a twelve-inch depth by a diesel tractor, this shank, and its eleven partners attached to the frame of the implement, had followed dutifully over thousands of acres. The tillage procedure is called, simply, "chiseling." Not unlike stabbing a pocketknife straight into a bare flowerbed and pulling it across the length of the window box, the tillage process breaks up hard and compacted soil and takes a lot of effort on the part of the horse or tractor. Unlucky enough to encounter a long-forgotten concrete remnant of a barn foundation, the metal shank lost a very quick tug-of-war. With a snap and a lurch of the tractor, my nascent tractor-driving senses told me to push in the clutch and see what had happened. I didn't think it was my fault, but, even if it were, the criticism would be mild, if at all. My uncle was the most patient man I knew. Mishaps like this were met with a cool reaction, maybe even a smile, and then a methodical solution.

Ever since I could remember, I idolized my uncle Alvin. When I was a teen, he was in his mid-forties, still a bachelor and living in the same big farmhouse as his folks. He diligently carried the responsibility of farming, yet was not a slave to the work. His northern Kansas accent, with an ever-so-slight western twang, was midway in the gradient between Texas drawl and the quirky Dakota manner of speaking. It was as flat as the land, and his words came out softly, even when he shouted, which was infrequent. The western characteristic only revealed itself with words like "cyows" for cows. He had a gentle way of looking right into you. Animals and kids just seemed to gravitate toward him. All of us nieces and nephews repeatedly begged to

Uncle Alvin.

hear the story about a youthful and mischievous Alvin putting a cow in the schoolhouse. With a tight-lipped grin pulled across his dentures, he would always stop the inquiry short by admitting only, "Yeah, that's what they say anyhow."

Though very likeable, there was something in his shyness that put a distance between himself and all others. He never married, and all my sisters and cousins agreed he would have been the best husband in the world. As I approached adulthood and spent more time around Alvin, I would search into his long periods of silence and occasional corny jokes; I began to catch glimpses of his inner workings. He would be the most rewarding of friends if known well, but I realized achieving that would take a long time. Committing his deepest personal trust seemed to be held in reserve for someone he hadn't yet met.

The kids enjoyed Alvin's bachelor status because we had him all to ourselves when we came to the farm. He happily loaded up the chest freezer in the basement with frozen pizzas and ice cream and bought a case of small green bottles of Coca-Cola when we visited. On every weekday, about mid-morning, kids would pile into the pickup and Alvin would take us on a leisurely, fanciful pickup ride for a mile and a half to the grocery store in Mahaska. He handed each of us a quarter to buy whatever candy and sunflower seeds we could afford. My six-year-old sister Judy told him, "You don't need any kids because you have all of us to spoil." My father said his brother "never was much interested in girls," yet as I became a teen I would watch him covertly ogling young and middle-aged women, and he quietly egged me on in my pursuits of girls. But he could be quite shy, especially around women. The prettier they were, the greater effort he made to conceal a bashful smile.

As the pickup barreled down the dusty road in search of a chisel shank fix, I attended to the most important task in that situation for a teenager: get a decent radio station to come in on the AM dial. Before Alvin purchased this truck a year prior, he teasingly suggested he might just come home with one minus the radio. "You gotta pay extra for them, for sure," as he shook his head in mock concern over the cost involved. But there was the radio, working just fine, in his new used pickup. It received the same stations as the blaring box he bolted on the fender of the tractor for me. Many farmers at the time objected to their hired help being distracted by a radio as they did their field-work; Alvin was smart enough to understand that an entertained young farmhand was more productive. Keep the boy in tunes and he would run that tractor all day long.

"Is that KOIL?" Alvin asked, not really wanting to know but feeling compelled to show an interest. "Yup," I shouted over the wind noise roaring through the open windows. The vehicle kicked up a rolling plume of dust; a quarter-mile long rooster tail followed the speeding blue pickup truck. "On some days the signal is strong enough from Omaha to get here." My uncle nodded in agreement. His concern was the broken shank and how he was going to deal with the old blacksmith, but as usual, he made me believe that my task of fiddling with the radio was of equal importance.

The six-mile drive on the dry dirt road led us across the Nebraska state line and into the tiny town of Hubbell. A typical rural village on the Great Plains, it contained perhaps 150 people. The main street was paved with low-quality blacktop that melted in small patches in the sun, and it speckled car and truck fenders with tiny dots of tar. It was far, far wider than need be—six lanes of width with only a smattering of cars parked on it, some parked diagonally in a row down the center. We drove past a small bank in a tidy little brick building and could see a grain elevator boiling with dust at the far end of the street. There was a beauty shop with two silver-haired women entering and a beer joint and steak house with large, hand-painted letters on a brick facade spelling out "Swede's."

On the rare occasion that my grandmother could be convinced to go out to eat, she would not have considered entering this restaurant because they served beer. "The Tavern," she called it. But she never scolded anyone else for going in. Grandpa would surprise me once in a while by quietly stepping into a pool hall while Grandma and I shopped for groceries on trips to the bigger grocery store in Fairbury or Belleville. He told me it helped keep his weight up, which made sense to me as I surveyed his five-and-a-half-foot, 130-pound frame.

The beer sign on the tavern exterior pictured a frosty mug with beads of condensation on the glass. I had only tasted beer a handful of times, but the picture appealed to my throat as I felt the blast-furnace heat come through the pickup window. The mirage of advertising disappeared from the windshield as Alvin slowed and wheeled the truck through a half-turn. We jerked to a halt in front of a faded galvanized metal building, and my attention was forcibly redirected to a sign on a walk-in steel door.

STRADLEY BLACKSMITH in big black letters. That was it. Title not followed by any unnecessary language, such as "Company" or "Service." His name was Stradley, and he was a Blacksmith. Whoever this guy was, he was likely straight to the point.

My uncle's larger frame provided protection as we entered the shop and he obscured my view of the building's interior. My eyes darted quickly about, taking in as much as I could gather without appearing too vulnerable. Something about this place smelled of danger and hazards, of hard work—something unforgiving. The walls were sooty and dark and crammed full of thousands of tools, iron pieces, and old coffee cans overflowing with nails and bolts. Despite the density of items, there was a neatness to it; the whole place had a crisp order, even as everything, including the air, seemed to be coated with a thin film of oily dirt. Every item in sight had its own little filthy place to rest. The smooth concrete floor was neatly swept, even into the corners. A massive anvil and other huge and menacing-looking machines intruded into any open space.

The owner was nearly overlooked. As I peered into the poorly lit shadows and the glare from the dirty windows, a giant figure of a man under a sooty conductor's cap was asleep in a filthy overstuffed rocking chair. The stuffing was escaping from the back and billowing over the cracked wooden frame. Both chair and occupant looked like something brought back from the garbage dump. The old man fluttered his eyes open with the close of the door behind me, and I felt a small wave of fear as I realized I had awakened him. His stout frame and fleshy face with a two-day gray beard stubble seemed to match his tattered button-down shirt. Blue jeans were stained in oil spots and full of burn holes and patches. Even slumped in his chair, his large size was obvious. He looked bigger than my uncle, and that put him at about 250 pounds.

A fat and wrinkled black-and-brown coon dog lay sprawled on the floor, asleep with his jowls silently flapping out a snore. A small puddle of drool leaked out of the side of his face onto the concrete. Even in the dim light I could see the dog was near the end of his useful days. His back was covered with scars from fighting raccoons, and his face was full of gray hair. His outer eyelids peeled open reluctantly, revealing bloodshot and translucent inner lids that followed suit. With casual notice, the dog shut both lids tight again to confirm that Alvin and I were not worth the trouble.

"What can I do ya fer?" The old fellow's voice sounded like gravel sliding out of a dump truck. He cleared his throat and blinked heavily. The dog attempted an opening of the eyes again. The man offered no apology for being asleep in the middle of the afternoon. Straightening his tattered hat and then raising his posture a bit, he sat up erect and waited for Alvin's reply.

"I got this broken shank that needs put back together, if you're not too busy," my uncle said with a hint of sarcasm, detectable to me but withheld from the blacksmith.

"Well, I may be hard of hearing as hell, but I can *see* that it's *broke*. And I am pretty busy today." I scanned the inside of the shop and could see no ongoing projects. No tools that were not hung up. It looked like someone had swept the floor yesterday and the coon dog hadn't moved since.

My uncle began to head toward the door and had a slight smile as he met my glance. He carelessly cast a statement over his shoulder in the old man's direction. "Okay, well, just thought I'd ask. Thank you."

I couldn't believe it for a moment. We had work to do! I needed to finish chiseling that field! We came all this distance to pay for a service, and this guy didn't even want our business. I wondered who else could weld things in this town. Why were we wasting our time in this place? Maybe Alvin could be talked into buying a cold bottle of Coke across the street.

Before I could start my exit, the proprietor raised his head to speak. "Wait a minute," with much greater volume, then a pause. The dog's eyes opened momentarily as the man's voice boomed through the metal building. "I think I can squeeze you in." My dad's little brother stood up a bit taller and concealed a smile. The blacksmith rose from the chair as Alvin walked forward and respectfully handed him the broken shank.

The blacksmith frowned as he examined the project. I anticipated harsh words, like "How in the hell did you break this?" or "*Who* in the hell broke this?" but instead he growled, "I suppose you wanted this done yesterday," exaggerating his already bent posture and casting an annoyed eye at Alvin. "No hurry," my uncle answered kindly. "I hear that you're the best. Whenever you get around to it." The giant paused for several seconds and then winked at me and gave Alvin a warm smile. His tone softened dramatically. "I'll have it ready for ya tomorrow noon."

As we drove away from the repair shop, I pondered the little exchange that had transpired. The beer sign on the tavern disappeared through the back glass, and I turned and looked at Alvin, who was shifting gears and wearing a pleased expression. "Quite a guy, huh?" he chuckled. "He sure is," I answered, grinning at a man who had once again found me in a surprised state of admiration. We rode on silently for a few minutes. Forgetting about the radio momentarily, I sat digesting a small lesson in human relations. I wanted to be more like my uncle. It was nice to be sharing the same ride. The rushing wind through the open window was the only sound until a new conversation topic arose.

Dad and Mom

Dad was raised during the Dust Bowl in the latter half of the Great Depression. He attended the Star School, the same building his grandfather had relocated, from the first through the eighth grade. I remember seeing a worn black-and-white picture of the pupils of the entire school, which probably numbered fifteen kids in grades one through eight, as they posed in front of the tiny wooden school building. Raleigh Cossaart, my father, shoulders back and eyes toward the camera, sported a shock of curly forehead hair tossed up by the wind as he stood in the back row with a half-dozen of the older kids. All the boys were dressed in striped overalls, the girls in shin-length cotton dresses. Dad's younger brother, Alvin, sat in front, crowded together with the other little ones seated on the concrete steps.

Dad's most vivid recollections were of the "Dirty Thirties." The area of our farm escaped the total devastation and "black blizzards" that occurred farther west in the heart of the Dust Bowl, but in north-central Kansas, it was bone dry from 1930 to 1940. There were many times when the March winds created blowing dust so heavy in the air that school ended at noon so the children walking home to their scattered farmsteads a mile or more away would not get lost in the dust.

My dad had the fortitude and skills to be a farmer, and from what my grandparents told me, he learned early to be yet another in a long line of Kansas farmers. But my father was ambitious and intelligent, and the lean times he saw as a child and young man convinced him to look beyond the dirt roads and wheat fields for his future. Dad was an excellent student and pursued his engineering studies with dedication.

After graduation from Kansas State University in 1944, he served a brief tour with the US Army Signal Corps in the Philippines and in the occupying forces in post-war Japan.

In 1947 he began what was to become a very successful forty-two-year career with Westinghouse Electric Corporation. Dad held a solidly confident view of himself as an engineer, and justifiably so. He was a great company man and an accomplished design engineer who even held two United States Patents for the manufacture of large power electrical transformers (the huge devices that convert raw energy created by the generating plants into usable electrical current and send it through the grid). Dad traveled extensively for his profession, as the gargantuan transmission equipment that carried his designs were online, meaning the power grid, worldwide. He knew his stuff. He was a great provider for his family.

When he began his career in Sharon, Pennsylvania, he reportedly still had a girlfriend back in Kansas somewhere, but, upon meeting my mother, she was forgotten in a heartbeat. Shirley Anne Shimp was a petite, black-haired beauty who worked as

Mom.

a smiling and efficient receptionist in a doctor's office, and Dad met her on a blind date set up by one of his Westinghouse coworkers.

My mother grew up in the eastern Pennsylvania industrial town, with even more modest means than my father. She had a sister and three brothers. When she was six years old, her youngest brother died of spinal meningitis, a fact she revealed to me with a serious face after I discovered a small crayon drawing in her cedar chest. Her father, overwhelmed, had more than he could financially and emotionally handle and abandoned the family without a word, but this was never elaborated to me in childhood. Mom was eighteen years old before her mother, Viola Mae Quigley Shimp, remarried a hardworking but eccentric carpenter with a glass eye who I would know as my Grandpa Albert Youngk. Shirley Shimp was full of "gumption." Printed beside her high school yearbook picture was, "Plays basketball with the boys."

In 1947, a year after my mother and father married, they made a fourteen-hundred-mile automobile trip from Pennsylvania to Kansas across less-than-smooth post-war highways, and my mother was introduced to a world she only knew about from the first movie she saw as a child, *The Wizard of Oz.* Upon arriving at the big farmhouse, she was met for the first time by not only Grandma, Grandpa, and Alvin but also a large, extended family of aunts, uncles, and cousins. As Dad was growing up, he had enough first cousins to fill two baseball teams at Sunday get-togethers, and at the time of meeting my mother, most of them, as well as their parents, still lived in the Mahaska area. Mom told me, "It looked like the entire state was there to look me over."

My mother gamely survived the introductions and charmed everyone, especially my grandmother. The two women formed a bond that seemed closer than that between Mom and her own mother. In 1954 my mother had a very difficult pregnancy that ended in the infant death of my sister, Diane Lynne, born two years before I came along. It was Grandma Cossaart who, in mid-farming season, came out to Pennsylvania from Kansas

Mom and Dad, 1973.

to help for a few weeks. Grandma Youngk, who lived only a few miles away, told her daughter that she was too busy.

Grandma Cossaart seemed to fill a small void in my mother, and when we would visit the farm, Mom fussed over Grandma and helped her with any house or garden task that needed to be done, which were labors worth more than gold to an aging farm woman. Grandma told me repeatedly that "Shirley was just the best daughter-in-law a mother could ever hope for."

Every little boy thinks his mother is beautiful; mine actually was to others as well, and none more so than Dad. He was one proud husband. At about ten years old, I remember seeing a *Life* magazine full-cover photo of Elizabeth Taylor on her fortieth birthday, and I thought Mom's black hair and flawless looks made her a pretty even match. She was a full-time housewife and looked to be the perfect spouse for my father. My sisters and I sometimes teased her unfairly about her intellect when compared to Dad, but she was quite bright and certainly capable of teasing in return. She was unfailingly cheerful and fully present for four kids while keeping her house spotless and efficient. I remember her humming happily as she would iron my father's white dress shirts. Dad treated her like a princess. I have always been a romantic and acquired it naturally.

My father seemed conflicted about the farm. Dad loved the farm on which he was born, but he also carried an equal amount of disdain for it. This always puzzled me as a boy, as the farm seemed like nothing but novelty and adventure, and I could not understand why anyone could ever view it with less than full enthusiasm. He himself was the teller of farm stories: adventures that he had lived through and skills that stuck with him for a lifetime. I could walk on the ground and see the same landmarks that he recollected. Despite his complaints of mud and bugs when we visited the farm, I saw something in his eyes that made me think he felt it was sacred. With time away from his job, he seemed more relaxed when we were there, and I loved it when he showed me around. He smiled a lot. I loved the farm because of that.

The Contract

Beginning at age fourteen, I began spending my summers on the farm as a half-skilled hired man. At first I hated it. But after a few weeks, I acquired some basic skills, and I began to feel useful and important. With each succeeding summer, I learned more: how to throw hay bales, drive the tractor for long hours in the fields, and become a good garden laborer for Grandma. The Cossaart farm began to be one of the tools used to carve out my emerging identity. My stays in Kansas became the high point of my year.

The summer before my freshman year in college my choice of occupations was yet undefined. Spending so much time with Alvin, I developed an intense interest in the business of crop farming. As we drove down the road, I constantly bombarded him with technical questions about fertilizer, seed hybrids, and tractors. He always continued answering until I was fully satisfied with the information. He never, ever got impatient or brushed me off.

Alvin, like my grandpa, was a quiet man. We often rode along in the pickup without any conversation at all. One day, at nineteen years of age, I broke the silence as we slowed down to turn into our driveway. "How would it be if you and I were partners some day?" Alvin sat up straight, looked over at me with wide eyes, and quietly reached forward and shut off the radio, without my objection. The silence asserted itself as I hardly believed what I had just said. The pickup slowed to a crawl, and he shifted into neutral and coasted to a quiet stop at the top of the gravel driveway. I bounced my gaze from his face to the floorboard. I looked back at him. After an interminable silence, his stunned expression relaxed and melted into a determined smile.

"Well," he started, and then paused wordless for a few more seconds. "Ah ... well ... that would be great!" His eyes glistened, and he burst out with an uncharacteristic belly laugh. "I don't see how two guys could make a living on a dinky operation like this, but we could figure out something." I looked over and watched his face brighten as I had never seen. "Maybe we could feed some cattle or something like that. Maybe we could rent some more land." He finally faced me directly. "This farmin', you know, ya never get rich but ya *can't beat the life.*" I nodded vigorously. For the first time, I felt the exhilaration of picturing, very concretely, my future as an adult. And it was with the most kind, honest, fun person in the world. My uncle Alvin Cossaart.

Uncle Alvin.

Crash

I had never felt such cold in my twenty years of life. I was lying on my back in the dirt, and the chilly eastern Colorado night in late May seemed to penetrate the deepest regions of my body as a frigid breeze blew over the skin of my bare chest. It was a desert chill; the arid High Plains are at an altitude where the earth's brief heating of the day quickly drops into the teens (Fahrenheit) by midnight. I could not seem to move any muscle, and my shivering came in involuntary waves. I could not move my head. When I opened my eyes, I saw only black, constant darkness with a few pinpoints of blurry stars. Three simple thoughts came slowly into my consciousness and repeated themselves, demanding simple answers: What state are we in, Colorado or Kansas? Is my friend, Jim, okay? Could someone call my grandmother and tell her we'll be late? All I was sure of was that we had crashed a car. Our journey had been interrupted. Self-concern stepped off to the side of curiosity. The three questions repeated like a skipping phonograph record, and I talked aloud and to myself: Jim okay? What state? Call Grandma. Cold. I am so cold.

I had been thrown through the windshield of a 1973 Plymouth station wagon at about sixty-five miles an hour. My unbelted body had been ejected from the auto as the big car did a side-over-end somersault. On one of the first revolutions, my forehead had smashed through the glass and my torso had followed; my big feet had impeded a clean exit while my legs were ripped forcibly through the broken glass. Hamstrings and ligaments were stretched and torn as the force removed both of my high-topped Converse basketball shoes, which were later found tossed onto the highway with both sets of laces fully tied. The skin on my back and shoulder blades was abraded off as my T-shirt was ground to a bloody thin strip remaining around my neck when my body skidded across the pavement and into the sagebrush median. My right arm had been pulled out of its socket and was lined with deep lacerations from hand to collar bone. The forearm was filleted like a steak at the butcher shop, the wound open the length and width of a pocket comb. I lay nearly naked, shivering and bleeding profusely in the median of I-70, fifty-some miles east of Limon, Colorado. The most sickening, lonely, cold sensation that I had ever experienced filled every cell of my body.

Earlier that evening I had arrived in Boulder from a ten-hour leg of driving from the farm in north-central Kansas. Grandma's food and my summer bedroom made for a welcome stop on my round-trip journey from Muncie, Indiana. I had driven Jim's family's station wagon to pick him up from the University of Colorado. My friend was anxious to get on the road and drive, and the plan was to drive through the night and make the return trip of ten hours back to the farm. We would rest for a day and night on the farm, load up on my grandmother's cooking, and finish the final fifteen hours back to our parents' homes in Indiana. Once there, I would recoup for a few days and then return again to Kansas and spend my usual summer on the farm.

After loading up the station wagon with my friend's luggage, we gassed up the vehicle and filled our bellies with Whoppers and fries. Jim and I had been great friends in high school in Indiana and had both completed our freshman year of college; he had a swimming scholarship to the University of Colorado, and I was attending Purdue University in Indiana. We chattered and joked and made it through the high-speed chess match of Denver's evening traffic. We also attempted a little capitalistic venture on the trip. We loaded the back of the station wagon with about ten cases of Coors beer in cans; that brand was not distributed west of the Mississippi River in 1975, and it would fetch a premium price in Indiana.

Jim was fresh and alert; he was enthused about arriving on the farm at just the right hour for Grandma's breakfast. I, on the other hand, was exhausted. After an hour of riding in the passenger seat, even our clever banter was no match for the need to close my eyes. As I sipped my bottle of orange juice, my barely conscious mind opted for comfort; I unbuckled my seat belt, contorted my body in a more sideways orientation, and fell fast asleep.

I remember the bang. It sounded like a gunshot. I groggily comprehended a swaying back-and-forth motion of the car. "A tire blew!" Jim shouted. I glanced at his wide-eyed expression of helplessness. The rear end was fishtailing too violently to control, and the youthful driver's panicked attempt to wrestle the steering wheel was precisely the wrong thing to do. The tail wagged the dog in ever more desperate swings until three or four sways back and forth gave way to a roaring of rubber and a plunge of my senses to the left. I felt the weight of my body reverse itself. The sound of exploding glass and the groaning of metal being crushed were beyond what my mind could process. My senses became a mix of silence and numbness. I felt only confusion and not a trace of pain. I was strangely concerned about the condition of my T-shirt, feeling the cotton fabric ripping, and worried about the damage to the Yamaha motorcycle logo printed on the front.

Jim rode it out unhurt, unstrapped his seat belt, and somehow found me in the dark. He was quickly joined by a Colorado state trooper, who had watched the accident happen as he drove in the other direction in the west-bound lane. Lucky timing: His nightly task was to drive from Denver eastward to the Kansas border and back. He covered the three-hundred-mile distance only once per night. He watched us crashing in the opposite lane and radioed the local community hospital and ambulance. While he and Jim kept me lying still and covered with a blanket, they slowed the flow of blood from my arm. The trooper confirmed that in spite of the torn and crushed beer cans scattered across the pavement, we were not drinking any of it at the time. The ambulance, located forty-five miles to the south, arrived in about the same number of minutes.

I remember the muffled sound of roaring tires beneath me as I lay flat on my back and strapped to a wiggling gurney. The ambulance sped down a gravel road at a steady one hundred miles an hour toward the small rural hospital. The gravel popped and sang in tiny tones as small stones hit the underside of the vehicle and echoed through my head. "Is he with us?" I clearly heard a man in the passenger side turn and ask another paramedic, who was hovering over me. "I believe so!" he shouted back, and I could feel the breath of his barking response against my face. His palm pressed on the solar plexus area of my chest. *Yes*, I thought, *I believe so, too. I don't feel anything, but I can hear you guys.* My labored responses were single-syllable grunts, and he acted like he couldn't hear me anyhow. I was alive, that much I knew. I was left with enough presence to surmise I was probably injured seriously.

Shock is a strange thing. It happens to the human brain during extreme physical trauma; a self-protection device designed to keep one from truly going insane. With mortality and bodily injury whispering a deafening, inescapable message into a person's ears, there is only so much the mind can handle. A sort of suspended animation takes hold, reducing the unfolding trauma to a cartoon-like event. The consciousness steps outside of the body and views the ongoing action like a detached observer. Brain function is slammed up against the cranial vault, where it liquefies and slides down like warm jelly thrown at a plaster wall. Intellect and reasoning coagulate in useless pools on the floor. Emotions like fear and horror slip into the background as if someone pressed the mute button, yet still they are discernible, chattering away incessantly and reminding the foreground of their constant presence. If a body can survive, the psyche that remains is never quite the same.

I was whisked out of the ambulance and placed upon a stainless-steel operating table in the Lincoln County Hospital, a two-dozen-bed hospital in pancake-flat eastern Colorado. The emergency/operating room probably had not been used for a month or more before I arrived. The old town doctor was disturbed from his sleep, and he drove to the hospital to sew me back together and attend to my other wounds. He was unwilling to administer any general anesthesia, due to my obvious head injury, of unknown severity at the time. An injection of Lidocaine under the skin near the forearm gash was administered as the state trooper and one of the paramedics steadied my body on the operating table and the bleary-eyed doc drove his first stitch into my skin. After remaining fairly quiet and passive up to that point, my fight-or-flight response awakened.

The hidden anger of a young man's subconscious burst to the surface; I was a solid little guy with an upper body developed with weight training and throwing hay bales every summer. Without warning, I lurched upright and swung a powerful left hook; my fist blasted the kindly old doctor directly across his jaw and nose, knocking the man into the corner of the room. Holding his own bloody nose, he gathered himself up off the floor, regained his composure, and instructed the two men to do a better job of holding me down. The quick surgery on my forearm was completed as I struggled, but my resistance soon wore down; exhaustion overtook instinct. The remnants of my clothing were removed, and my wounds were cleaned and dressed. I was placed in a hospital bed down the hall and slept for a few hours.

I woke up midway through the next morning, slowly comprehending a foggy, surreal consciousness. I could not believe the pain. No movement failed to elicit a stabbing or tearing sensation unlike anything I had ever felt. I was propped up at a forty-five degree angle as my eyes looked down to the foot of the bed. It took several minutes to figure that my feet and legs were still attached, and I haltingly wiggled toes, one foot at a time. The shoulders shrugged. *I'm not paralyzed*, I thought. *This is good.* Tape and cloth surrounded my chest and wrapped up my right arm tightly to my chest, prohibiting all but slight movements.

In TV scenes there is often the injured hero, lying in a hospital or day bed at the ranch house, following a gunfight or combat. Despite his pain, the hero suffers with good nature and iron resolve. The attentive and attractive nurses place cold rags gently upon his forehead, and friends gather round and express kindness and concern like the hero had never seen before. As a boy, the tale had a certain draw to the melodramatic musings of a young male. It always appeared to me that you need only endure the pain with dignity and the world attended to your every need.

As I gained consciousness and experienced the pain, live and in color, it was definitely not TV. Nothing I had ever felt in my young life had prepared me for this. Every part of me hurt like hell with each breath and twitch. My inability to move was not due to paralysis. Whatever slight movement I made hurt far too much to repeat it.

The doctor returned the next afternoon and quietly formed an upper-body cast on me that immobilized everything from my lower ribs to my neck, with only my left arm hanging out. He formed the plaster with gentle movements and kind glances into my eyes. I noticed the black-and-blue area on his cheekbone; he paused momentarily and frowned slightly when I asked how he got it.

Thus began my convalescence, a progression of days blurred through a concussion-scrambled brain bobbing in a fog of Darvocet. Restlessness took control, and I began taking slow steps, haltingly at first, then becoming more measured. I began limping, without crutches, up and down the shiny hospital hallway floors, disoriented and bored. There were only a few nurses on duty in the nearly empty facility, and it was no problem escaping my room. The drugs had masked the pain in my knees and ankles as I ignorantly damaged my legs further with each venture up and down the halls.

It was decided that I should be flown home to my parents as soon as I could tolerate the trip to the Denver Airport, four days post-trauma. Mom and Dad were not informed of the true extent of my injuries. Somehow my mother was convinced, by both my friend's father and my own false reassurances by telephone, that I was healthy enough for her to stay put and wait for me to fly home. She was worried sick but resisted her maternal instinct based on my phoned-in perjury. My memory of the time has always been incomplete, but I will never forget her face as I shuffled off the jetway in a plaster upper-body cast and into the waiting area at the Indianapolis Airport. I was startled at the sadness and guilt in her eyes. I was more beaten up than had been described to her.

After I arrived home, my injuries were attended to more definitively by my parents' general physician and then referred to a young and progressive orthopedic surgeon who believed surgery was a last resort. I was immediately ordered to get off my feet and restrict myself to a wheelchair, unless I was in water. Intense rehabilitation began, starting with modest exercises like light leg lifts: My mother ingeniously filled up an oversized handbag with soup cans and steadied it over my ankle as I did several sets of repetitions daily, sitting on the kitchen table in my thin, aqua-colored hospital gown. I remember yelling at her one time when it slipped off. I am so sorry I did that.

The illusory bubble of a young man's invincibility had burst, and I was mad as hell. It took me one day to despise my wheelchair. I was sitting in it next to the garage, trying to soak up the mid-May Indiana sun. Acting on an angry impulse, I hopped out of the chair, aimed it toward the road, and gave it a push. It rolled into the street as I prayed for a speeding station wagon to come down Beechwood Avenue and smash the goddamn thing like a pancake. My mother bounded out of the house and into the open garage, asking, "What's the wheelchair out *there* for?" I just stared, mute and without expression, at the upturned chair at the bottom of the sloped concrete drive, one large wheel still spinning as it lay helpless in the gutter.

The physical therapist at the hospital shook his head as he surveyed my injuries and held two wooden crutches in his grasp. "It won't work," he said definitively, refusing to release his hold on the crutches. "Fine!" I snapped back at him with my glare of rage. I seized one crutch out of his grasp and struggled to position it under my good left arm. After forcing it into my armpit, I lunged forward in a giant step, suspending my injured left leg off the floor and taking an equally exaggerated step with my right. "Don't tell me what I can't do!" I yelled back. Down the hall I went, despite the protests, rising to shouts, coming from behind me as I careened toward the outside hospital door. My mother tried frantically to keep up, certain that I would fall on my face with each vaulting step. Hopping up and down on my good leg and striking the panic bar on the glass door, I galloped out onto the sidewalk and into the sunlight and tried to catch my breath. Mom told me later I looked like a baby giraffe.

As the weeks went by, depression and helplessness smothered the anger. My father plumbed in a hand-held showerhead and placed a metal stool on the tile floor of the stall. He got on his knees to wash me, reassuring me in the same soft tones that I could recall hearing as a little boy. Unable to wash myself, still dazed and with little ability to remember from one moment to the next, I felt like a sick little child. A month prior, I was stocky and cocky; suddenly I was helpless, skinny, and weak. As the water poured down my back, I began to tremble and cry uncontrollably. My whimpers echoed off the tile walls of the shower. "It will never be the same, and I'm right-handed..." I sobbed while gazing into the floor drain. "Sure it will, sure it will," my dad whispered, delicately lifting the useless appendage at the elbow and washing my armpit.

After a month, it was an enormous victory as I raised a glass of milk to my mouth. Exercising three times a day began to pay off, along with plenty of bed rest and a good diet; my body began to heal with the speed specific to twenty-year-olds. I assembled the stacks of jigsaw puzzles that were placed before me, but reading was impossible; my eyes would not focus on command, and my attention span was a few seconds long. I could not read more than a few lines without losing my place. I still used the crutch, and probably before I was ready, insisted on traveling back out to the farm. Alvin interrupted his planting tasks and drove out to take my seat for the Indy 500 as I listened, fuming, on the radio in my parent's living room. My patient uncle drove me the eight-hundred-mile trip back out to the farm, making frequent stops while I dealt with constant car sickness and a damaged bladder.

After a few days' rest and Grandma's cooking, I began sitting on the tractor for a few hours at a time. Still stunned and mostly mute, I literally wasn't sure who I was. The slow and automatic movements of engaging hydraulic levers and steering the Case tractor slowly across the dry soil gave me a sort of whole-body exercise in recall of my acquired skill. With monotonous, endless hours to think, I let my mind wander about in a disjointed stream of consciousness. At the end of a long afternoon I drove the tractor and disk home, rolled triumphantly down the sweeping gravel driveway, and pulled to a stop in the barnyard. I killed the roaring diesel engine, removed my earmuffs, and the tiny *tink tink* sound of hot engine parts was an astonishing contrast to silence. After a few minutes, my uncle or grandpa walked up to the tractor, spread out the legs of a stepladder, and steadied me as I struggled back down to earth.

Getting hurt is easy. Healing is what takes the work. I walked, swam, stretched, and lifted increasingly heavier weights daily as I settled back into the farm work routine. My body began to recover, but my mind lagged behind. Thoughts were exasperatingly hard to form, and I was filled with sadness most of the time. What beliefs and hopes I had before, I could scarcely remember. Old friends started giving me puzzled looks and quickly began treating me with resentment from our verbal exchanges that could no longer sustain my interest. It was difficult to be in anyone's company, as it took far too much concentration to hold up my end of even a light conversation. My mind would wander off, and my body often wandered away as well, in a limping, halting walk. By the end of the summer I was avoiding social situations entirely. I had, and needed, abundant time to think, time to reflect. Life is a tenuous thread, only to be used once.

It seemed as if someone had taken a videotape of my life and chopped out several chunks of that year. At the time I knew I was head-injured; I had read the list of symptoms and knew they described me well. But I didn't want to be looked upon as brain-damaged, and I worked very hard to stay silent and hide my lack of concentration.

Later in the fall as I went back to college at Purdue, I realized how difficult academics were going to be. But with a lot of help

Jim and the Case 830 tractor.

from my roommate and endless studying and memorization, I managed to make fairly good grades. By the end of the 1975-76 academic year, as a sophomore, my mind was finally working better and studying was easier. People who knew me both before and after the accident insist that my personality underwent a marked change. I was much quieter, more reflective, and much less prone to anger or impulsive outbursts. I emerged from the fog to feel and think differently. I wanted no more of anything that was not on that patch of Kansas soil.

❊ ❊ ❊

As much as I would try through the years, I could not reassemble an exact sound to my memory of the accident; I tried to imagine what all that violence sounded like but could only conjure up silence. One chiropractic adjustment was performed on me a few years ago, and quite unexpectedly I heard the tearing of steel in my ears for a second. It was a horrific sound, even just for that tiny moment, and I promptly tumbled off the adjustment table and vomited in the trashcan. To the present day, on the rare times I experience a fever, powerful waves of chills overtake my body and I become terrified beyond rationality. I cannot control my shaking, and often I begin to weep and feel like I am dying.

A full twenty years after the accident, I had a vivid nightmare. I felt a giant hand grasping me tightly by both ankles, hoisting me into the air, and slamming my body to the ground over and over again like a rag doll. I woke up believing I was lying in the dirt, terrified to make even the slightest movement, naked and freezing, with a bloodied body full of broken bones.

To conveniently forget we are mortal is among the most human of traits. The little aches in my bones and the caterpillar scars on my right arm remind me that this is my second chance. Yoga and a good chiropractor keep me moving. My right shoulder has been surgically repaired, finally, after twenty-some years of constant dislocations and, up to then, a lack of health insurance.

Throughout childhood and adolescence, it seemed I was constantly afraid of so many things, real or imagined. Now I can think of very little that frightens me. My habit of refusing to ride in the passenger seat amuses me at times. I am one of the few dentists who willingly violates the long-sleeve OSHA requirement while practicing; the feeling of the confinement still lingers faintly from a plaster cast. The aches and pains that reverberate in my frame actually make me smile. Trite as it sounds, every day is a gift.

Billy

When we were teenagers, Billy's path and mine seldom crossed, which was just fine with me. He was definitely a bad boy. In the rural area with a limited cast of characters he stuck out like a sore thumb, and I avoided him, especially without any good-sized buddies in my company. He was a big Czech kid with shoulder-length blond hair, and he walked through the world with a mean and menacing look. Harry the blacksmith once summed up his assessment of Billy. "When that kid was born, they shoulda knocked him in the head and throwed the milk to the pigs." The summer after my car accident, I went to the Republic County Fair in Belleville, Kansas, about thirty miles from the farm. The fair was a big social event, but typical of that summer, I went alone. After a season of hard work in the waning days of summer, the fair was a good place to find friends and, of course, to try and meet girls.

Ever since I began coming out to Kansas in the summers, the limited social contact I had with other young people my age was never easy. Because I did not attend school in the area, I was looked upon as an outsider, and at that age, I was wise enough to avoid any situation where I could be ganged up on. Post-pubescent young men are, by nature, territorial, and the country boys guarded their limited selection of available girls. In all modesty, my looks attracted the eyes of some girls, but I had to be careful about which one I was talking to, lest it turn out to be some big farm boy's girlfriend or intended future one. I was easygoing and quiet, so I did manage to make a few key friends, and that usually allowed me to socialize without getting into a fight.

The beer garden at the fair was a garage-sized tent with a roped-off area around it to keep the beer drinkers corralled. I was still using a cane at the time but was so self-conscious about it that I left it in the pickup parked a few blocks away. Walking was tough after shedding my casts. Before the crash, I was 155 pounds of weightlifting-developed muscle with a blue belt in TaeKwonDo; a few months later I was down to even less than Grandpa's size: 110 on a five-foot-seven-inch frame.

I did my best to walk confidently through the beer garden. A formidably large guy with long blond hair stopped directly in front of me. "What's *this* shit?" Billy sneered down at my face, a good half-foot below his. He was drunk and feeling mean, and I was dating a pretty girl that, at the time, he coveted. She wasn't there, but that made no difference to Billy. I looked up at his face and thought of how any blow to my body would break me again like a toothpick sculpture. My shaky pride was mashed underfoot into the muddy, beer-soaked grass as a noisy tent full of eyes stared at me. I limped aside a few steps and replied, "I'm not stoppin' you, man," and I walked away in humiliation. Had this happened before the accident, my muscles and confidence never would have allowed such an affront, even from such a big, tough guy like Billy. My thinking was still cloudy and slow, but I boiled in anger and labored back to my pickup truck and vowed that someday I would make that big, overfed Bohunk pay.

A Kansan

While formulating my college plans in high school, I chose Purdue University because of its strong programs in agriculture, and the cheaper in-state fees for Dad's benefit. One of my father's life goals was to pay full tuition and expenses for my three sisters and me in all our college years, which he did, and he prohibited all of us kids from working even part-time jobs like he had to. Purdue was a mammoth campus, full of very smart and often colorfully crazy people, and the energy was amazing. I always kept a small Kansas state road map pinned to my dorm room wall. "Stairway to Heaven" played repeatedly on FM stations and blared through the thin doors of dorm rooms as I passed; it had a line that stuck in my ears: *There's a feeling I get when I look to the west and my spirit is crying for leaving.*

Five months post-crash, I began devouring a book as my comprehension improved. *Zen and the Art of Motorcycle Maintenance* had captivated my imagination because of the curious title and my fascination with motorcycles. It wasn't about motorcycles. What it presented was a philosophy of quality, cleverly told in a metaphor about simple mechanical maintenance.

Quality is equated with truth, and truth is reality. To do any task half-heartedly or without commitment to quality was ultimately a lie. And so there should be a Zen, or love, in life's necessary work. The choice is to be false or real. That clinched it for me. I relinquished myself to the gravitational pull of the farm.

Kansas State, like Purdue, is one of a handful of major ag universities formed under the Land-Grant Act of 1862, and the moderate-sized town of Manhattan is tucked into the rolling and grassy Flint Hills of Kansas, one hundred miles south of the farm. My father found my wish to attend his alma mater too appealing to resist. It was a third the size of Purdue and spoken of favorably by one of my favorite professors as I finished up my final semester. He longed for relief from the crowded Purdue campus himself. "It's more of a cow college than this place. You'll like not having someone a foot in front of you all the time."

After finishing my sophomore year at Purdue, I spent a week at my parents' home in Muncie and packed a duffle bag full of summer clothes to strap to my Honda 550 motorcycle. I tried hard to be irritated with Mom to cover up my sadness and anxiety about leaving Indiana, and her, and I tried not to cry as she displayed a smile and a pained look simultaneously. I rode the quiet and smooth-riding road bike across Illinois, Iowa, and southern Nebraska, across the Kansas line, and rolled down the gravel drive of the farm. Grandma came out of the house in a shuffling run and hugged me before I even got my helmet off. I was proudly cognizant of finally being a true Kansan.

I plunged into the routine of farm work with Alvin with more energy than ever as I looked to the future of collaboration with him. In 1976 the nation's Bicentennial celebrations were in full swing everywhere, and in rural north-central Kansas there were lots of street dances, fireworks, and parades all through the summer. Alvin and I attended these when the work schedule allowed. We went to the sprint car races in Lincoln, Nebraska, whenever we found a weekend that was too wet for fieldwork.

My uncle Alvin was a fun guy to be with. He had a quiet, clever sense of humor, with just enough mischief to accent his likable personality. I can't think of anyone who did not genuinely like the man. He knew how to work hard; he could put in long days on the tractor and throw sixty-pound alfalfa bales halfway across a hot barn all afternoon, but he could also interrupt the toil with a humorous diversion. One afternoon he wanted to get a picture of his dog Scotty, "who was so smart he could drive a pickup." Alvin stood in front of the parked pickup truck, focusing a camera as I hid inside the cab. An insurance salesman drove into the barnyard to see my legs hanging out the pickup door and a collie behind the steering wheel.

I have hundreds of memories of his playful side. My younger sister, Judy, and my parents came out for a few days during the summer, and Judy and I were walking through the backyard. We heard Alvin's voice, calling from behind the screen window in the upstairs bathroom. "Judy! Jimmy! Come over here and look at this for me, will ya?" We walked over and stood two stories beneath the window. As we scanned the ground to find the item that he supposedly had dropped, a bucket of water came down upon us. After I left my boots out on the front step during a noon meal, he put a toad in one of them. One July day, he and I quietly drove away like saboteurs after placing an "auto-fooler" noise maker on the starting mechanism of a neighbor's car parked uptown. While going after tractor parts in Belleville, we would rarely pass up the A & W Root Beer stand, and then talk each other into buying a gallon to take home. He would grin with delight as we watched the dark-haired, big-bosomed weather woman point out the highs and lows on the evening broadcast. After the long summer workdays, he and I would dish ourselves out two big bowls of ice cream and stay awake long enough to watch Johnny Carson, after Grandma and Grandpa had long gone to bed.

There was a day when I was driving the tractor and pulling a harrow across a field. Alvin came up to check on my progress and slowed his pickup truck alongside my tractor as I traveled in a parallel path to the dirt road. I was just about done with the field and about twenty feet from the road, making my last few passes. As he slowed to match the speed of my tractor, he looked over to see me rhythmically banging on the steel fender with my gloved palm as the tractor radio blasted Elton John's "Saturday Night's Alright for Fighting" through my earmuffs. He watched me through his open window and waved. I waved back, both pickup and tractor still going at the same rate. He smiled and nodded; I smiled back. Then he pointed backward with his thumb, and his face burst into laughter as his truck sped up dramatically and into the distance. I looked back to

Alvin and Jim's sisters, Jean and Elaine, with Grandpa barely to be seen.

discover my oversight from the previous pass down the length of the field: The drag harrow was parked unhitched nearly at the opposite end.

The job of picking up the hay bales in the field had become more infrequent after he bought a machine that made large bales, handled with tractor hydraulics instead of by hand. But we would still gather up a limited number of small bales, and as I matured, I began to do most of the heavy lifting. This job that seemed so terribly hard as a fourteen-year-old became enjoyable, and I could throw the small, round fifty-pound alfalfa bales with ease. Alvin drove the tractor as I stood on the wagon and stacked the bales. The bale elevator, hitched tandem to the wagon, gathered the bales from the ground and lifted them to me as I deftly walked about the moving wooden floor. On that clear morning, as I stood upon the empty wagon with my hay hook in hand, I shouted, "Come on, man! We ain't got all day!" With an obedient nod of the head, Alvin popped the clutch, and my body flipped off the back of the wagon. As I lay on the ground and gathered my wits, he drove forward, pretending not to notice my absence. I ran and caught up, leaped onto the moving trailer, and tossed a dried cow pie toward him that sailed over his head and landed on the tractor hood. He never looked back but instead lifted his middle finger behind his back so I could see it clearly. He maintained his steady pace while I shouted curse words in between laughter, and he threw back his head and cackled.

Now that I was older, he began to open up more. He finally revealed the details of the cow-in-the-schoolhouse legend. "Well, yeah, we locked the poor thing in the principal's office, and of course it shit all over the big desk and everything." I asked whose cow it was. "Old man Taylor's," Alvin chuckled. "The principal had me by the collar as he yelled out at the street. 'Hey, mister, come here! This young man has something to tell you.' 'Not now,' old man Taylor said with a dismissive wave. 'I'm busy lookin' for my cow.'"

Later that summer Alvin stopped to chat a few minutes with his friend Smitty at the Mahaska filling station. Alvin answered a question with a phrase that his friend had heard more and more lately. "Aw, I'll just wait till Jimmy is with me to do that..." His friend looked at my uncle. "You're gettin' pretty dependent on that kid, aren't you?" Alvin gave Smitty a tired and grave look. "More than you can imagine," he replied.

As the summer wore on, I noticed my uncle's mood turning darker. He looked weary and was often uncharacteristically grouchy. When I announced that my friend Frank and I were going on a trip to Colorado for a few days, his angry reaction stunned me. "When do you think *I* get a vacation? Why don't you stay here and look after these old people and *I'll* go somewhere?" I drove off in a huff.

A week after I returned from my trip, Alvin helped me load up my stereo and clothing, and on a hot and windy late August afternoon, I moved into a high-rise dormitory room at Kansas State. The crisp lines of the limestone buildings at K-State filled the expansive campus and blended into the surrounding rocky Flint Hills in the deep Blue River Valley that cradles Manhattan. We dropped the cardboard boxes onto the floor of the empty and sterile room with two single beds. As the staff resident gave me all the orientation details, Alvin sat off to the side bashfully. He looked quite out of place and fidgeted in silence, but finally gave in to the need to say something to the other man. "Boy, you folks are a lot drier down here than we are up north." The blank look from the nonfarmer made Alvin even more uncomfortable, so he quickly excused himself and went back to the farm.

As the heat of August abated, the first chilly days followed in mid-September. On a Sunday in the middle of fall harvest, and before I headed back to Manhattan, Alvin urged me to stay the next weekend at school. I had spent every weekend up to that point helping him plant the fall wheat crop and begin the grain sorghum harvest. We called it by the common name, milo. The rows of stalks supported a cluster of deep maroon seed heads containing BB-sized grain. It constituted one-third of Alvin's yearly income as a farmer, and the weather risk of an early snow grew with each autumn day. Heavy snow would flatten the crop and make it a miserable, muddy mess to retrieve, so he was worried and working hard. But he persisted in trying to convince me to stay in Manhattan. "You have things to do down there," he said, trying to hide a forlorn look. "Enjoy your college years while you can." His words drifted off in the chilly wind as I got on my motorcycle and headed back to K-State.

The next weekend I took his words at face value and followed his suggestion to stay on campus. That Friday afternoon, I showered in the dormitory common bathroom and looked forward to going out with some friends and having a few beers for a change. For once I could indulge in some sort of social life. I felt the relief of not having to make the weekly road trip; Alvin was grumpy most of the time anyhow.

My shower was interrupted by a tense voice calling to me: "Cossaart, you have an emergency phone call." I stood dripping with a towel around my waist as I put the hallway pay phone to my ear. "Jimmy, this is your uncle Bill." I recognized the voice of Grandma's brother. "Alvin is dead." My fifty-two-year-old hero had climbed down from the grain bin and had collapsed and died in the arms of my eighty-eight-year-old grandfather. He'd had a massive heart attack.

I dressed with automatic movements, staggered out of my dorm room, and walked down the street to find a friend I had made a month earlier. Without hesitation, he handed me his car keys, and I drove back to the farm through a cold, steady rain. I cried until I was numb, and my thoughts turned to my Grandma.

Alvin still lived on the farm with Grandma and Grandpa, and their bachelor son took care of life's matters in their old age. Out of nowhere, it felt as if an invisible finger had interrupted the happy silence and pounded out a deafening E flat note on some piano, resonating through our heads thereafter. "Never in my darkest dreams did I think Alvin would beat me to the grave," my grandmother told me, looking as if she had suddenly aged twenty more years. Uncle Bill met me as I arrived with my friend's car on that drizzly and dark night. He heaped the burden upon me as I walked up the sidewalk to the house. With the characteristic Davenport lack of tact, he barked, "You have to farm this place now, Jim..."

That night, after several exhausting hours of consoling my grandparents and chatting with various neighbors and relatives, I collapsed into my bed in my little basement bedroom in the farmhouse. I fell into a vivid dream, and even dreaming, Alvin's sudden absence was front and center. I was sitting out on the front cement step, starting yet another routine day of farm work. There were muffled wails coming from inside the big white farmhouse, and I had grown tired of listening to the constant bursts of sobbing and watching the dour expressions of the neighbors who came and went to express their condolences, so it was a relief to be out in the fresh air while the morning sun came up. I tied my bootlaces, petted my butterscotch-colored kitten, and wondered just what in the hell I was going to do with myself to try to escape the stench of grief for a while, and more generally, how I was going to manage all this.

In my dream, the screen door slammed behind my back as I sat slumped on the step. I felt the heavy footsteps of work boots on the concrete, and my uncle Alvin, once again alive, stepped forward a few feet and turned toward me. As I looked through my long hair hanging over my eyes, he towered over me in his worn overalls that were crisp and clean to begin another day. His pudgy face was clean-shaven, and a hint of Lectric-Shave lotion floated away in the soft breeze. He looked off to the horizon as if assessing the weather and planning out the workday in his mind. This particular morning, he looked even more relieved than usual to be out and away from those a generation older than him. My grandparents and their contemporaries were numerous; hence Alvin, who I viewed as my near contemporary, seemed to be always in the presence of a bunch of eighty-year-olds. He was good at it, but it looked like a real drag to be doing it constantly.

My uncle Alvin turned to me and made his usual brief and occasional eye contact. He seemed anxious to get going. "Well," he said softly, as he gestured with a thumb to the sorrow behind the screen door, "That's enough of all that crap. Let's go check those cyows."

I awoke and stared at the cobweb-laden floor joists above my head, nearly catatonic, for a long time. Days later, I staggered through the funeral proceedings in a fog. All I can recall to this day is picking out the baby blue casket, his favorite color.

Dad's sister, Ruby, and husband, Wilbur, were an enormous help during this time. They made the four-hour trip from Wichita many, many times. I always did like them in the past, but we bonded even more closely while sharing the loss. I came to understand there are few people on earth finer than Ruby and Wilbur.

I began a weekly one-hundred-mile commute from the farm to college. I altered my class schedule from five days down to three and a half. On Thursdays at noon, I would jump in the pickup and drive to the farm, tend to the cows and my grandparents until Monday morning, then drove back to K-State to resume my studies. I did this nearly every week for my entire junior year and only failed one class—differential equations. Something had to give, and I didn't have the patience to decipher the broken English from the prof that came from God-knows-where. My dad tried to reprimand me, but any harshness was tempered by concern. "I don't want you failing any more classes, Jim." I swallowed hard on the other end of the phone.

Grandma and Grandpa lost their youngest son, and I was around to watch them deal with it. They had both grown hard of hearing, and whispers from their upstairs bedroom could be clearly heard in the night. Grandma would weep, and soon Grandpa's voice would answer in the darkness. "I know, Mama,

I know. I'm just hangin' on for you..." At times, usually in the afternoon, they shouted angrily at each other, and it echoed through the house. My worry soon got the best of me, and I asked Grandma about it one evening. She gave me a smile as she dismissed it all. "After sixty years of marriage, dear, we holler if we need to."

My father, who was still at the apex of his career at Westinghouse, took all the vacation time he could and made many trips to the farm from his Indiana home. He provided me with moral support and served as my hired man when he would show up at the farm. It was fun telling him what to do. It was a time when I got to see what my dad was made of, and he stepped up to the moment when we needed him. It was the first time I had witnessed Dad in a crisis, and I would be indelibly and forever impressed.

As spring approached, I committed myself to the job of planting the 150-acre milo crop, even though I had no experience performing the most critical farming task of the year. A prominent neighboring farmer and lifelong friend of Alvin's, Russ Long, gave me advice and encouragement. He educated me about fertilizer, herbicides, and ground preparations needed to plant the rows of milo that Alvin had been putting in the soil for years. Everyone in the community seemed to look at me with sadness and pity when they addressed me, and Russ's otherwise stoic face was no different. But he seemed to stay around after the others had made their awkward exits. The horizontal corrugations in his brow gently shaded his eyes and gave him a worried

Dad and Grandpa.

and sad expression. But the look in his eyes made me feel that I could make it all work.

As the soil warmed through March and April, Dad was back on the farm at the time. Grandpa was trying to be of help, and viewed himself as the new boss, a role he had given up long ago. He questioned my every move, criticized whatever I did, and walked around like one grouchy old son of a bitch. His eyes were filled with desperation. In his late-eighties, his thin features and years of working in the weather made him look a hundred. I recalled my dad's assessment of Grandpa as we both watched him on his hands and knees, feebly chopping away with a corn knife at the weeds growing next to the barn, a task that kept him busy for days could have been completed in ten minutes with a weed eater. My mind went back to a year earlier, when Grandpa had looked like he thoroughly enjoyed his weed-chopping job. Now it just looked like hard work. Grandpa looked up at us both as we piled into the pickup truck and barked out an order about something he thought important. Dad and I nodded our heads in patronizing agreement and drove away. "Just a harmless old man," Dad smiled and repeated again while he shook his head at me. "A harmless old man..." He told me his view of his own father's accomplishments: "You know, Dad was a great guy and all that, but he never expanded his business beyond what he was given."

Indeed he had not. Grandpa had been willed 160 acres on his tenth birthday, and in old age had the same land and another poor-laying quarter section we called the north place. He bought it cheap after his youngest brother didn't want it: It was one of those farms that Great-Grandpa had bought and was unarguably the worst one. In Grandpa's defense, I pointed out that he had hung on to it all through the Depression and even built a big two-story home. But Dad was correct; indeed, Grandpa was always content with the status quo as the world of agriculture went from mules to tractors with air-conditioned cabs. Alvin had confided to me that at one time he was frustrated as his father stubbornly clung to horses while the neighbors began using tractors. As Alvin matured, his own threats of leaving the farm were the final reason that pushed Grandpa into relenting and buying a tractor. Both Alvin and Dad had told me at separate times, and used identical words: "If Dad had his way, we'd still be using horses."

Recalling a considered measure that Alvin and I had discussed the previous crop year, I decided to narrow the dimension of the planted rows of grain sorghum from thirty-six inches to thirty; changing the planter box spacing to a narrower width would provide better protection against weeds and conform to what guys like Russ had been doing for some time.

My father and I began rather covertly working on the grain sorghum planter. Changing the dimensions required sliding over the heavy seed boxes on the large iron frame, as well as moving the huge rear wheels on the tractor to straddle the rows. It was noisy business as we pounded away at it in the garage. One morning as we were assaulting the planter with sledgehammers and pry bars, Grandpa walked into the garage and looked on in horror. To him, it looked like we amateurs were changing what Alvin had established. Unknown to him was the fact that Alvin was planning to make the same change that season.

"What do you boys think you're doin'?" he asked excitedly, the veins protruding on his bony neck and fire flashing in his eyes. Dad stopped hammering for a moment and tried to be authoritative and firm in an environment that had long ago ceased to be his own. He attempted to elevate my legitimacy. "Dad, we're changing this planter so it will do a better job. Jim's going to school to learn about these things, and he says this is what we need to do." I was very flattered but at the same time alarmed at an impending confrontation. Grandpa's face twisted with puzzlement and rage. "Alvin didn't need to go to school to know anything about farming! *Leave it alone!*"

A few more exchanges were passed between the two regarding the value of education. Dad's normally patient manner with his dad evaporated, and his face burst with anger. "Aw, for cryin' out loud, Dad! Here we go again with this crap!" My heart rose up into my throat. Holy Moses, I thought. It looked ridiculous to me. At twenty years old, I figured that father-son arguments somehow dissipated with the years, especially one looking so trivial when measured against time. Dad was clearly a success story with his life, and any need to justify his education and career choice seemed, well, stupid. A brilliant engineer was arguing the merits of his own education with an obsolete farmer who had not progressed past the eighth grade. I hadn't been alive to hear their arguments thirty-five years earlier, but it all sounded like an echo.

I tossed my crescent wrench onto the dusty cement floor while they escalated their shouting match, and I walked far up the driveway to leave behind something that was not my issue. But then again, it was. It struck me that I had now been thrust in between these two men. I fumed and kicked the stones on the driveway as I walked up toward the mailbox to check on mail that I knew wasn't there yet. The ever-patient and authoritative Alvin was nowhere in sight to tell Grandpa to go back into the house. Never in my life had I heard anyone even try to push my father around. As far back as I could remember my dad was tough and fearsome, and now he was being treated like a foolish kid. I had the urge to reach out and strangle my grandfather.

I recalled my grandmother telling me about the hard times of the Depression. "I pray that you will never live through as hard a times as them were. One year in the thirties, after the grasshoppers ate everything that was green, I had a little life insurance policy I had to cash in to survive. I also had to tell Raleigh we just didn't have any money left to send him to school, and he sure was disappointed." With less help from his folks, Dad's determination and brains carried him through Kansas State, and he accomplished it by being frugal, working part-time, and fulfilling his ROTC obligations. It became obvious why he was so adamant about me not having to work while I was in college. It was also clear why he resented the farm's sudden demands upon me, and the interference with my education while I helped to look after his aging parents. He felt Grandma and Grandpa ought to be off the farm and living in town like the rest of the retired farm couples; instead, they were now a huge problem imposing on the rest of the family. Years later, I found out the absurdity was at a level higher than I knew. My grandparents actually suggested my father curtail his own career to take over the farm. I can only imagine his response to that.

Later that evening we all sat down for supper, and the mood was dark and subdued around the squeaking oak dining table. Grandma had help fixing the meal from my ever-cheerful and optimistic mother, and Mom seemed to be the only one at the table holding her head up. Grandpa quietly coughed and rose from the table, retreated silently to the kitchen, and soon reappeared with a face full of desperation as he gripped the wooden door-frame with his shaking hands. Mom cast an alarmed glance at my grandfather and blurted to my father, "Jim! I think he's *choking!*" Grandpa stood clutching his throat with both hands and wilted to the floor. Dad and I took frantic turns performing the Heimlich maneuver, having only the slightest idea of how to do it, while exchanging panicked looks at each other. Grandpa lay crumpled on the linoleum floor as he finally ejected a piece of ham with a gasp and began breathing again. I cannot recall if it was me or Dad who finally met with success, but we carried Grandpa to the couch and eventually to his bed. The next day, Mom, Dad, and I shared a private moment of squelched laughter when we learned my ever-practical Grandma wanted to serve leftover ham for supper again the next night. "It's still good. We need to eat it up."

Grandpa spent a lot of time over the next several days lying on the couch. His legs were numb, but he steadfastly refused to go to the hospital. Frustration and guilt filled my father's eyes for days as we all sank further down into sorrow and exhaustion. Grandpa regained his ability to walk by the end of the week, and by that time the planter was finished. Ruby and Wilbur arrived again to take over being with Grandma and Grandpa, and I felt relief for Dad as he and Mom finally drove up the driveway and headed back to Indiana.

❊   ❊   ❊

Six weeks later, I began planting the grain sorghum crop. I cursed and struggled with plastic herbicide hoses and pumps and finally began the planting. I was clumsy and tense at first, and my rows meandered and wiggled worse than Oliver Douglas's on *Green Acres*. I began on the fields that were tucked away in the far corners of the farm so no one would see them. The word was out in the community that the kid was indeed going to plant the crop, and it seemed as if all eyes were upon my work. Day by day, my confidence grew and my hand steadied upon the steering wheel as Russ Long would stop twice daily to check on my progress and even offer a gruff sentence or two of advice and encouragement. By the time I had planted for five days straight, I had progressed to the last field, thirty-four acres adjacent to the house and next to the paved road. My rows had become bullet-straight, and the ground was uniform and smooth. Two weeks later, I looked upon my work and felt triumphant. The huge fields of healthy and green milo plants three inches tall were exhilarating to behold. For the first time in months, feelings of joy leaked out of me. Russ's daughter and son-in-law teased him about taking lessons in planting from me. The wife of a prominent farmer tapped me on the shoulder as I was in the grocery store uptown. "Your uncle would sure be proud of those rows."

One day I was driving back home from the grocery store after picking up milk and bread on an errand for my grandmother. Russ's truck slowed in the opposite lane, within sight of my newly planted grain sorghum field. Russ puffed on his pipe and removed it from his mouth to speak as our open windows drew beside one another. Those kind eyes twinkled in the mid-day sun. "That sure looks good, Jim. Looks like you've been doing it all your life." Russ was a local farming icon with over fifty years of experience. He rarely doled out any praise to anyone.

The rains began in earnest, and the growing weather turned ideal. The crop thrived, and my confidence grew as I went about tending the cattle and maintaining the farm. My days were filled with nonstop work, and I was deadly serious about it. To be constantly on the move helped me cope with missing Alvin. In spite of my success, the daily criticisms from my grandfather continued unabated, for he never left the farmyard to see my work. We rarely spoke through the days, and I was usually moving too fast around the farmyard for him to catch me, or I would be off doing fieldwork or checking cows in the pasture. At mealtimes, I kept my head down, ate my food quickly, and dashed out the door to get back to work. Only with the sharp words of my grandmother had Grandpa grudgingly begun to open his eyes. I heard Grandma's angry voice projecting from an open window as I was out in the yard. "Reuben, that boy is killing himself out there, and all I hear from you is discouragement. *He will never be Alvin. We can't bring Alvin back.* Jimmy is doing just fine, and if it wasn't for him, we'd all be in big trouble." Grandma had an iron will and a fiery temper. I heard no response from Grandpa.

As summer progressed and the raw edge of grief dulled, Dad, Ruby, and Grandma began discussing the future. Hard choices had to be made. My practical grandmother served as the final decision maker in the process. Up to that point, she had lived all of her eighty years on or near this farm. It must have been an unimaginable change in her life, but she decided to do what was best for everyone involved. The cattle and machinery must be sold, and my grandparents had to leave the farm.

My father offered to buy the line of machinery from Alvin's estate and set me up as a beginning farmer. It was an incredibly selfless offer. Every parent wants something a little better for their children and to enable his only son to be a farmer must have flown in the face of all his life's ambitions. But he knew I loved the place and that I had found a new propensity to farm and to do it well. I was grateful beyond expression for such a proposal. But it wasn't right: The farm was too small to have a future. Larger and larger farm units of American agriculture were creating an increasingly competitive environment in the seventies. The farms like Russ Long's dwarfed our little place, and the capital required to play the game properly was beyond my ability to find. I had one more year of college to attain a degree. I was tired of all the work and responsibility and knew that if I stayed, my grandparents would also want to stay. If I went, they would have to leave, and that was the only realistic option for them. I surprised myself by making such a clear-minded and definitive decision so quickly; a year and a few months post-head trauma and twenty years old, my thought processes were at last working well. I passionately wanted to farm but realized I could only do it on my terms, without the entanglement of my grandparents. I had to do what was best for them and me. My gut told me so. Despite my father's touching offer, I declined.

Finally one day Grandpa caught up with me in the yard; he had talked a younger brother into driving him around to look at my growing crops. "The place sure looks good, Jimmy." He surveyed the neat farmstead around us. "I wish you would stay." I recalled all the criticism and felt angry. Now he tells me, I thought. My defenses were up, but his words were genuine. I loved Grandpa with all my heart, and those few kind words seemed to make all the bad feelings vanish.

I looked at him and recalled the fun times before the burden of losing a son fell upon him, like the secret pact he and I shared once while fixing fence: We laughed until we were in tears after tumbling ass-over-appetite down a ten-foot embankment, after we both tugged on a fence wire and it snapped in two. He and I diligently cleaned the dirt off each other before tiptoeing into the house like two mischievous boys, evading Grandma. I recalled all the time I had shared in his company and how peaceful it felt just to be around him when I was a little boy. He was a good guy, in his day a good farmer and stockman, unfailingly honest and kind, and I was intensely proud to be his grandson. If I could live a life like his, I could call myself a success. I felt so sorry for him and wished things were different so he could stay on his homestead the rest of his days. I couldn't think of anything to say, and I fought back tears and toughened my face. "I'm sorry, Grandpa. I really am."

A unique opportunity arose in Wichita, home to Dad's sister, Ruby, and Uncle Wilbur. My grandmother boldly wrote out a check for a house located immediately next door to Ruby. Grandma definitively announced the plan to Grandpa, and Grandpa reacted with silence. Days later he confided to one of his younger brothers. "Ruth is moving to Wichita. I hope she will be happy there."

But in due time Grandpa accepted the reality of extreme old age and the security and semi-independence of living with family next door. We all were dreading his move and made dire predictions of his impending depression and death, but he adapted amazingly well. He quietly held his head up, appreciated the visits from his new neighbors, and spent his last five years reading the papers and watching Grandma tend her small backyard garden. "There's a young girl on the other side of the fence that talks to me," he described to me with a wink. His rocking chair was placed in the garage, and he sat with a long-haired white cat in his lap, a worn survivor brought from the farm. He smoked an occasional cigar, but after he was discovered unconscious and slumped over the iron front porch rail like a rag doll, he quit smoking them. His appetite remained strong, and Grandma still cooked solid meals complete with desserts for his undiminished sweet tooth. He drank coffee at his meals, and upon lowering his cup with trembling hands, winked at me and said, "This ... invigorates me, you know." Equally predictable would be Grandma's response as she placed the back of her hand next to her face in a confidential whisper. "It's decaffeinated, you know."

I carried around a lot of guilt and grief for not wanting to stay on the farm with Grandma and Grandpa. Even if I knew their moving to town would be best for everyone, I could not imagine trying to do that after a lifetime on the farm. As I returned to an apartment in Manhattan, Kansas, for my senior year at K-State, I found myself sliding downhill into serious, unprecedented depression. Alvin was gone, and with him, apparently any dream of being a farmer. No amount of hard work or selfless act of love could give my grandpa another sunny afternoon in the barnyard to chop weeds. For the first time in my life I carried a heaviness that I could not shake.

My girlfriend at the time, Missy, was relaxed and easy to be with. However, she was inexperienced in dealing with grief and just generally unavailable for me to talk with at any depth. So the sorrow and confusion turned in upon itself and roosted in my psyche. I knew I needed to talk to someone. Counseling would have saved me a lot of trouble; fear and resignation are lousy motivations, and clinging to a relationship that offered less than what I needed violated what my gut was telling me. But my head told me it probably was the best I would ever find, so I had better settle for it.

I diverted myself into my studies for my senior year at K-State. In a burst of determination one semester, I busted my tail and got straight As, the first time ever in my life. I told myself I would use my learning to fit into the world of agribusiness or banking after completing a degree in agricultural economics. My roommate, Randall, and I excitedly chattered about our future employment; we tossed around names like Purina Mills and Ciba-Geigy, and it made us feel like we could become important. Large-scale agribusiness looked like the place to be for an ambitious young man. It would have been an understandable choice to follow my father's path and work for a large corporation.

But much of me lagged behind in the memory of the dirt beneath my feet. My crushed hopes of farming began to stir again.

I admitted to no one, not my girlfriend and then fiancée, not even to myself, that there remained a hypnotic pull back to the soil. After a few airplane trips and interviews with Cargill and DeKalb, my secret prayer was answered: I found a job in the Republic County area as a direct feed salesman for Moorman Manufacturing Company. In May of 1978, I graduated with a BS in agricultural economics, got married to Missy, and we moved into a ramshackle house a mile south of Mahaska because the Cossaart farmhouse was being rented by another family until September. Missy and I raised a litter of Doberman puppies and had absolutely no idea what an adult relationship entailed.

I soon viewed the sales job as woefully uninspiring. It was a poorly paying affair, replete with moronic sales meetings and one hell of a lot of driving, as I spent my days zooming up and down gravel roads in my bantam-yellow Chevy LUV pickup truck, visiting other people's farms. I did chores and fieldwork for my own farming neighbors to supplement the meager sales commissions. Another sales job selling hog buildings, requiring more travel to areas several hundred miles out, filled up my next year and was even more of a drag and little money. I was constantly second-guessing my refusal to join the corporate world. Such a choice would no doubt be smiled upon by my dad, and that is one heck of a strong incentive. A job in agribusiness, complete with buttoned-up collar and tie, meant certain residence in a large metro area somewhere; ironically, there were very few opportunities out in the country. I tried to picture myself in the daily commute, jockeying for position on a metropolitan beltway, and shuddered. A song by The Police popped into my mind: Sting's shrill voice wails out, "Packed like lemmings into shiny me-tal BOX-es ... contestants in a su-i-ciii-dal raaace."

I quit the sales job and then worked for the "Alaskan Queen" in the southern reaches of Republic County, who needed a herdsman for her purebred Shorthorn cattle operation. She and her common-law husband had the best breeding cattle money could buy. Rita, her real name, retired after making a small fortune in the office supply business during the construction of the Alaskan pipeline. She moved back to the area of her childhood, about a thirty-mile drive from my place on the southern edge of Republic County, and bought several adjoining farms around an old stone flour mill, which she turned into a modest mansion.

As an employer, she was fair and paid well. On Friday afternoons she wrote out my paychecks, and the diamonds on her hands looked to be worth more than I could earn in a year. I don't know if it was her intention, but she resembled Katherine Hepburn: elegant, cool, intelligent. But always down-to-earth and sincere. I learned from Rita that even when you're rich, you can still be a nice person. I had worked a year for her when Russ Long approached me about a job.

Russ

———————

Russ Long was held in high respect for his honesty and successful farming methods. His crops always looked healthy and weed free. He drove decent cars, and his machinery was well maintained and current. The silhouette of his farmstead, with gleaming metal grain bins, a tall silo, and expansive feed yard, loomed a half mile away on the western horizon as something greater than ours. When Russ grudgingly gave his opinions on what wheat variety to plant, everybody shut up and listened. His timing, that critical and artful attribute so key in making crop production decisions, was right on the money most of the time, and the more jealous souls described it as luck. He was a big man, six foot three and perhaps 260 pounds, and was intensely energetic and nervous for a seventy-year-old. The thick hair on his head was black, with a little help from a bottle, combed back close to his scalp under a clean seed corn hat or a black felt hat on Sundays. He could be seen puffing on his pipe as he hustled into the post office, distracted and deep in thought, the gears in his head churning anxiously as he processed a solution to his latest challenge with growing grain crops. Despite his revered social and professional stature, he was bashful and had a comical clumsiness to him, and his reputation for distraction and dented fenders was well known. When I was twenty-four, he asked me to come and work for him and be his lone full-time hired hand. My mood turned meteoric. It was an honor and an opportunity to work with the best. I could also see in him a faint light of my dream that had been derailed by the death of his old friend, my uncle: the possibility of establishing my own farm operation.

My ambition to farm full time was a sleepless drive that never left my mind during the next few years. When I began the discussion with Russ, he verbally left the door open for a future buyout of his operation, and that was all I needed to commit to his offer. I had entertained the idea of becoming a lawyer, and Missy's hopes of finally leaving the area were buoyed with the idea of being married to an attorney. I even took the LSAT, the entrance exam, and did well enough to qualify for two different law schools in Nebraska. But as soon as Russ and I began talking, I threw the results in the trash. As far as I could see, the world needed no more lawyers. Time was a-wasting to get inside the cab of that nice new John Deere tractor.

In late summer 1978 Missy and I moved into my farmhouse after the renters moved out. She really didn't want to be married at all, but I tried to treat her like my dad treated Mom. We were pals. We had the same tastes in music. Living together out of wedlock in the farm community was unacceptable in those days, and since we didn't know what else to do, we entered the legal relationship like two wandering kids. She was beautiful, tall and slender, with a broad and easy smile, and eye-catching straight and brilliant blonde hair, bleached from summers spent riding her horse around the empty streets of Mahaska. She possessed an amazing two-handed set shot, far and away the star on the girls high school basketball team. Quiet and down-to-earth, she refused to wear makeup, and in my opinion didn't need to. Amidst our playing house for three years was a solid friendship, even as the undercurrents of her life's frustrations increased in volume. She wanted more than Mahaska could offer, and becoming a farmer's wife was her vision of a dead-end life. Her consumption of cheap canned beer increased as our time went on. Her eyes lit up in empathic joy when I described the possibility of farming with Russ, then suddenly turned to the floor in sorrow as she faced the incompatibility. I loved her, to the extent that was possible in my early twenties, but ultimately the truth surfaced: When given the excruciating choice between her and the farm, I chose the land and all that machinery. We split without any argument, legal or otherwise. Then, in the deathly quiet aftermath of the big house without her in it, I learned what a broken heart felt like. I quickly learned to keep in constant motion during the days with hard-driven physical work. But the nights became a never-ending search to fill empty space. A few beers in the evenings became a habit, and drinking alone became common. When I walked outside and peed in the front lawn, the night air and the billions of stars in the dome of black sky blanketed me with suffocating loneliness.

Best Friends

In 1980, Frank Fiser, pronounced FISH-er, was my best friend
and had been so from the time I began spending summers on
the farm. He lived across the one-mile-square section to the
south. Frank was a good-looking, energetic young farm kid with
a broad smile and sense of humor to match. He was a true country boy with a large intellect and an insatiable curiosity. As we
entered our adulthood, I came to love him like the brother I had
always wished for. He gleefully teased me about my urban upbringing; whenever a situation revealed my lack of experience
in rural life, he shook his head and gave me a mocking glance.
"City kid. Jeez..." We were often mistaken for brothers to the
casual acquaintance; the association flattered me.

Frank's dad was a hard-driving, fun-loving, full-blooded
Czech farmer. He worked incredibly hard at raising hogs and
grain crops, and he instilled in Frank a near-manic zest for life.
I admired his farming skills and ability to hold his money together, and he enjoyed life more than anyone I had met. Frank's
mom had the personality of sunshine; she wore a constant
smile while acting as a gracious recipient of her husband's

teasing and was so cute you just wanted to squeeze her like an adorable little doll. As a teenager, I soon developed my first crush on a middle-aged woman.

After Frank and his sister had both reached adulthood, Frank's parents moved to town and left the home place for Frank to live on and start his farming career. Frank lived by himself for a year while his future wife finished up her schooling at Manhattan. Much like Frank's mother, Donna was smart, pretty, hardworking, and a true friend. I would often ask myself why I could not have such luck as Frank, and as I grew to know them both, my admiration for the couple solidified. With the backing of his father, Frank began crop farming and raising hogs, and I spent a lot of time helping him set up the facilities and doing chores in the winter. After we stood as best men in each other's weddings, our wives carpooled on weekdays to their jobs thirty miles away. On the weekends we all partied together, went to dinner and movies, and explored old abandoned farmhouses in the area on Sunday afternoons, when us two farmers felt justified to quit working for a while.

One winter night Frank called up and suggested the four of us drive into town and see a movie. He and I were typically short on words in our conversations, and I answered, "Okay, see ya soon." We both hung up the phone, and both couples jumped into their respective cars and drove around the square-mile section to each other's houses. It was just after dark, and I could see headlights on the other side of the section piercing the endless Kansas sky, traveling in a direction that was a mirror image of ours. We had driven to each other's farmsteads, and at

Young Frank Fiser.

both locations, no one was home. So each of us turned around, backtracking around the section, and I could see the headlights across the section again, traveling the opposite direction. We each arrived again at our own homes. Shaking my head at the ridiculousness of the situation, I got out of the car and walked back into my house as the phone was ringing. I picked up the receiver, and the familiar voice on the other end was choking with laughter. "Okay ... who's going to drive?"

On a cold winter day while our wives were at work, Frank and I decided to have some fun after finishing his morning hog chores. The conditions were unusual: There was a six-inch-deep layer of snow on the ground, freshly fallen and undisturbed by the howling north wind that was sure to follow such a storm, which would inevitably scour the open areas bare and blow the snow into huge drifts. We took advantage of our rare sledding opportunity and improvised a saucer sled out of a damaged hog feeder lid, a perfectly smooth four-foot circle of sheet metal shaped like a giant dinner plate. We attached the lid to a long piece of rope and tied it to Frank's four-wheel-drive pickup truck. Somehow, I talked him into being the first passenger.

As I drove the pickup across the smooth ground adjacent to the house, I peered into the rearview mirror and decided that my friend's ride looked too easy. A frozen plowed field beckoned to me through the windshield. In the mirror Frank's eyes widened, and he began to shout something, which of course I pretended not to hear in the warm and quiet cab. As I bounced across the rough ground, my passenger and his sled were battered violently by the frozen dirt clods hammering away at his butt. He was being vibrated so hard that he could not hang on, and yet he could not gain enough stability to simply lean over and bail out. Frank looked like a piece of popcorn bouncing around on the bottom of a hot pan. After about forty-five seconds of the punishment, my conscience and a small remnant of sense overtook my laughter.

With gritted teeth, Frank stomped up to the truck and said, "Okay ... now your turn!" I jumped on the hog feeder lid and braced for the revenge. I will say one thing for Frank, he was creative. As I gamely hung on to the edges of the saucer, he drove the pickup slowly back across the smooth part of the field, lulling me into a false sense of assurance. Then he swung the pickup out onto the dirt road and accelerated toward the Rock Island train track crossing. The rail bed was banked up a good three feet higher than the dirt road, and the last thing I saw was the back axle of the pickup leaving the ground as Frank hit the ramp at about fifty miles an hour, a split second before the air caught the underside of the saucer and I took off like an airplane.

I recall seeing blue sky for a few seconds, a feeling of myself flying, and then a decisive pummeling of my body into a five-foot-deep snow bank. When I finally figured out which end of me was up, I wiped the snow off my face in time to see my friend's insane grin a few inches from my face. "Now *that* was *really* cool! Ya wanna do it again?"

We each had Doberman pinscher dogs. They were littermates, the last two that got too big to sell out of a litter of pups born a year before. My dog, Tyler, seemed to reflect my more laid-back personality, and Frank's dog, Nemo, was full of extra determination and free spirit like his owner. In those days it was a common practice to trim the floppy ears of Dobermans when they were puppies, brace them for a few weeks while they healed, and then remove the splint, standing the ears up permanently and giving the dog that traditional Doberman look. Frank left Nemo's splint on a few weeks too long, so his dog's ears not only stood up, but the tips actually crossed each other like a rabbit-eared TV antenna. It gave Nemo a goofy, almost alien look. The dog was famous for digging after rats that would burrow under the buildings with full commitment to his task, and Frank's various outbuildings were surrounded by large holes dug up by his singularly focused dog. The smallest building was a feed shed, a shabby little wooden structure the size of an outhouse. Nemo dug so long under it that it finally tipped over like a fallen tree. Incredibly, he even dug a large hole directly in the center of the gravel road in front of the farmstead that served effectively as a speed bump.

❊   ❊   ❊

One bitterly cold day during a low-level blizzard, I was enjoying a quiet morning in my own house while catching up on the news and sipping a cup of instant coffee. Frank burst through my kitchen door without so much as a knock and said through clenched teeth, "Gotta use yer phone." The look on his face told me to forgo any questions, so I just pointed to the rotary-dial telephone, which by that time he had already snatched off the receiver. He was standing on my linoleum kitchen floor, snow melting into a puddle surrounding his overboots, and the steam was rising off his sweat-soaked head. His dialing motion jerked the phone around on the table while I retreated to the living room and sat down to catch the weather forecast on TV. I figured he would tell me the story after he cooled off a bit.

Frank had traveled by tractor on a three-mile trip from his farm to Mahaska in order to purchase a trailer load of hog feed, which he needed to get back to his hungry animals in a hurry. He quickly returned with his load, only to find the tracks blocked by a locomotive engine, stopped dead center on the crossing and making it impossible to return to his farm. The Rock Island Railroad, once a proud passenger and freight train giant, had slowly decayed into near bankruptcy, and the haphazard scattering of rail cars and engines on the dilapidated rail bed had become commonplace by 1980. From our perspective, it looked like when lunchtime or a coffee break occurred, the demoralized employees simply shut down the engines wherever they sat at the time. Frank had crawled up onto the engine to find that nobody inside the locomotive would answer his furious pounding on the door. This was apparently the third time that week Frank had been detoured. He was in no mood to negotiate.

I didn't listen closely to the conversation, but evidently he got through to someone at the railroad. All I could make out was "...gonna pull that son of a bitch over with my tractor..." and with the size of the tractor, the degree of his anger, and his knowledge of cables and chains, he just may have been able to do so. Frank slammed down the receiver, gave me a very determined "Thanks!" and stomped down my sidewalk to his idling Allis-Chalmers tractor. He roared up my driveway, and a few minutes later I could see the profile of the locomotive, a mile in the distance, lurching ahead slowly as the diesel smoke poured out of the smokestack. His pigs were fed an hour later than usual that day, and his path was never blocked again.

In my ambition to farm I had envisioned my friend and me farming side by side as the years unfolded, trading chore work and swapping the use of equipment. We would mature and hold each other up as peers. His presence comprised the bulk of my social life. But unlike me, Frank had lived all his life on the farm, and after several years of getting paid pennies for sorting pigs and driving tractors, he decided that he wanted more than to fight the uphill economic battle that was required of a beginning farmer. He enrolled in school to become a machinist, and he and Donna moved to Salina, a fair-sized city about a hundred miles to the south. I understood his reasons and admired his courage to undergo a difficult change, and I supported him openly, all the while silently and selfishly hoping he would not go. He sold his machinery at auction on his farm, and I helped him move his possessions to the city on a warm autumn day. It truly broke my heart. After unloading the last of his furniture, it was a sad two-hour drive home. My friend and only true contemporary was now far away, and I could find no suitable substitute for him. Farm life became many degrees lonelier, especially after Missy had moved out. In a time and place where the young people were steadily moving away, winter afternoons turned noticeably colder, and I felt a thin slice had been cleaved off of my person. Frank and Donna's house remained empty for a few years, and I purposely avoided driving by it from that point on. Soon thereafter, Frank's dad had the house, tree windbreak, and outbuildings bulldozed under, and all that remained was some scattered rubble in the middle of a wheat field.

Russ, Continued

Russ Long's father went bankrupt during the Dirty Thirties, and the neighbors gathered for the public sheriff's sale of the bank's land collateral. Not uncommon at the time, the surrounding neighbors got together and collectively agreed not to bid. They let Russ buy it back for a minimum price. Russ gambled big in 1942 and planted fencerow-to-fencerow crops of corn, risky to grow in dry weather but of great yield potential. "If you don't sow," he once said with a spit of pipe tobacco, "you'll never reap."

Coming off of a ten-year drought, the skies abruptly opened up with abundance, the price of commodities spiked during World War II, and Russ harvested more corn than he knew what to do with. He piled it in enormous mounds out in the fields and ingeniously contracted with a struggling grain elevator company that was just starting out in business. They both made a lot of money that fall. From that point on, he was off and running in the farm business. Through the years he bought the most productive land and good machinery, worked smart as well as hard, and always kept up with the times.

Russ had a deserved reputation as a stickler for detail, and he was demanding and often impulsively difficult. I found this out quickly in the first few days I worked for him, but I had observed him for years as a close friend to my uncle Alvin, and I could look beyond his occasional odd screwups and constantly changing mind. At the time, my first marriage was recent history; Russ had been a widower for ten years or so. We slowly grew to enjoy each other's company, and he began taking me with him to socialize briefly on an errand to the grain elevator or the gas station; it felt good to be treated as a near equal among the other farmers. As a result, I worked hard and eagerly learned just how he did things. Russ respected my abilities and diligence, and he found it easier to drive to the county airport, fire up his Cessna 190 airplane, and fly off to visit his grown children in Kansas City or elsewhere while I stayed home and took care of the farm.

The small prop plane made the long trips across the flatlands quick and enjoyable for Russ. Unlike his car and pickup, the plane was meticulously maintained. If I ran out of things to do on rainy days, we would drive to Belleville where the hangar was and I would polish up the Cessna. A seasoned pilot, he loved to fly even more than he loved to drive the dirt roads and worry about his crops. On clear days my time was always taken up with the necessary fieldwork, and he was not instrument rated to fly in less favorable weather. So I never got the chance to go up in the air with him. Anyone who had ever flown with him reported an uncharacteristic calmness and confidence he practiced in no other area of his life. "That's the only place where

Russ is cool," Alvin once told me. On many Friday afternoons he would fly his plane over the farm as I was passing up and down the field in the tractor, swoop down to five hundred feet above me, tip the wings once as a salute, and disappear into the horizon.

He rarely drove a tractor. I always thought he was wise in hiring someone else to drive the tractors and thus minimize the repair bills. Fieldwork and driving grain trucks were left for the hired help, and Russ paced up and down the country roads in his pickup, monitoring conditions and stopping to bark instructions to me or whoever else was doing the work. His pickup truck had a mangled rear bumper and a driver-side door that couldn't be shut all the way; the hinges were sprung from colliding into a utility pole with the door open, and tobacco spit ran in stains down over the dents in the faded red door. I kept the tractor cabs vacuumed and the outsides washed, and at the rare times Russ would run a machine himself, I would shake my head in irritation at the mud and burnt pipe tobacco on the upholstery, marveling at how such an intelligent and ambitious fellow could be so incredibly careless.

Everyone had a Russ story, whether they had seen it firsthand or heard it from someone else. In the years when his oldest son was still on the farm, the two men had a dozen or so young heifer calves contained temporarily in an area of lush grass adjacent to the barnyard. A single-wire electric fence, powered by a car battery, was suspended two feet off the ground with flimsy steel posts that were pushed into the ground by hand. Electrical impulses coursed through a wire the diameter of a piece of spaghetti. Discovering that several animals had broken through the fenced area and were tromping down the tender young milo crop in the adjacent field, Russ burst from the barnyard and took chase through the rows of plants. As Russ shouted and waved his arms, the calves scattered in all directions as the big man churned through the muddy field, pipe stem still clenched firmly in his teeth. In his excited state, he forgot about the wire. The thin strand snared his boot, and he stumbled and landed heavily in the mud. The broken wire looped around his leg while a twelve-volt charge pulsated through his body at precise one-second intervals. "TURN OFF!!! ... THE SON!!! ... OF A BITCH!!!" he yelled at the sky as he lay in the mud, his body jerking with each shock. Twelve volts cannot deliver serious bodily harm to a big adult, but he was still pretty hotheaded long after someone switched off the power.

Even after only a few months of working with him, I grew wise enough to always park my pickup out of Russ's path. Certain that my small yellow Chevy LUV would be safe, I parked it off to the edge of the yard under a shade tree next to the fuel barrel. Sure enough, Russ hit the accelerator in reverse gear after he hurriedly jumped into his pickup truck. With the tailgate left thoughtlessly down, he backed up without looking and speared the back of my innocent little truck with a direct hit. I watched it happen and could not believe the odds he had defied in the space of the huge barnyard. Sputtering and cursing, he leaped out of his pickup after hearing the bang behind him. "Well, damn it, you'll have to go and get that thing fixed," he blurted, as if ordering me to do yet another task. His demanding yell disguised his embarrassment, but my response surprised him and myself as well. *"The hell I will!"* I shouted a foot from his face. *"YOU'LL go get it fixed."* From then on, we seemed to be on more equal footing.

Despite his type A personality, he could be a real softy. I still carried a lot of gratitude from his encouragement a few years prior, when I'd planted my first crop without Alvin around. On any given Sunday one could look down the side street in Mahaska and see Russ dressed in a suit, taking his ninety-year-old widowed mother by the arm and escorting her to his car, and they would both go to church. His tough exterior belied a generously charitable side and a kindness to all. I cannot recall him ever saying anything demeaning about anyone. Beneath Russ was a bedrock of optimism and positive energy. His favorite conversation filler was, "Well, it's a fine old world, don't ya think?"

One time during wheat planting, it began to drizzle lightly as I was finishing some fieldwork on an open-air tractor, and Russ walked an eighth of a mile out into the field. I pulled to a stop and wondered what he wanted. I jumped down from the seat, and I told him I wanted to finish the small area that was left. He nodded in silence, took off his coat and hat, wrapped the coat around me like a child, and smashed the cap over my head. He looked off into space. "Well, that's fine," he snorted, "but it's gettin' wet out here." He turned and slowly walked back across the field to his pickup, and by the time he got to it, he was soaked and cold. I was warm and dry.

Russ suffered a mild heart attack a year after I began working for him. Predictably impulsive, he surprised me one day by bursting into the shop after a visit to his physician. "What'll you buy me out for?" he boomed without preface. As time passed and rationality returned to his thoughts, we crafted a purchase agreement of his machinery and a verbal promise to lease all his lands to me. Now *this* was the chance to farm on a level that would constitute a full-time occupation. I was flattered by his faith in my abilities, and although I was lacking in experience at running such a large operation, I eagerly embraced the idea, knowing that Russ wouldn't go far without giving any necessary guidance.

I was deeply moved upon discovering Russ had turned down several offers to lease his land to other, more experienced farmers. The competition for prime farmland was fierce, and in order to keep the social pressure off of him and me both, he kept our plans under his hat for almost a year. My desperately needed capital from the Farmer's Home Administration, the only source of financing available to a beginning farmer, was held up by the usual government budget wrangling and a regional director who was a real stinker for paperwork details. In 1980 the prime rate was hovering around a barely believable 20 percent, and the only viable option for financing was the FmHA, which charged 7 percent to a beginning farmer. September arrived, and it was time to plant wheat. Russ was chomping at the bit, as always, but seemingly more so about my first crop. One afternoon he drove fifty miles to Concordia and thundered into the FmHA office, pounded his palm on the counter, and told the director to "get off his ass and get the young man his money." When that yielded nothing, Russ went ahead and purchased all the needed inputs of fertilizer, fuel, and seed—roughly twenty-five thousand dollars in 1981—on his retail accounts, and let me use the machinery for nothing. When my line of credit finally arrived, he quietly turned all his open accounts over to my name, and with a loud voice, instructed the vendors in no uncertain terms to listen to me from then on. By the time most had learned of the change in operators, my crops were growing in the ground and were halfway to harvest. A few neighbors who had been kissing up to Russ for years in expectation of his retirement were very disappointed.

Russ had a hard time relinquishing control of something he had done so well for fifty years. One of our more colorful arguments happened out in the middle of a sixty-acre wheat field, with an idling tractor as background noise and a final scream from me, "*Dammit, Russ! Which one of us is retired?*" He stomped off, spitting and cursing under his breath. But if I was patient enough to let it pass, he usually apologized the next day after realizing he'd overstepped his bounds. Ironically, he now began to put in more time driving the tractor for me than I had ever known him to. If he had trouble sleeping, I would find out the next day: Many more acres had been covered by the tillage equipment in the middle of the night. And he didn't seem to make as big a mess of the cab interior.

It was a difficult spring to plant the crops; the unusually wet weather delays drove me stir-crazy as we would stand by the tractor and planter in the shop and look out at the unceasing and steady rain. My sister, Judy, was midway through her college career, and I talked her into coming to the farm for the summer and helping me out. She became my full-time hired man, and, after a few scary moments as I first watched her pilot the large John Deere, soon became one hell of a tractor driver. We bonded in our first opportunity to work together as adults; she rose to the occasion and did every task I assigned her. The crops were put in the ground in a timely fashion, and Judy's sense of humor often helped bounce me out of my worrisome funks. And it was good to have another human in the big house.

Dad showed up for wheat harvest, which was to become an annual job for him for the next several years. He drove my big two-ton grain truck, a 1959 GMC with a Pontiac V-8 engine and an oversized carburetor, and for extra challenges, it had a split-shift axle and absolutely no power steering. On two separate occasions I was off with my timing of the distributor spark, and the backfire blew open the muffler like a tin can. When timed correctly, it ran flawlessly and roared like a hot rod. Wheat harvest went on for about ten days, hopefully without a rain, just before or during the Fourth of July holiday when it is generally hotter than hell. Dad put a lot of heart into the task, and he never got paid for putting in long hours at such a hot, dirty, and noisy job. After a few short lessons he quickly mastered the old beast, and he certainly didn't let any grass grow under the wheels as he shuttled my full loads of wheat to the grain elevator in Mahaska. During good cutting days, I would thrash away with the twenty-foot combine until about ten o'clock at night, when the dew would begin to settle out of the atmosphere and

The combine.

make the straw too tough for the machine to handle. We were often the last load dumped; the elevator guys would be anxious to close down the scales but would dutifully wait to hear Dad coming from off in the distance. "We could hear Raleigh comin' with a load on that truck of yours," one of the guys told me after harvest was over. "He'd turn out of the field onto the highway, and we could hear him puttin' the hammer to it, I'll tell ya."

I had a fifteen-year-old boy named Jon helping me do some tractor work now and then, especially if there was tillage needing to be done while Dad and I were busy combining wheat. Jon was a mouthy and headstrong kid, and he was full of eagerness to operate the big machinery. I was teaching him to dump grain from the combine into the large truck that Dad drove. Dad sat on the cab roof of the old truck for a clearer view as Jon sat in the operator's seat of the combine and cautiously drove the machine forward. I moved out of the operator's seat and watched closely as Jon eased the hydrostat lever forward. He flipped a switch and the ten-inch-diameter dump auger poured a waterfall of golden grain, falling eight feet vertically and pounding the wooden bottom of the truck box. A jittery Jon pushed the lever a little too far, and the auger spout jerked to a stop directly over Dad's head. The grain fell heavily over Dad's body for about ten seconds as Jon fumbled with the lever. I intervened and pulled the lever back, and Dad jump to his feet on the roof of the truck, shaking grain out of his underwear. Jon got on his nerves already, and that sure didn't help things.

Several days later Dad got his revenge. I sent Jon and Dad out to fuel up the large tillage tractor one morning while I was doing daily maintenance on the combine. I had a one-hundred-gallon fuel barrel in the back of the pickup to refuel tractors in the field, and it had an old hand pump as a means to force the diesel fuel through a hose that was about twice the diameter of a garden hose. Jon was holding the nozzle into the open fuel tank on the tractor while Dad powered the pump with back-and-forth motions. Jon said, "Stop," as he began pulling the nozzle out of the tank opening. Dad gave the pump another half-stroke, and Jon was showered with a half gallon of number two diesel fuel from head to toe. It's pretty skunky stuff, so he dashed off to his house in Mahaska to take a thorough shower. Nonetheless, he stank for days. Dad said it was an accident, and while ordinarily I knew him to be an honest guy, his grin gave him away.

History repeated itself in Russ's presence. The fall of 1982 was a record-breaking, "bin-busting" year for my first grain sorghum and soybean crops. The huge cash inflow enabled me to pay large amounts of overdue debt, and I was suddenly established as a successful young farmer in the area. On a visit to the local coffee shop, Russ and I walked in and heard, "Hey, there's Jim Cossaart and his hired man, Russ Long!" Russ grinned silently, and I felt like a big shot.

Dignity

Once or twice per year Ruby and Wilbur brought Grandpa and Grandma up from Wichita and to the farm, usually for family reunions or funerals. The last trip of Grandpa's life was to attend the funeral of his sister-in-law, my Great-Aunt Bertha and Grandpa's brother Leslie's wife of sixty-two years. Grandpa was so frail at the time that it required a person under each of his armpits to support his weight as he walked. And walk he did, with determination and nonchalance that would make onlookers stop and gasp. My uncle Wilbur and I provided the support as we guided him up the sidewalk toward the church in Mahaska. The pastor stood at the entrance and smiled broadly. "It's so good to see you here, Mr. Cossaart." Grandpa had made eye contact with him a few steps prior to his greeting as we all negotiated the short stairs. His mind and humor still sharp, he acknowledged the Presbyterian minister's welcome with a crisp "thank you" and shouted loud enough for the people sitting in the pews to hear, "I've always said it takes two men and a boy to get me into one of these places!"

A month later I drove down to Wichita and shared a secret with my grandmother. I had agreed to purchase Russ Long's equipment, and he had quietly rented all his farmland to me. The verbal agreement was made while I was waiting on huge sums of borrowed operating capital from the government, and I was nervous about letting the word out for fear that some more competitive neighbor would offer Russ a better deal. It was a dream come true for me—the chance to farm that I thought I had lost forever—and I wanted to share my good news with Grandpa while he could still hear it. Despite Alvin's death, a Cossaart would continue on with the farming tradition.

"Oh, I don't think that would be a good idea, dear," Grandma cautioned. "He has been so confused and weak lately, I just don't want you to say anything that might upset him. Please be still about it." I nodded in agreement. Grandpa sat silently in his overstuffed chair, dressed in clean overalls and a faded button-down denim shirt, just as he did on the farm on Sundays. He slipped in and out of a doze. His lucidity was diminishing by the day. Grandma went next door to borrow some cooking ingredient while I sat with Grandpa in the living room.

I listened to the door slam shut as she left and wasted no time. "*Grandpa!*" I shouted at his face. "I am going to *farm*. All of Russ Long's ground and the Henderson half section too. I am going to be a *good* farmer, just like you!" He snapped to attention, placed his hands upon the arms of the big chair, and leaned forward. Looking directly into my eyes and smiling in gratitude, he spoke clearly. "How about that! Well, it was always a good life for me. I wish you luck. That's just great, Jimmy." He

Grandpa at ninety-three.

leaned back into his chair again, where a smile remained on his face as he drifted off to sleep once more.

My sister Jean also lived in the Wichita area and gave birth to a son, Cory, a few weeks later. When the baby was several days old, she brought him over to my grandparents' house. As Grandpa sat quietly in his living room chair, my sister asked him if he would like to hold her baby. Grandpa brightened momentarily as the infant was placed in his lap. His eyes widened with amazement as he gazed at the sleeping baby. Two identical tears ran down his wrinkled and shaking face as he looked up at Grandma. "Mama!" he shouted in hoarse whisper. "Isn't he a *dandy!*"

Several days later Reuben Comfort Cossaart died peacefully in the night at the age of ninety-four. He made his final trip to the church in Mahaska, and I watched my own father's face smile with pain as he waved his hand and said softly, "See ya, Dad..."as the two undertakers closed the casket. Grandpa was buried next to Alvin in the prairie cemetery in the same township in which they had both been born.

I have a picture that has been on the wall of whatever dwelling I have lived in. The five-year-old boy that was once me is sitting on Grandpa's lap, both of us sharing the seat of the old Farmall H tractor, on the farm that eventually was passed on to my care. His battered corn knife hangs on the wall of my garage. His old oak rocking chair rests in my living room now. When I get agitated or worried, it helps to sit in that chair.

Part-time Job

In late fall, after a tremendous harvest, the grain bins were full of soybeans and grain sorghum, and my first hard red winter wheat crop—five hundred acres of it—was safely planted in the ground, asleep in winter dormancy and patiently awaiting the coming spring rains. I cleaned, painted, and repaired until Russ's farmyard looked like a showplace. Equipment was washed and parked in neat order in the machine shed. Scattered piles of junk were cleaned up, brush and trees trimmed, and the shop was organized and tidy. It was a happy time; I had never seen Russ so unburdened, and I had never felt such optimism and energy since Alvin's death. The farming work was finished for the winter, and I found seasonal employment working for Harry the blacksmith and his son, Carl, in Hubbell, while Russ was free to fly his airplane more. As the winter days grew short, I began to work every weekday and Saturday fixing chain saws and working in the sawmill at the blacksmith shop. At the end of the day, I would drive home after dark, weary from the hard labor, and pass Russ's house. If his kitchen light was on, he was gone somewhere. If the living room window was illuminated, that meant he was home. I often stopped in and chatted for a few minutes as he sat in his recliner, smoked his pipe, and happily read from a stack of Zane Grey novels.

Alvin used to have enough cattle to keep him busy in the winter and was financially secure enough to not require supplementing his income. Russ worked part-time in his earlier years, farmed large acreages when near retirement, and spent his winters relaxing and traveling. I had to work hard to survive the winter, and the job in Hubbell was the best I could find. It sometimes struck me as perverse that I had borrowed and sunk the equivalent of a year's salary, twenty thousand dollars, into the soil a few months prior for my growing wheat crop, yet I needed to work an exhausting minimum-wage job to cover my meager living expenses. Farms all around me, as well as across the farm belt, just kept getting larger and larger; the capital requirements, mostly borrowed sources, kept rising as well. Yet at the same time the thin income margin kept shrinking. Other farmers and I often shared a joke: If the trend continued, someday only two guys would be farming all of Nebraska and Kansas, and their wives would have to work in town so they could buy health insurance.

✻   ✻   ✻

I was sorting the inventory of nuts and bolts for Carl, and Harry was busy working on his baler. I watched him patiently for a time and resisted the temptation to interfere with the repair process, but he was fumbling repeatedly with a small bolt. Finally he noticed me standing a few feet away and looking over

Harry in the sawmill.

his shoulder. "Here, dammit!" he shouted to me over the noise of the accompanying tractor. "You got little hands like a woman; see if you can get this bolt to go in..." It was a plea for help disguised as an insult. It was also a veiled admission of the facts: His two hands were grotesquely disfigured. A thumb and one index finger made up one hand, and a thumb with half of the first finger, plus a full second finger, made the other. There were no third and fourth digits on either hand. Huge opaque and fleshy scars covered the backs of both hands. They looked bizarre, scary even. Despite all the damage done, Harry still had a powerful grip. He usually avoided handshakes, but when he did participate in the custom, it was with gusto, and the strange feel of his grip startled anyone meeting his acquaintance. He took great delight in watching people recoil.

Harry loved machinery of any type, and he spent a great deal of time on the finer adjustments. "Listen to that!" he yelled over the quiet clatter of the baler as it went through its process. "If you get 'em timed just right, they sound nice and smooth, like sewing machines." The greater the mystery and complexity of an item of farm machinery, the more loving attention his analytical mind gave it. The type of machine that would leave most owners stymied with frustration fascinated Harry. In his many years of using and repairing farm machinery, he could always get two types of machines to run well—hay balers and corn pickers.

He was a hardened man who rarely displayed affection or concern. But one winter day, a half-inch of the tip of my right second finger was cut off by a spinning pulley and fan belt on an engine—an absent-minded mistake that resulted in a goofy-looking fingernail that still gets in the way of decent guitar-picking technique. I showed my newly shortened and bandaged finger to Harry with my story. His words came out softly. "Hey, now." He put his arm around my shoulders, and his cataract gaze found its way into mine. "You gotta take good care of those hands of yours, young fella."

Before the development of the modern combine harvesters that fully processed standing corn crops into grain, corn pickers were commonly used. A corn picker is powered and pulled down the rows with a tractor at harvest time. Alternating steel fingers snatch the dried plant into the machine and twisting barbed-steel rollers rip the ears off the stalk, stripping the leaves off of the cob. While the machine is operating, there is a real hazard of getting loose clothing caught up into the mechanism, and as long as the machine runs, it will keep tearing away at whatever is being fed into it.

One day in 1965 Harry had been making adjustments to a running corn picker in the yard outside of his shop. He got his right work glove caught in the gatherers as he tried to free a wad of material from the pickup mechanism. Reaching to pull his ensnared hand out, he suddenly found both of his hands sucked into the machine, and the mechanical beast ground away at them without mercy.

He was able to yell for help, and someone finally ran over to stop the machine. Several men pried with crowbars and pipe wrenches, taking clear instructions from a still-conscious Harry, who was the one that kept the others calm. After thirty minutes of effort, they pulled his mangled arms from the corn picker. Two of the men took off their shirts and wrapped his hands as they carried him into the back seat of a car. They sped to the hospital, a full twenty miles away, as Harry bled profusely. "Dumb-like," he recollected to me, "I put my arms down in my lap. If I would have held them up, then maybe I wouldn't have lost so much blood." He was unconscious by the time they carried him into the emergency room.

He was treated for shock and blood loss and then transferred to Kansas University Medical Center in Kansas City the following day. He underwent what limited repair they could perform on his hands, and the skin-grafting process was excruciating, even for a toughened workingman. He pointed to his crotch area and recalled with tightly closed eyes, "When they pulled that skin off the insides of my legs... well, if I hadn't a-been strapped down, I would-a run from that hospital and just ... kept on a-goin'." After a month of surgeries and lying on his back in the hospital bed, he came home and could be seen sitting on a chair in the shop, work boots on bare legs spread wide, still wearing a hospital gown. His arms were wrapped in huge billowing bandages as, day after day, he had his wife drive him to the shop, where he sat off to the side of the working area, mute and staring into space. He acknowledged only the most persistent greetings of old friends and customers with expressionless grunts. For four weeks he sat silent, consumed in his deepening depression.

One day, to everyone's astonishment, he broke his silence and made a rare request of his son, who was taking a break from his own repair work. Harry instructed him to peel away at the huge bandages with scissors and cut a hole so each working thumb could escape out of the wrappings. He sat down again, and for the next hour intently manipulated both of his thumbs like the wings of an awakening butterfly. "Now," he instructed Carl, "go wheel that cuttin' torch over by that son of a bitch and set a chair by it. Light it and turn the flame up good and hot."

Over the next two weeks, Harry exacted his revenge upon the evil monster of steel that had taken his fingers and nearly his life. He clumsily but meticulously dismembered every iron component of the corn picker into several hundred small pieces, and with the acetylene cutting torch he carved out ragged chunks of sheet metal and iron into sizes no larger than dinner plates. His white bandages grew dark with soot and molten metal slag. He began taking occasional breaks and waddled across the street to the tavern for coffee and renewed conversation as the pile of iron pieces grew larger, and Harry's mood brightened with each day of labor. The small mound of scrap metal rusted further with each rainstorm and lay untouched for many years thereafter. At sixty years of age, Harry made his hands work again and had returned to reign as a fully functional blacksmith and welder. The tragedy he endured probably would have killed most men, and the devastation to the most critical parts of a workingman would have emotionally broken anyone else. It just seemed to make him stronger. He rejoined the process of living and continued to enjoy his work well into his eighties. Whenever anyone would ask how his hands were feeling, Harry would reply, "Goddam' thing won't hurt nobody now!" and he would point with his remodeled hand to the pitiful-looking pile of rusted scrap iron across the street.

Again

At Christmas Russ was concerned that I would spend the holiday alone and offered to take me to Kansas City with him. I declined and told him I needed to drive out to Indiana and spend the holidays with my parents. Since Alvin's death, I had existed in a constant state of mild depression that had never been properly dealt with. It was taking hold with even greater force leading up to the holidays. I went to Blue Valley Behavioral Clinic in Fairbury and talked with an impatient and half-interested staff psychologist. He prescribed a daily dose of an antidepressant. It helped a little.

It was a miserably long car ride on my way to Indiana, but it helped to have my dog, Tyler, along. I-70 was walloped with a snowstorm through Missouri and part of Illinois, and what would have taken sixteen hours in good weather turned into a thirty-hour trip through foot-deep snow and black ice. Most of the time I was going thirty miles an hour, following someone else's bumper and tire tracks through the deep snow.

I had lots of time to think. A favorite piece of music by Dan Fogelberg was in the cassette player, and some haunting words came from the speakers accompanied by rich and dramatic orchestration: "...And where do you go when you get to the end of your dream?" Farming was glorious; a goal that once seemed so far off and formidable had suddenly been fully attained. But after the tractor was shut off and the sun went down, it got very quiet. The easy company of my first wife was gone. Family members who had helped me hold the farm tradition together after Alvin's passing reappeared for short visits now and then but soon retreated back to their urban lives. My best friend had given up farming and moved a hundred miles away, and now my nearest young contemporary lived six miles north, and the self-centered bachelor could only be tolerated for a few hours at a time. I lived in a cavernous two-story farmhouse with no one around but my dog. At times a few tightly held tears dropped to the soil as I paused to survey the moonless Kansas night sky. But I made myself feel better with the fact that Russ was around for friendship and guidance.

Upon arriving at my folks' place, I rested for a day, and on the night before Christmas Eve, I went out to visit my old high school friends. It pretty well confirmed what I had suspected before leaving my parents' house that night: I no longer had much in common with them. My attempts at conversation with my pals elicited a lot of blank stares. I wasn't the same, they insisted. I could overhear side conversations about my concussion and behavioral changes. I walked out into the chilly suburban Indiana night feeling glum. This was no longer home, and my friends all looked like a bunch of shallow, city dumb asses.

When I got back to Dad and Mom's house, Mom met me with a frown as I opened the front door. "Your dad has some bad news for you." I walked into the family room and could see Dad with his back toward me—sobbing in the corner, something I had never seen in my entire life. He faced me and choked between words as I fell headlong into the dark void of a dream: "Russ Long crashed his plane and was killed."

Apparently Russ flew into some thick fog while fighting off engine trouble. It was speculated he was searching for a landing strip close to that area on a path he had flown so often. Another pilot told me that if thick fog is encountered and you don't have instruments to tell you, you can't tell up from down. The impact and fire burned Russ's body beyond recognition, and Christmas presents were found scattered far from the wreckage. One of them was for me. The day after Christmas, I boarded a flight to Kansas City that Dad had arranged. I landed at a snowy Kansas City airport, rented a car, and drove back to my farmhouse.

I left Tyler back in Indiana, so the cold farmhouse felt even lonelier. I hastily showered and dressed in my church clothes. I drove up to the Presbyterian Church in Mahaska, a place that held warm memories of sitting side by side with my grandmother during church service when I was a teenager, and the site of my informal and quick marriage to Missy. As I pulled my rental car into a parking space in front of the church, I got out and met an older couple, Victor and Leah Wall, who owned a large piece of prime farm ground that Russ had rented for many years. They were my new landlords.

Vic and Leah had known Russ since childhood, and they often gave me kind advice over the phone on how to deal with his strong personality. They had become my good friends in short order, and visits to discuss farm business at their place in Clay Center, Kansas, were always a pleasure. Vic was the son of the local doctor in Mahaska, when there was still a doctor in town, and my father would hitch a ride in Vic's brand-new 1940 Chevrolet car when they both traveled to college.

My father elected to delay his college entrance by one year, raising hogs with his brother Alvin to make some quick money, which they didn't, and also working as a temporary hired man for Russ Long. Dad told me of driving tractors for Russ on one side of the road, while his own father was working with horses on the other side. Dad's one-year delay effectively put off his active military service until after the Japanese surrender.

My association with Vic and Leah had renewed their communication with Dad, and often the subject of conversation was me. Having my dad's old high school friends keeping tabs on me had a nice feel to it. As I struggled with starting up my farm business, and sometimes struggled with Russ, they had been like an extra set of parents. In the front yard of the church I fell into their arms like a child and wept. "I just don't get it..." I sobbed repeatedly.

I turned to the local minister in the search of some comforting words. "Tom, I'll be damned if I understand the reason for this." He looked at me with a determined expression and did his best impersonation of reassurance. "I can't tell you, Jim, but I know God has a plan. He has a plan." I appreciated the effort, but I really didn't want to hear about any damn plan. The words rang as hollow as a casual good-bye. Sitting in the crowded little church, I listened to the out-of-tune organ play and felt like an orphan. Again.

I stayed for the post-funeral dinner served for families and friends by the church women's group, shook hands and did the usual funeral socializing thing, and felt numb to the core in my sport coat and tie. I checked on my farmhouse and made arrangements with some friends to look after the place. The next day I made the return flight to Indiana and spent a few somber days with my parents. But I needed to get back, and I left their comfort to drive the eight hundred miles back to my farm.

The winter sunset came early on my first day home, and after doing my evening feeding chores, I jumped into my pickup to go get some supper in Hubbell. I turned out onto the gravel road and up the slow rise a half mile to the west and, out of habit, glanced a quarter-mile north to see if Russ's kitchen light was on. At that instant it felt as if a fully loaded grain truck hit me head on. I pulled my pickup to a stop in the middle of the gravel road and wept a rainstorm.

Russ had two children who were both past forty at the time of his death. A year or so prior to my appearance on the Long farm, Russ's daughter and her husband had lived with Russ for several years and farmed with him in a loose partnership. It worked reasonably well, but then they had a child with special needs and moved to suburban Kansas City, where Russ could fly and visit them on weekends. Russ's daughter was always warm and supportive, and when we were neighbors, I would occasionally coax her husband, Bill, out of the house to share a few beers in Hubbell. It was Bill's daughter from his first marriage who had caught my attention as a teenager when Grandpa asked about my ripped blue jeans. Bill was one of the nicest people I had ever met, and we shared the odd commonality of being former city boys.

Russ's son had tried to farm with him many years before I arrived on the scene, and Sam had an ego the size of his huge buckskin Stetson cowboy hat. His propensity for big dreams and impulsive spirit had cost Russ dearly in terms of dollars and mental anguish. After several financial disasters from which Russ bailed him out, and the expected tension of a father and son doing business together, Sam moved away to western Kansas and found employment as a cattle buyer in one of the region's enormous cattle-feeding operations. Russ never spoke ill of his son's travails, but the tales of deals gone sour were local legend. Everyone who was around at the time had a tale to tell about the red-headed cowboy with the big ideas.

Even as we were burying Russ, I could feel the family dynamics at work and the power begin to shift. I could see Russ's kind and sad eyes in all three of them as we shook hands. "Russ thought a lot of you, Jimmy," his daughter, Eleanor, said to me. Her husband, Bill, added, "He sure told us about all the wonderful things you did." He chuckled, "That's sure a lot more than any of us ever got out of him." But I soon felt a faint shadow of jealousy and bitterness in the son's stare, and his new presence left me feeling uneasy.

Less than two months after the burial, Sam showed up in my living room one day with a proposal. Three semitrailer loads of young cattle would be trucked in and, over the period of ninety days, placed out in two of the large fields of growing winter wheat that I rented from Russ. Instead of allowing the crop to mature and be harvested as low-price-per-bushel grain in July, the cattle would graze on the lush, growing wheat, and this new landlord and I would share in the proceeds of the weight gain. The USDA would pay landlord and tenant a modest amount for effectively destroying the crop so as not to add to the already bulging national surplus of wheat. Sam's utilization of the growing wheat crop to produce beef was not an outlandish idea by any means, but the work and worry of keeping the cattle contained in the fields, watered and otherwise cared for, would fall entirely on my shoulders. Sam owned the cattle and administrated Russ's estate as well, but he lived five hours away in the western Kansas town of Larned. The income from the weight gain wasn't a great deal more than keeping them off and just harvesting the grain. But I had to go along with it. And he knew that.

At the time I had about twenty cows out in my pasture, and most of the season they pretty much took care of themselves. They were the same familiar group, year after year, and came to know me as the source of their food. Brood cows, especially mine, are docile and easily contained behind a modest barbed-wire fence. They require a minimum of attention, especially when there is plenty of grass to eat in the growing season. After a while they all become like a bunch of large pets. New cattle, young and confused, brought in for one-time grazing periods are a whole different story.

Two hundred and four six-hundred-pound heifers, arrived one afternoon. They were packed like sardines and terrified from a three-hundred-mile trip from a western Kansas feedlot, and they exploded out of the banging aluminum semitrailers amidst shouts from three cowboys on horses. Cattle scattered in all directions in the muddy seventy-five-acre wheat field, and the only thing keeping my responsibility from disappearing to the four corners of Kansas was a thin single-strand electric fence wire and some very good cowboys on speedy horses. I looked on in horror and cursed the Lord and Russ for flying his damn plane into the ground.

Thank God for the horses and cowboys, who circled and contained the animals until they calmed down a bit and coalesced into herd behavior on the lush, growing wheat field. The cowboys tipped their hats, loaded up their horses, and were gone. From that point forward, it was my job to make sure all those heifers stayed within their confines and had enough water: Eight gallons per head per day amounted to a daily three-mile haul of just over sixteen hundred gallons to be poured into two gigantic metal tanks out in the field. The sympathetic neighbors helped round up the few strays that would get out on occasion and didn't seem to get too upset with me, even though it was leading up to planting season and they certainly had better things to do.

After six long weeks of lousy sleep, four semis showed up one day with the same cowboys, and they rounded up and loaded the calves. They were trucked back to the feedlot in western Kansas. I got paid 40 percent on the gain that the animals put on during their brief stay; I had no idea if I had been cut a fair deal or not, since they were weighed under the auspices of a red-headed cowboy. I was just glad it was over with.

The spring crops were planted with a dark cloud of emotion parked over my head; it was the first time I had put a crop in the ground without Russ hovering about. The weather cooperated and the crops grew well, but as they matured Sam seemed to find more reasons to frown during his unannounced visits as he and I looked out across the fields. It was about mid-August when he told me that my lease on Russ's former farm ground was to be terminated. It was a crippling blow to my business and a blind-side shot to my young psyche. I found an obscure law about landlord-tenant relations that required him to pay me several thousand dollars for the severance, but it was pretty meager compensation. Since Russ's death I had carried a bit of empathy for his son; reading between the lines led me to think there was much left unresolved between Sam and Russ and taking control of his father's holdings dulled the grief. The bitterness took control in my final verbal exchange with Sam, however. "I bet your daddy is real proud of you now," I sneered, as he donned his Stetson and got into his big fancy pickup truck. He looked like he was going to jump back out and take a swing at me, so I figured I hit a nerve.

The three universal human motives of greed, lust, and greed showed up right on schedule. Russ's ground was immediately leased by a large and heavily capitalized operation owned by a middle-aged couple with influential political connections, about the age of Russ's son. The woman was a flashy blonde in skin-tight blue jeans who struck a high profile in the area and had a history of great friendship with the big cowboy. Again, the community was sympathetic. "Jimmy, you ain't got the proper plumbing to compete with *her*." Gleaming new John Deere tractors and combines paraded through Russ's fields in the next growing season as I drove to and from my remaining lands.

Carl

_____

As the winter approached, once again I went to work for Harry and his son, Carl. Carl was the one I usually worked for, as he ran his own welding and repair business in the same shop with his dad. Several years earlier, he had left me with quite a first impression.

Carl sometimes worked in the evenings at Swede's, the tavern across the street from the blacksmith shop. The town of Hubbell had roughly one hundred official residents, yet in a rural region with so much distance between small towns it drew a lot from the surrounding area. People would come from a long ways to eat or have a drink at Swede's, and no more so than during a Saturday night dance.

Swede's catered to all ages old enough to drink, and since the 1940s, the little tavern in Hubbell had been the place to party. Until the '70s and the acceptance of "country rock," most celebrations were Saturday night dances with regional polka bands furnishing the music. The most memorable name recalled from the polka genre was "Bob Blecha and the Bouncing Czechs." But by the time I was old enough to drink, polka music was infrequent and the dancers were usually moving to rock-and-roll standards.

Many families in the area were first-generation descendants of immigrants who funneled through Ellis Island after leaving their homeland surrounding the present-day Czech Republic. During the settlement of the region, they coalesced in small and cohesive communities scattered across Nebraska and Kansas. "Bohemians," they called themselves. The middle-aged adults that I knew spoke fluent American but with occasional and amusing butchering of the King's English. Their humor was full of self-deprecation. Czechs always told the funniest Bohemian jokes: When the pickup truck full of Bohemians drove into the lake, why did the ones riding in the back drown? They couldn't get the tailgate down. Why do Bohemian farmers like the old two-cylinder John Deere tractors? They like the rhythm, "oomp-pop-pop, oomp-pop-pop." Our regional Czechs seemed to share a propensity for drinking too much alcohol, almost as if it were a directive handed down through the generations. Drinking was not only tolerated but even encouraged for adolescents. It was not unusual to see a young teen of Czech descent openly tipping up a can of Coors, often in the company of their parents. It was just understood that if you were born a Bohemian, you drank beer. "Pevo" was the Czech word for it, a term still used proudly by the second generation. Alcohol use was high in the area, and Hubbell and its bar was the location for a good old-fashioned beer blowout about every month in the summer and fall. After wheat harvest was over around the Fourth of July, the party was huge. An observer walking through

Hubbell at dawn the next day would find a thick smattering of crushed, empty beer cans strewn across the pavement, and no one seemed to be embarrassed about it.

Now and then a fight would break out between two young men, usually fairly harmless stuff over a young woman and fueled by the predictable combination of testosterone and alcohol. Usually this was settled out in the back alley or in the street out in front of the bar if the participants were looking for an audience. When any sort of trouble happened in the bar, a code was generally honored by the combatants to not damage bystanders, tables, or wall fixtures and to take the debate outside.

To say Carl was big and strong would be understating things. He was the only child of Harry's second marriage and had inherited his strength and size from both parents. Carl was six feet five inches tall and carried about 280 pounds of muscle. He was loud and very good-natured; his high voice would bark out greetings and questions that would startle his friends and downright terrify strangers. I was grateful that such a large man was blessed with such a friendly demeanor. He worked hard, and he looked like he did. As he came of age, his skill as a welder put him in high demand for erecting grain systems, building iron feedlot fences, and repairing farm equipment in the field with his portable welder. His strength was evident even back in high school, and I have vivid memories of driving past the football field in the fall and hearing the coach yelling, "For God's sake, Stradley! Don't *kill* him!" A friend of mine witnessed Carl break a mounted bench vise with his bare hands as he tried to bend a hefty piece of steel pipe. Sometimes, during busy nights at Swede's, Carl tended bar and served as a bouncer who was seldom needed. If anyone was thinking about making trouble, a quick glance at the towering figure behind the bar or a look of warning from his face was all that was needed to keep the peace. No one messed with him.

One hot summer night, the crowd was especially devoid of inhibitions after a successful wheat harvest. "Tank" was a large bully from outside the local area who could always be counted on to fully participate in a drunken argument. He sat at the near end of the bar, close to the cash register where Carl was trying his best to count change and place it in the outstretched hand of a customer. Tank unexpectedly took a clumsy swing with his open hand at the head of his neighbor on the barstool. Carl leapt into action so quickly the money never made it fully into the palm of the customer, and coins bounced off the hardwood floor.

Before the swing could meet its target, Tank's arm was firmly in Carl's grasp. Carl twisted Tank's forearm violently up against his back and threw his entire weight upon him, throwing him off his stool and making him reel for balance. The two giants became one tangle of bodies with Carl's massive legs providing the locomotion, huffing and puffing with huge stomping steps, and barreling headlong for the front door. The floor of the old building shook under my feet, and I stepped aside as they rolled by. Some very alert person opened the large wooden door, and the two men crashed at full speed through the screen door and into the street in a tumble. If the door had not been opened, it was my guess their inertia would have sent them through it.

I never saw what happened in the street, but there really wasn't time to walk out and look. Thirty seconds passed and Carl stepped back into the bar, without accompaniment, wearing just a scuff of dirt on his clean white T-shirt and sporting a wide smile. To the crowd of patrons with their mouths and eyes agape, he simply flashed his big friendly grin, and his good-natured announcement broke the silence of the astonished barroom air. "Just a little discussion about the seating arrangements!" he shouted as he strode over to the cash register and began picking up coins from the floor. His voice softened to conversational volume. "Sorry about throwing your money around, Everett." He resumed his bartending duties without fanfare, and without any evidence in his breathing of the struggle. Slowly the din renewed itself, and life inside the tavern returned to usual. When I would ask him about it years later, he shook with a roaring belly laugh and said, "Yeah, old Tank and I cleared a path, didn't we?"

Fathers and sons have done a strange emotional dance, vivid and predictable, since time began. Carl and Harry's duet looked like the whole thing was scripted from mythology. Harry loomed as an aged legend in the area and possessed an amazing wealth of knowledge and skill, albeit about the old stuff. He cast a large shadow upon his grown son, and it was a Herculean task for Carl to garner legitimacy when working in the same shop as his dad. It was painful to watch Carl ask questions of his father; when he simply asked for information, it ended up sounding like he was seeking approval. Shop customers and bar patrons sometimes equated Carl's large size with a small intellect. But working near him, I knew differently. I watched him figure out blueprints and do quick calculations that would challenge any college graduate I knew of, including myself. And in regards to emotional intelligence, that ability to relate to other humans and instantly adjust his behavior and communicate effectively, he was one damn smart guy. Lots of people thought I was smart because I did well in college and spoke the language of my middle-class upbringing. But I looked up to Carl in the brains department.

Every month or so in the warmer winter days, we started up the old John Deere B tractors and loaded our large cottonwood logs onto the log ramps, large iron sawhorses that stood outside of a low and tin-covered shed. Harry had assembled and refined a small homemade sawmill and placed it fifty feet from the main shop building. The sawmill was incredibly loud and equally dangerous. A forty-two-inch diameter blade without any type of safety shield was directly mounted to a clutch mechanism and coupled to a Ford V-8 engine, all inside the tin building. The blade had replaceable teeth that Harry hammered to trueness by methodically striking a die to each tooth after a sawing job was done. He patiently fashioned the delicate behavior of the blade that would course through giant logs of green cottonwood.

The log was rolled from the ramps and clamped tightly to the carriage, or a miniature rail car of sorts, and the car and log moved along a short section of railroad track with a series of steel cables, pulling the log through the spinning blade. Back and forth the carriage and log would travel, and a man was

Carl, present day.

required to ride the carriage and advance the log over toward the blade before the next pass. Each pull of the lever slid the log the distance of the width of the finished dimension lumber. If two-by-fours were needed, the log would be pulled over two inches with a full stroke of the lever by the rider on the carriage.

Sharing a ride with a log next to the angry blade was, to say the least, unnerving. Over the deafening scream of the V-8, the giant blade showered out wood chips and sawdust, and with cottonwood logs, a lot of water spray. Safety glasses and earmuffs were necessary to keep one's hearing, eyesight, and sanity. Of course, behind the control panel and engine, Harry wore neither.

With each slice of lumber peeling off the carriage, another man on the ground was required to quickly remove the fresh board, without pinching the long and heavy slab back into the blade, which was a cardinal sin with Harry. Outside of the open shed door, the same man placed each board in a neat pile to be bundled together for shipment. This particular work position was the most physically demanding, and Harry often assigned newcomers to the task to see if they would quit on the first day. When all the mechanisms were timed well, and Harry was pushing the controls to maximize production, it was difficult for the stacker to keep up.

There was a joke around town, told with a degree of seriousness, that if government safety inspectors ever spotted the sawmill, they would hang Harry from the rafters. If the blatant hazards were ever pointed out to Harry, the old man dismissed it all with a wave and a few curse words and pointed to the crudely written sign hung on the wall of the sawmill shed: "Not responsible for accidents." If someone was afraid of being hurt, he barked, they oughta go work somewhere else or become a preacher. To an old man who had worked around danger all his life, the concept of liability suits and OSHA regulations was beyond comprehension.

Usually, I rode the carriage. My short frame lent itself to the position, as the rafters of the shed hung low enough to be a hazard to the head of most others. I did not have to bend much to clear them, but Carl certainly had to crouch on his haunches.

The sawmill.

Nevertheless, Carl had put in lots of hours riding the carriage as he grew up, and he knew how to handle it well. For some reason that day, I was out behind the shed, loading logs onto the ramps with the tractor, relieved to be away from the incredible noise and grateful not to be the stacker for a while. Carl was riding the carriage, and a middle-aged man whose name I cannot recall was doing the stacking, and having a hard time keeping up. He was working part-time, new to the process, and quickly growing tired. The fellow was slightly overweight and used to sitting on a tractor most of the time; the sweat ran down his face in fifty-degree weather as he hurriedly wiped his brow with his shirtsleeves between trips. Falling behind meant boards falling off the table onto the sawmill floor and a verbal thrashing from Harry. Getting chewed out by Harry was the ultimate punishment, particularly if he had to stop the process, idle down the engine, and bark like his old coon dog, with a "you dumb bastard" thrown in for good measure. People entering the tavern across the street stopped to watch, and sometimes the audience would grow to half a dozen. Only a brave few would venture across the street to get a closer look at the process.

On one of his hurried trips back into the shed, the weary man stumbled over his own feet and his momentum carried him toward the blade. At the same time, the carriage and log was making its trip forward with Carl astride it. As Harry recalled later, the man was headed directly into the path of the blade, which was spinning at full speed. As he clung to the half-cut log and the carriage traveled forward, Carl took a full swing, directly over the blade, with his huge arm at the man's face and hit him as hard as he could. His giant fist struck a direct blow to the man's head, lifting the victim off the ground and driving his body backward, without so much as a nick from the blade. The poor fellow laid on his back, halfway through the open door, arms at his side, completely motionless. Carl had knocked him unconscious with a broken jaw and nose, but quite alive and in full possession of all his body parts. Someone drove him to the hospital, and he recovered well, after several weeks of sporting a black-and-blue face with swollen eyes. I don't recall him ever coming around the mill again.

Cowgirl

In no moment in my life was my thinking process more clear than when I looked directly into the barrel of a gun. I had just jumped into my little yellow pickup parked in the dimly lit shadows of the garage, hurriedly started the engine, and out of habit looked behind the truck while I pushed in the clutch and deftly placed the gearshift on the floor to reverse. I felt a slight rock to the vehicle as I faced forward to turn on the headlights, and I discovered a .22 caliber rifle aimed directly at my forehead with Glenda spread-eagle on the hood and holding the gun in a rock-steady aim on the other side of the windshield. Glenda's facial expression was incensed and fiercely determined while she held the gun in her outstretched arms. The end of the barrel wavered slightly, but her bull's-eye was focused on a three-inch piece of real estate centered between my eyeballs. Her eyes were wide open with seething rage, and one corner of her down-turned lower lip twitched slightly.

Through the windshield I was looking at my father's gun. When Dad was ten years old, my grandmother bought him a small Winchester "Little Scout" .22 gauge rifle for his birthday over the objections of my grandfather. Dad was a responsible farm kid in the 1930s, and Grandma's gift provided him with a means to take target practice on empty tin cans and hunt rabbits to feed his dog before the days of manufactured dog food. When I was in my early teens, Dad took me out into the pasture and gave me an afternoon tutorial on gun safety that stands in my memory as one of the greatest teaching jobs ever performed. Normally distracted or tired and often impatient, he was never my choice of someone to help with homework. But on that afternoon, Dad spoke clearly in quiet and meticulous tone about a tool that, in careless or irrational circumstances, was lethal. Never look down the barrel of any gun. Never, ever, point a gun, loaded or unloaded, at a person unless you are fully prepared to use it. And if someone in your presence violates those simple rules, get away from the situation as soon as you can.

This was my second marriage. The cowgirl and I had married about three years prior, and she had been trudging into the wind and dragging along her shaky self-image since we met. She was a charming, bright, and attractive young woman who grew up on a small farm near the Republican River about thirty miles to the south. She struck a high profile in the area, and she was likable and energetic. Vivacious, I guess you would say. Those who did not know her certainly knew of her; she was a head turner. Her flirtatious wink would grab and hold a man's attention, and it held mine for a short while several years after my first marriage ended. She had worked her way through college and was a capable social worker in Salina when I met her at a party. She was eager to return to farm country near her parents;

her stalled social service career accelerated her courtship with me, and by that time my farming future looked bright with three years of successful farming experience under my belt. This young woman was a former rodeo queen wannabe, and her makeup was carefully applied each morning, even when she was to be sorting cattle or driving a tractor. She worked hard at styling her big yellow hair and chose her clothes with a great deal of thought. She drove herself wild with her struggle to keep off the weight, and I never got the courage to tell her that her affinity for sweets, beer, and a light cigarette habit might have something to do with it. She craved and cultivated compliments from men to store up like ammunition; it would be used to shoot down the voices in her head as she looked in the mirror with predictable disappointment. One night some drunken guy told her she resembled Marilyn Monroe, and she wore the statement like a medal for months.

There could not have been a worse partner for her than me. Deep within me I had probably not let go completely of my first wife. I still considered my first spouse an old friend, much to the discomfort of my new partner. Missy had been a slender, natural beauty, and that really bothered wife number two. I was a cross between a hick and a hippie, a self-described hybrid I referred to as a "hickie." I reveled in my role as an individualist on the border of being an oddball: a city kid who became a country man, and with luck and determination, a large-scale farmer. While my cowgirl companion listened to Haggard and Jones, I preferred Pink Floyd and Yes. My politics were liberal, and with the exception of Ronald Reagan cutting the social service budget, she thought conservative Republicans were the only people worth electing. I was not one for hiding my association with the pot smokers who were shunned and derided by the redneck cowboy crowd; the former were far more interesting to talk to. Any whiff of marijuana would have sent her running the other way and perhaps calling the cops, so I eliminated that little vice from my routine. Some of our most spirited arguments were about music and the social value of the 1960s. I never donned a cowboy hat in my life and wore sneakers most of the time. My hair was always longer than most other guys. I was easygoing and tolerant to a fault, sidestepping and absorbing the conflict to keep an uneasy peace in my new marriage. No man could have ever satisfied her need for attention regarding her looks, and I grew weary of fabricating compliments. She seemed to dazzle every other man with her appearance, so I felt it wearily redundant to heap on any more praise, of which she needed an unlimited supply. At the outset of the relationship I harbored a lot of jealousy, but after a while I just wore out and gave up. The marriage soon became a lot of hard work to keep afloat, and when the arguments began stretching into months of duration, I fell in upon myself and plunged off into depression deeper than ever. The more depressed I became, the more sullen and withdrawn I behaved, and the more exasperated she got. And the more depressed I became.

She was one hell of a polka dancer and loved to drink beer. I could never keep up with her beer-drinking capacity; the two or three that I would consume made me even more moody and quiet. As for the dancing, I would try to lubricate myself with a few cans of Coors, but my sneakers would not slide on the gymnasium floor and my stiff and battered farmer legs refused to relax. Some other guy would whirl her across the emptied dance floor with her red gingham dress flying in the wind as the crowd clapped in unison. All eyes were on her flashing smile while a few quizzical glances would be cast at me as I lingered off to the side and tried to sit up straight. The only thing worse than trying to dance with her in public was the impromptu rehearsals for such social events: a dance lesson in my own living room at the hands of an impatient cowgirl who insisted on leading. She surprised me with a pair of dress cowboy boots for my birthday, but after a week of stumbling and having my fat toes pinched, I tossed them into a dark corner of my closet.

Why we married in the first place was a mystery to me at the time, but in retrospect it was the result of loneliness and hormones, catalyzed by alcohol. At the time we met, it seemed like we were the last two attractive young single people in Republic County, which was a wasteland in the selection of available women. I had lived several years alone in my farmhouse with nothing but oppressive loneliness and my Doberman. What looked like the best prospect for companionship jumped behind the wheel and started driving. I sure didn't want to follow my beloved uncle's path: unmarried and dead at fifty-two. This woman, who was not my type, became the only foreseeable option, and a marriage was a practical way to hang onto her before she followed all the other ones out of the area.

Even in the early 1980s living together was still not socially permissible in the area, especially in my grandma's house.

Glenda was raised in the next community to the south and was hyperaware of my community's perceptions of her. At first, like all love affairs, there was excitement and happiness, but it didn't last long. My black locks and her poofy blonde hairdo made for a nice contrast in photos; we looked good together as long as we kept faking the smiles.

She repainted and wallpapered my old farmhouse to copy the photos in the *Country Living* magazines. A compulsive house cleaner, she accented my plain home with dust ruffles and hand-knitted doilies; as my father snarled to my sister Judy, "that frilly crap scattered all over Jim's house." We spent money that we did not have on elaborate decorating that would cover up the muted tones of paint and paper that were always good enough for the uncomplicated tastes of my first wife.

Glenda was born and raised on the Republican River bottom, where irrigation and rich soil created crops that were impressive nearly every year. The small community of Clyde, Kansas, was cohesive and more prosperous than Mahaska by a long shot. Farmers on the flat river bottomland didn't need to practice conservation tillage or terraces to keep the land in place. One afternoon, after she had been driving the tractor and making endless turns to accommodate the French-curve-like terraces on one of my larger fields, she stomped into the house, complaining bitterly about "this godforsaken land up here." On one hand, I found it amusing there could be a measurable cultural and class difference between two ends of the same dry Kansas county. On the other, it made me madder than hell. God did not forsake my land. You just have to work with it and hold your horses in terms of your expectations. And, goddamn it, cursing it is the height of blasphemy.

I liked her folks; they treated me well, and they appreciated my tolerance of their daughter's more difficult attributes. After getting to know them, I always wondered how such a high-strung woman could come from such broad-minded and relaxed parents. Glenda was named after the good witch of the north in *The Wizard of Oz*. During a particularly tense time after she threw a tantrum in front of her parents and me, her mother asked me confidentially, "What was the name of the witch that had the house dropped on her?" After hiding our growing marital conflict from her parents for over a year, Glenda unleashed a laundry list of complaints about me one night at her folks' dinner table. Her father listened in silence as if he had heard it all before, pointed a finger in the air, and released a long-held thought. "That's all very well. But it takes *two* to make a deal..."

Quiet depression became my daily state, and she became more desperate. My irrationality turned inward to consume myself as hers turned outward. A single mother who lived in the nearby town knocked on our door one Sunday morning with apologies on behalf of her teenage son, who had driven off the gravel road the previous evening and smashed a hole in our pasture fence. The car was stuck in the field, so I drove out to the crash site with my smaller tractor and pulled the dented vehicle out of the mud so they could drive it home. I refused to take any money for compensation and told the poor woman the fence was no big deal. As I returned to my house, I was met with a barrage of angry questions and accused of having an affair with "the skinny woman" I had helped. There was no convincing Glenda otherwise, so after an hour of yelling, I gave up and fell asleep on the couch. I was awakened violently a half hour later with a blow to my face; Glenda had delivered a direct kick to my right eye with her bare heel as I slept. I stayed close to the house or hidden in my tractor cab for about a week as the black eye faded.

One hot summer night she had been drinking too much and picked yet another fight with me. Demanding "total honesty," she screamed at me to confess my first impression of her at the time we met. "What did you think of me? What was going through your mind when you first saw me?" She wanted two things at the same time: reassurance that yes, indeed, I thought she was beautiful and to root out her suspicions of my deeply held and guarded perception of her, as if to scare the demons from her male partner so she could grab hold of them and throttle them good. After three years of this exercise, I was exhausted. *The hell with it*, I thought. She wanted her truth delivered, and I was tired of witholding it. "I thought your ass was a bit too big," I quietly enunciated as I stared blankly into the dining room table. Her face turned to stone, and she stomped off with her boot heels pounding across the wooden floor of the dining room. I wasn't sure what she had in mind, but I figured this farmer should probably just get out of the insane asylum and go take a short drive. So I headed for the garage.

I studied the machined round end of the gun barrel through the windshield. And I was strangely calm. I began making a clear and rational list of options in my mind. The first possibility was to shift gears, pop the clutch, and stomp on the accelerator with the hope of driving her body forward through the back wall of the wood-framed garage. It would certainly injure her badly, maybe even kill her, but then again she might get a shot off in the process. Or, I could keep the gear selection in reverse and hopefully throw her aim off as she tumbled off the hood when I suddenly backed out. That might not work either; I could see her finger gently resting in front of the trigger. Man, she looked pissed. Was the gun loaded? Would the sheriff believe my claim of self-defense? It was only a .22 caliber barrel, but at two feet away, could I survive it? Bobby Kennedy sure didn't. An hour of pondering was compressed into ten seconds. I opted for a third idea: I simply looked deep into her eyes, searching for her soul. *If you can kill a man while looking him in the eye,* I thought, *you are far braver or crazier than even I know you to be.*

We remained in the standoff for about a minute. The engine idled, and our eyes locked together in unflinching stares. Finally, grudgingly, she slowly lowered the gun and carefully slid backwards off of the hood, still in uninterrupted eye contact. I ever so gently backed out of the garage and drove up the long gravel driveway.

The adrenaline faded as I processed the event for the next few hours and wandered the back roads of my farm in my pickup. Sometime after midnight I pulled into one of my wheat fields and walked across the ground in the full moonlight and realized I felt more fully alive than I had in three years. Even though I did not have the courage to end the relationship, she did it for me. I was completely alone and safe, and my energy had changed from terror to exuberant freedom. I felt the tilled soil under my feet and was filled with pride: I was still a damn good farmer, a healthy young man, and I was alive to feel the cool summer night breeze upon my face. I raised my clenched fists to the stars. Finally at about two o'clock in the morning, exhaustion took hold and I fell asleep inside my truck with my tennis shoes dangling out the passenger window.

The next morning I went to a friend and rented an empty house in Mahaska for thirty-five bucks a month, and I moved in with only the clothing on my back, a new sleeping bag, and a few pots and pans hastily purchased. I did not attempt to go back into my farmhouse for another two months, not even to gather any items. My machinery and shop were located at Russ's place, the next farmstead west, and as I drove past my home-place one day, I could see a stock trailer and shiny new pickup parked at the bottom of my long gravel driveway with several people loading up furniture. The word uptown was she had found herself a cowboy, and he had offered to help her move out. When I finally moved back into the old two-story farmhouse, it echoed with the void of every scrap of furnishings, pictures, and curtains gone. She'd removed all the light bulbs as well.

Years later I made peace with her. I drove to her new place where she lived by herself and her young daughter after another failed marriage. She still had the gleam of fire in her eyes, and it confirmed my lesson I had learned: Watch the burn from a distance. I thanked her for the good times I could remember and apologized for not having the guts to terminate our relationship before so much damage was done to both of us. She was pleased with that. I wished her well.

Eddie

The operation that assumed my lease on Russ's ground was a cold, business-like family consisting of a blonde woman, her husband, and an only son who was finishing up his animal science degree at Kansas State. Eddie was a big and good-natured kid who usually wore a smile as he drove around in his new Trans-Am. Though obviously well provided for, he never seemed to have many friends. The other young men would comment about his privileged status, and his shyness was misinterpreted as snobbery. His father, the son of a prominent and long-time state representative, seemed to be quite skilled in finding outside money to finance their farming interests. Eddie's dad was an articulate fellow who never seemed to get dirty or have his neatly trimmed hair out of place. They had the biggest and best machinery around, all current-model John Deere equipment that left me mystified as to how they could pay for it with dryland wheat and grain sorghum crops grown in a climate of constantly declining commodity prices, while the rest of us common dirt farmers fixed our own weekly mechanical breakdowns and drove around in battered pickups. Admittedly, they were efficient; they could be timely and seize those rare opportunities to plant or harvest that are so critical in crop farming and move their harvested grain to the elevator with speed in huge grain trucks. But I shook my head in dismay when I calculated the interest and principal payments on so much machinery. Some of our fields lay side by side, or at least we traveled down the same gravel roads to access them, and it was always a challenge to the more enlightened corner of my soul to watch them work ground that was once promised to me. I would steam with resentment. Their current-model gleaming grain truck carried about 750 bushels, while my old 1959 GMC two-ton truck would haul about 350. But my mechanical genius cousin Charlie put a four-barrel carburetor on the huge Pontiac 370 engine in the old red beast, and in his words it ran "like a striped-assed ape." And indeed it would as I would take great delight in blowing past my successors on the way to dumping our loads at the elevator, both of our trucks loaded to the gills. I sat in line and watched in my mirror as they would slowly pull to a stop behind me.

All farm people waved to each other. It was just common courtesy. I refused to wave to any of *them*, and most of the time the one going down the road in a tractor or truck was Eddie. He lived in Russ's house by himself after a broken engagement from a young woman whom he met in college and who, upon surveying her future of living out in the middle of Republic County, changed her mind. I spent almost an entire year avoiding my new neighbor, who in an area full of old people was certainly the nearest guy even close to my age. I dragged my bitterness around like a leg iron, and it was renewed now and then with a snide comment of support from one of the other neighbors. But time went by, and I grew tired of all the emotional work it required to maintain it. One day it occurred to me that the young man might just feel as lonely as I did, and I surprised myself by giving in to a gentler notion. I banged on Russ's old screen door one night with a small cooler of ice and a six-pack of beer. Eddie was stunned as he came to the door, invited me in, and we began to thaw things out. The beer tasted good after a hard workday, and it was nice to have someone to talk to that evening. We both came to the conclusion that the arrangements were out of our control; each one of us was playing a hand that we had not really asked for. We were farming side by side and trying to outsmart the weather in a crashing farm economy. Both of us had grown weary of our respective roles in the local soap opera centered on our farm operations. My parents lived halfway across the country, and his kept him at an emotional arm's length. Our women were gone. He was doing his best to live his life, and so was I.

My grandpa used to tell me about the practice of placing "hobbles" on the lower legs of horses to slow their spirit and impede their progress. Around midnight, all the beer was gone, Eddie and I had each cautiously made a new friend, and I walked out into the clear night air to my pickup truck, unhobbled.

The next Fourth of July we were all deep in the heart of wheat harvest. The temperature read over a hundred degrees, and the wind was blowing hard out of the south—perfect weather for ripening and harvesting the mature wheat crop. But there are few things on this earth more terrifying and fiscally crippling than a wheat field fire, especially in a mature, tinder-dry, un-harvested field. Once the blaze starts in that kind of weather, an enormous amount of money and effort can be incinerated in ten minutes. While cutting wheat on my very northern field of seventy-five acres, my combine burst a diesel line and set the engine on fire, dropping grease flames onto the edge of the wheat field. The wind caught it, and it began its march to the north with an entire field ready to be consumed, along with the neighbors' additional eighty acres. The fire built slowly, as if contemplating and poising for the big breakout.

I scrambled up the ladder and into the cab and shoved the hydrostatic lever forward to move the machine out of the field and onto the dirt road. Killing the engine, I climbed down the ladder of the machine, ran to the rear ladder, and scampered up to the platform. I unfastened the clamps and threw forward the sheet-metal cowling that covered the engine, just in front of the fuel tank. I unloaded the powder from the fire extinguisher on the blazing engine, but it merely paused for a few seconds and then reignited in a flash. The fuel tank was between the engine and me. I leaped off the back of the machine and tumbled as I hit the dirt road, a good eight feet down. As I struggled to my feet, I could see a monstrous and shiny John Deere tractor racing toward me, dust flying from the enormous tires, and towing a twenty-four-foot wide disc harrow that was hoisted up on its transport wheels.

"GET IN!!!" Eddie screamed over the engine, roaring at full throttle, while pushing his foot in on the clutch and holding the glass door open. I scrambled up the ladder, and he pulled the cab door shut. I seized the back of the upholstered seat as he popped the clutch, and both tractor and implement dove headlong into the two-foot-deep grader ditch that separated the dirt road from the field. Through the ditch we bounced as he slammed the throttle lever forward. My body was bounced violently and thrown against the side glass window.

The shiny soil-turning blades of the disc were sucked into the ground and began peeling off giant ribbons of fresh soil that buried the standing wheat into moist black soil. Repeatedly hammering his fist upon the hand throttle to its full limit, Eddie geared up progressively to catch the speed of the racing flames as the black smoke shot forcefully from the exhaust stack and the engine was taxed to its limit. He ran a parallel path to the ten-foot-tall flames, and the heat on my face through the glass made me turn my head away. Hanging on to the bouncing seat with both hands, I looked with astonishment upon the determined young man behind the wheel. He was trying to race my wheat-field fire with his $150,000 tractor and implement. "I'm gonna try and cut this son of a gun off!" he shouted, and we overtook the rate of burn. That was a very risky idea: A large diesel engine running at full throttle requires about five thousand gallons of air for every gallon of fuel, so plunging the tractor into a potentially oxygen-starved environment next to the fire would run the risk of the engine dying at a very bad time.

Gaining some distance between the tractor and the fire, Eddie turned a hard left, and we bolted forward directly across the path of the approaching wall of flames. He buried the disk into the ground to its full depth and pounded on the steering wheel, urging the machine on. *"GO, YOU SON OF A BITCH, GO!!!"* we both yelled. He had about a twenty-second window of opportunity to get around the fire and escape before it engulfed the tractor. "For God's sake, don't burn this thing up for three-dollar wheat!" I screamed. He successfully maneuvered around the fire's path and headed back into the wind and on the other side of the fire, containing it totally.

The entire amount burnt was about five acres. I had purchased the standard crop insurance package for the year, but wheat crops cannot be insured against fire. Even at three bucks a bushel, I figured he saved the equivalent of about a third of my yearly income. The local volunteer fire department arrived and put out the sporadic flare-ups, finally extinguishing it altogether. My combine was completely destroyed; when the diesel tank burst, the entire machine was consumed within minutes. Dripping with water, the warped hulk of sheet metal sat smoking in the middle of the road. The seventy-five gallon fuel tank was peeled open like a tin can, and the radiator was a pile of melted lead dripping over the giant right-side wheel, nothing remaining but the charred rim. A friend of mine who lived thirty-five miles north, near Hebron, Nebraska, could clearly see a tight and dark plume of smoke coming from a spot on the south-southeast horizon.

Eddie and I exchanged honest smiles and waves thereafter. Two years later, his parents and their farm operation went bankrupt. The nice equipment and cattle were liquidated to satisfy the creditors, and an even larger outside farming corporation made a cash offer to purchase the farm ground from Russ's kids.

By that time they were relieved to be rid of the source of conflict between all the players. Russ's home sold for a few thousand dollars, and it was jacked up and moved by a house mover twenty-five miles to the north. The rest of the grain bins, the garage, scrap iron piles, and the long shelterbelt of mature cottonwood and pine trees were bulldozed into a hole, set on fire, and buried. All that remained was a short gravel driveway with his old implement shed and a sodium-vapor streetlight. The entire four hundred acres that comprised Russ's home farm became one giant soybean field, planted in one day by a large farming interest. I don't know what ever happened to Eddie; with a college degree, good interpersonal skills, and the wisdom that forever remains in a farmer, I am sure he found plenty of opportunities to do his own thing. I hope he is doing well.

Schnapps

A swirl of snowflakes followed me into the blacksmith shop as I fought to keep the metal door under control in the bitter northerly wind. The darkness and cold of a long winter workday had begun to settle into my bones, and as usual, the old blacksmith was still inside. Next to the woodstove, Harry was finishing his daily tasks, putting away his tools in their perfectly ordered places above the smooth concrete floor that he had swept clean. He loved his work, he loved his precious shop, and he seemed to deliberately put off any retreat to his home and wife at the end of the day. After several winters of working with him, I had earned his respect and become his friend.

It always appeared to me that while his marriage was a thing of convenience and even survival, he really did not love, or even like, his wife, Frances. The couple had met late in life, each well into their forties. The early death of each of their respective spouses in the 1940s led them to meet through acquaintances; two rural working people entered into a marriage of necessity with evidently muted enthusiasm. Compatibility took a back seat to practicality. Romance was a distant memory buried with their previous partners. One time during a coffee break, several other men were seated at a table with Harry and me in the restaurant. Harry had given me a goose and a gander several days earlier, and their welfare was being discussed. One of the men asked, "Whatcha gonna name your geese, Jim?" I grinned as I answered, "Harry and Frances." Harry immediately piped up as he shook his head slowly, "Hell. They'll never breed."

The old man was always glad to see my weary, coverall-clad frame enter on those cold winter evenings, and the heavy metal door would slam shut and echo through the cavernous blacksmith shop, built of iron framing and covered with corrugated tin. It would serve to announce my presence to one so hard of hearing. After exchanging a few jovial shouts and small talk on that night, Harry ceremoniously opened his fat wallet, stuffed with hundreds, fifties, and on down in descending order, and looking like they had been in the exact same place for years. "Growing mold," as his son had sometimes described. He plucked out a five with his battered old fingers, shoved it in my face, and shouted, "It's colder out there than a well digger's ass in Alaska. Go get us a bottle of schnapps. The cheaper stuff." Harry had held a lifelong love affair with peppermint schnapps. He told me how his mother made her own brand of liquor, a regular treat as he was growing up. He held his mother in deep reverence; her homemade schnapps recipe, and her occasional enjoyment of her product, was a source of pride in her son.

Harry's second wife, however, was a strict Lutheran teetotaler, and it irritated him greatly. He was not permitted to drink a drop in his present home, but his tidy shop was his undisputed

Harry and Frances.

domain. After the day's work was completed, it was there that the old man could take a drink, out of sight from a strong and very large spouse, who would rarely keep her disapproval to herself in her own territory. If she ever made an appearance in the shop, it wouldn't be for long, especially in the bitter cold away from the woodstove. Harry claimed the real estate next to the stove.

Returning from the bar across the street, I dutifully delivered the bottle and change from the five dollar bill. Harry always carefully scrutinized the change returned to him, with a quick calculation in his head to see if an honest transaction had been made. His humor had a hard edge. Once in a while there came an opportunity to throw it back in his face, and this was such a moment. I carelessly flipped two crumpled dollar bills and a dime onto his metal workbench, as if throwing down a gauntlet. His eagerly anticipating face immediately turned to a disapproving frown, and I felt the heat of his glare. "Problem?" I asked, faking mild surprise.

"You damn right this is a problem," he snorted. I braced myself and prepared for another lecture on how to act, how to work, and how to be the kind of person worthy of a crusty old blacksmith's respect.

"These guys that treat money like you do will never have anything to show for it," he barked. "Now, I have a little money and property, and I treat my money like this..." he continued, fumbling for his overstuffed wallet and opening it so I could get a good look at the contents. I feigned curiosity and admiration as I watched him flip through his perfectly aligned and hard-earned currency. He stiffened his posture, triumphantly returned the fat wallet to the back pocket of his overalls, and prepared to drive home his point. A man who came of age in the Great Depression was an expert on thrifty living. Frugality was his sole lifelong religion.

"I take care of my money, and so I will always *have* money." He puffed his chest up with exaggerated pride. He pointed an ungloved and wavering finger at the abused bills on the desk. "If you don't treat your money with respect, you never will accumulate it like I have." He paused and looked to me for a humble apology of my slovenly ways. In Harry's eyes, the succeeding generations were recklessly free spending and wasteful, and he never missed an opportunity to point it out. Reverence for a dollar was a lesson he intended to hammer into me as forcefully as he beat on plowshares. I had heard it a hundred times.

But I seized the moment, leaning back and pointing my finger at the wadded bills. "That's your money, Harry." He glared at me as I continued. "I don't *give* a shit about your money." I opened up my wallet and proudly displayed the ten, a five, and three ones all arranged neatly and sequentially. I gave him a big grin and announced, "This is *my* money."

Harry was at an uncharacteristic loss for words. The silence remained for a moment. With a concealed smile and palsied shake of his head, he leaned menacingly close to my face and snarled in a whisper, "You son of a bitch." I accepted his capitulation in our little battle of wits.

Turning his attention to the freshly purchased bottle of schnapps, his phony scowl vanished and he sported a satisfied smile. "Oops!" he blurted and comically unscrewed the cap, tossing it over his shoulder into the dark void of the shop floor. "Lost the cap," he said as he examined the bottle. "Guess we gotta drink the whole damn thing."

The schnapps went down warm and easy, even if it made my eyes water a bit. We talked about the winter workday, and all evidence of pretend animosity was gone from Harry's face. We passed the bottle back and forth for a few minutes, further cementing a friendship that crossed a wide generational and social gap. While away from his wife's house, Harry kept a small wad of Copenhagen chewing tobacco in the vestibule of his right cheek, and I could see tiny brown speckles floating in the liquor bottle as I tipped it up to drink. A mix of respect and fear prevented my objection to the pollution; exhaustion and cold at the end of the day made me grateful for the warming effects of the liquor. "Never look a gift horse in the mouth," he always preached. Besides, there could be nothing more futile than to try to teach manners to Harry. He also said once, "If a fella ever wants to give you something, by God go ahead and take it or you may insult the guy."

The bottle was about half gone when a vigorous young man in insulated coveralls, arriving with an armload of logs, burst through the door. We heard it flying open, and Martin quickly slammed it behind himself. His breath came out in steamy puffs as he shouted his greetings. Harry held out the bottle, and Martin joined our circle with wide eyes and a large grin. In a few moments three-fourths of the bottle was gone.

Martin was a quiet, hardworking man in his thirties whom Harry held in deep respect. They knew each other well, and the old man would sometimes defer to Martin's intellect or ability to solve problems quickly. Without warning, the shop door flew open once again with its familiar violence. With his back to the door, Harry read a dire nonverbal warning from Martin's face. Harry halted his drinking motion in mid-swig. His eyes widened in genuine terror as he hurried his final swallow with great effort. The old man's fearless exterior evaporated in a heartbeat, and he quickly and discreetly handed the bottle to Martin at belt level. Martin smoothly tucked the bottle, the cap long gone somewhere in the darkness, into an equally dark and small shelf on the wall above the workbench. We all tried to look nonchalant, which was not easy when startled by one large old woman.

I always thought Harry's wife, Frances, to be the biggest old woman I had ever seen. She was always kind and sweet to me, and I enjoyed our short conversations that were hurried through as she dashed about her days. Her height and breadth seemed incongruous with a woman in her early eighties—when she stood up straight, she was tall, but she was certainly not fat. I would watch her approach on the sidewalk, and she looked as if she could pick me up and throw me right through it. A lifetime of hard work—hanging out the wash, cooking meals, mowing lawns, and feeding the woodstove in their drafty home—had bent her upper back to give her a constant, exaggerated stoop. In the winter, her appearance would make me laugh out loud: a fuzzy pink winter wool hat, cream-colored long coat, and insulated white stockings painted a feminine exterior that contrasted with a body so large. I could see why Harry didn't give her too much lip. Harry would often use her as an example of the wonderful individuality of humans, when he would quip: "It's a good thing we're not all the same. Or we'd all be in love with my wife."

Frances shouted a subdued "Hullo" to the group of men halfway across the shop. She apparently knew her place in her husband's environment. She could not resist her need to be useful, and the only way she was tolerated in the shop was if she was doing something akin to work. So she quickly cast her eyes to the floor in deference while busily searching for the broom that leaned against the wall. The broom made quick jousting motions as puffs of steam billowed around the face in the pink hat. But no matter how fast she moved the broom, it was never appreciated by Harry. Her attempts to contribute only seemed to irritate him, and her tense presence served to upset the long-established balance of power in the blacksmith shop.

We all went about our business, although it was hard to find just what that was. Each member of the drinking circle began straightening tools, emptying trash, checking the woodstove, or just posturing as if in the middle of something important. None of it looked very convincing, but obviously Frances wasn't going to upset the awkward silence by questioning anyone. She went about her sweeping, and everyone else went about their acting.

The door flew open yet again. Into the shop darted a small boy, a grandson of Harry and Frances, who was in his grandmother's care that evening. Ryan shouted a short greeting to his grandpa. Frances swatted the boy's feet away from her accumulating pile of dirt on the floor, and he danced about the shop to amuse himself. Everyone was minding their own business as the uneasy and unspoken truce settled in. Suddenly, Martin grabbed Harry's dirty coat sleeve and frantically motioned toward the tool bench while Frances intently swept, her back toward us. The five-year-old had a firm hold on the schnapps bottle with both of his little hands, tipping the nearly empty bottle up toward his mouth. Imitation of Grandpa was occurring at a very bad time. Everyone knew that if Frances caught a glimpse of the boy in such a pose, the roof would blow off the shop. None of us tough guys, especially Harry, had the courage to be witness to the consequences. If there was ever a time to panic, this was it.

I sprang into action. I took several sprinting paces toward her as she emptied her dustpan into the trashcan. "Frances, can we look at something on your car? I thought I saw something to worry about earlier today." I dominated her attention and opened the shop door. She looked puzzled but trusted me enough to believe in my concern for her 1963 Chevrolet Impala parked in the street directly in front of the shop.

I escorted Frances out to the car for a few moments. Because she appreciated my concern, I felt a bit dishonest. I examined the air pressure in all four of her tires, which were all properly inflated. Frances and I chatted quickly in the cold wind while my coconspirators covered up the crime. I insisted that she leave the little boy with us, and we would see that he was delivered to her house before supper was ready. She welcomed the relief while the large evening meal needed to be made. Most of all, she appreciated being acknowledged in the hallowed halls of noise, dirt, and men, for through the years she had grown accustomed to being snubbed there. I could easily and genuinely be her friend, in spite of whatever Harry thought about her. And to his credit, he respected that bond between us.

The crisis had passed, and I retreated back into the shelter of the shop and was greeted with a hero's welcome from the drinking club. The energetic little boy was happy to be in our company where he could be roughhoused and cajoled in a way specific to a gathering of men. The drama bonded us all in a very small way, and the détente of marriage, solidly in place over the course of thirty-some years, remained intact for another night.

Scripture

After the loss of Russ's land, I leased more ground in the area to try to make up for it. I still farmed Vic and Leah's and three other pieces of farmland besides the tracts belonging to myself, my dad, and my aunt. But it was necessary to refinance my machinery payments for several more years, and I also worked more part-time jobs whenever I could find them, even in the midst of cropping seasons.

I was surprised one day when the local John Deere dealer in Fairbury, Nebraska, offered me a part-time job. They were temporarily short-staffed with their sales department, and they needed a face to represent the dealership in a lucrative area in Nebraska, fifty miles north of my place. Over the course of a year, for two days out of the week, I would go up into the area and call on the more prominent farmers. Officially I was a salesman, but in actuality just a professional visitor. My quiet manner and knowledge about farming and John Deere tractors let me fit in well. I really wasn't a salesman; I was one of *them*. Occasionally I even sold something, but usually I spent my sales calls in enjoyable conversations and met a lot of fine people as

I traveled around Plymouth, Nebraska. It was an area of heavy irrigation that yielded tremendous corn and soybean crops and was full of neatly maintained and modern farms that were well equipped with mostly John Deere equipment.

I never knew the guy's name, but there was one very eccentric older fellow who walked around Plymouth, Nebraska, angrily spouting Bible verses. "Thy God shall smite thine enemies..." The town was a tidy place of about four hundred people, mostly of German heritage, and I often ate lunch at one of the taverns. The man with the deeply furrowed brow and set jaw looked to be in his sixties at the time I knew of him, and he spewed his fundamentalist ranting at patrons coming out of one of the two town bars or at a diligent homeowner raking leaves on a Sunday. "This is the Lord's day! Thou shall keep it holy or suffer the wrath of the Almighty!" I witnessed individuals cross to the other side of the street when they saw him coming up the sidewalk.

He had a small acreage with a two-story white farmhouse by the main highway on the edge of town. A large billboard stood in his cornfield depicting an Anglo-Saxon version of Jesus complete with shepherd's staff and golden halo with a painting of a fetus, sharing the white background with a disturbing anti-abortion message. The yard around his house was planted with eight to ten large white signs with Scripture verses painted upon them in bold black letters. An occasional syntax or spelling error was large enough to be easily read from the road by even the nearsighted.

One early spring day the grass had turned a lush green, the birds were singing, and the daffodils around his house were opening into full bloom. The man was walking through his yard on his way to get the mail, and as he passed in between two of the signs, a lightning bolt struck him directly, blowing off both of his shoes and killing him instantly.

Leslie Joy

In 1985 my great-uncle Leslie Joy Cossaart appeared to be the oldest man on earth. I had known my grandpa's younger brother since I was a young child but came to know him well when I was in my early thirties. Joy was his middle name and was actually his mother's—my great-grandmother's—maiden name: Nora C. Joy. The middle name fit him well. To meet him in person would make anyone gasp in amazement that a person could be so old and yet so alert, cheerful, and present. He had leaned into the unrelenting Kansas wind for ninety-some years and appeared ready to topple forward with the slightest gust upon his back. He never was a very big man, even in younger years, and when I knew him he was probably five foot two inches tall and 130 pounds in muddy boots. Six days a week, Uncle Leslie wore old and worn, but always clean, overalls with a long-sleeve blue denim shirt buttoned up to the neck that billowed out of the side openings of his Big Smiths. Sunday morning he put on a coat, tie, and jacket for church and stocked the pockets full of candy to give to the little kids.

His most striking feature, besides his appearance of extreme old age, was his constant closed-lip grin, sunken deeply within the large wrinkles and bony caverns of a face that had spent nearly every day of his long life working in the sun. When he smiled, which was most of the time, his eyes would stretch to two narrow slits with only a thin hint of a sparkling gleam that squeezed through the lids. I always wondered how in the heck he could see anything. The skin on his tiny head was stretched so thin you could discern every outline of his skull, and he sported a small wisp of two-inch-long hair combed over his otherwise bald head. His farmer skin was leathery and tan with sun blotches up to the size of dimes. At the risk of offending his spirit, I always possessed a mental picture that could describe his face and head: a jack-o'-lantern made from a shriveled-up apple. To look upon his facial expression would elicit almost automatic, unintended laughter in anyone he would meet, and would always guarantee the same in myself, no matter how often I would see him. I imagine he understood how funny he looked as he peered into the mirror himself. Laughter to him was the tonic of life, and his clearly thought-out speech was peppered with chuckled exclamations. His little frame shuffled through the world with enthusiastic kindness, gratitude, and such dignity that I had never seen.

At around his ninety-second year I was going through the predictable legal and emotional exhaustion from a divorce. It was my second one in ten years, and the idea of being a two-time loser had my posture reflecting the fact. Suddenly I had become a bachelor farmer again, living alone in a big, sparsely furnished farmhouse with no one to hear my thoughts but the dog. This was before the Internet. With the accelerated exodus of broken farmers from a marginally productive farming region, I seemed to awaken that decade and look around to find a spouse gone along with most of my friends and neighbors. Unless I made a conscious effort, human contact beyond a telephone call could be absent for weeks on end. Looking for someone to talk to, other than the cows or my dead tractor battery, took extra work and a drive somewhere thirty miles down the road; the social venue was usually limited to a bar. After a long hard day on the tractor or fixing fence and working alone immersed in self-doubt and anxiety, I could be with my old uncle and just be myself. We always had far too much to talk about, mostly him doing the talking, to be bogged down by my legal and emotional troubles. He was unique among the other limited cast members in my life, in that my problems, ripe for the workings of the local gossip and great material for ponderous and empathetic analysis, were never openly discussed by him. In the soap opera of ultra-small town life, my more interesting personal episode at the time made me feel scrutinized like a bug under the community's magnifying glass. Uncle Leslie's huge farmhouse, with its high ceilings and dusty unused rooms, was one truly safe place where I could enter and escape any disapproval. No one should judge, but if any human could get away with it at the time, it would have been a clear-thinking ninety-some-year-old man. But he would not, did not, and I felt that because of his goodness, he could not. We liked each other. He was fun to be with.

Uncle Leslie and I both lived on Section 1. Leslie was the brother immediately younger than my grandfather, and at the time I knew him well, Leslie had lived almost as long as Grandpa had. My grandfather Reuben, born in 1887, was the oldest child in a family of eight, all born in the house that Leslie still lived in through his old age. Five daughters and eight years later, Leslie arrived in 1895. He reminded me, in appearance as well as in spirit, of my grandpa. This was good in all respects; Leslie was as easygoing and kindhearted as my grandfather, in constant good humor, and nothing delighted him like sharing someone's company. But being more energetic and extroverted than my grandfather, Les was an enthusiastic and at times incessant talker and storyteller. If I happened to be in a hurry on a particular day, stopping by Leslie's farmhouse for an intended five-minute visit to check in on him could stretch into a full hour. The only effective way to stop his talking was to raise my hand to signal a halt, announce my need to get back to work, and go. I learned to stop over at his house in the early evening after my work was done for the day.

His culinary abilities he developed late in life, and these became valuable as he and Bertha grew old. My spitfire great aunt actually survived seven separate mild strokes over the course of about ten years. In spite of that, I always remember her standing upright and never in a wheelchair. Since she had been gone, Leslie's skills had become much simpler in his old age. Nevertheless, he presented a three-course meal with trembling fingers—warmed tomato soup, a very well-done fried hamburger patty, and a package of Little Debbies in the cellophane

Uncle Leslie in a parade.

wrapper—served with all the pride and love of a gracious host. It became his major task of the day to fumble with can openers, battered pans, and a temperamental propane stove that would confound his arthritic fingers. He never offered apology or embarrassment for such laughably simple meals. He simply stood back from the table, assessed his bounty set before us, and gave a hearty chuckle. It made his day to know he was providing nourishment for me. His three grown children, all in their sixties and living in the area, checked in on him often and looked after him well. With me at his table, he got his chance to take care of someone. I felt grateful for his efforts but also appreciated not choosing between the two options of cheeseburgers and fries from Swede's or an empty and silent house surrounding me as I cooked a convenient impostor of a meal, for which no one but the dog would thank me.

Bertha and Leslie had been married sixty-five years when she finally passed away. I had heard stories that Les and she often had a stormy time of it. When I was a teenager I could recall my grandma's face as she hung up the phone from her daily conversations with her sister-in-law. "Leslie and Bertha," she would mutter. "They have their troubles..." I was saddened to hear that he had at times been mean to her, emotionally and physically. I did not pry into the details from his granddaughter, my cousin, but she told me Bertha kept a gun handy in her bedroom drawer. Aunt Bertha had a constitution of iron and only took so much shit. She was a tiny, hardworking woman, and I recalled watching her quick movements and wiry figure carrying two five-gallon buckets of heavy kitchen waste across the farmyard, in a rapid and purposeful walk, to throw into the hog trough on the other side of the barn. Like her husband, she seemed to shrink with age. As my grandfather and I would drive past their place and see Bertha pinning bedsheets to the clothesline, he would comment, "Any windier and they're going to have to tie Bertha down." Uncle Leslie would tease his wife about having a tapeworm. A great cook all of her life, she loved to present huge meals for any neighbor, especially kids who would stop by. As a teen, I sat at their table, already stuffed to the gills, as she worked her way around the table and questioned each member if they wanted more mashed potatoes. Holding a large aluminum kettle of spuds against her hip and a huge spoon in the other, she barked out her question two inches from my ear. "Jimmy!" she snapped in a shrill staccato. "Want more mashed taters?!" I could not find room for another bite. "No, thanks," I mumbled in protest, patting my stretched belly and vigorously shaking my head from side to side. Her expression unchanged, fully sure that a growing boy needed to be sufficiently fed, she forcefully delivered a giant glop of mushy potatoes that buried half of my plate. "Sure you do!" she retorted and proceeded on to the next guest. Her sharp focus help herd a more scattered Leslie, and in the days of corn that was hand harvested, he would not shuck corn without Bertha by his side. My dad told me the only reason Uncle Leslie got his work done was Bertha.

In my company, Leslie would sometimes reminisce about his courtship with her. When he was twenty, he would borrow his dad's single horse and buggy to visit his sweetheart in the evenings. Bertha lived about six miles south, and Leslie would invariably stay far too late in his romancing. Her parents would finally tell him to go home, and Leslie would snap the reigns as the horse trotted out the drive. More often than not, Leslie nodded off to sleep as the horse went down the road, a trip made over and over as their courtship progressed. Unguided, his trusty mare would make the trip from memory, and Leslie would awaken to find himself, buggy, and horse safely halted in his parents' front yard.

Uncle Leslie was always a show-off. When every young man in the community sought a horse to ride around on, Les purchased a bona fide thoroughbred racehorse so he could be fastest among his peers. The problem soon became evident, as the horse would run the distance of a mile as if it were on fire, break to a halt, then refuse to go anywhere at more than a slow saunter for the next half hour. Uncle Leslie was a man who was never rushed, but he still loved to go as fast as a horse or vehicle would propel him—not for the sake of saving time, but to impress any onlookers. His fieldwork, particularly in places next to the road where others could see, was laid down for show; even with a pair of meandering horses, his rows of corn were so straight they looked like they had been laid out with a surveyor's sight and transit. And he let everyone know about it too.

Leslie's remarkable age was hard to fathom, even as I listened to him from my adult perception. His first historical recollection was the rural mailman dismounting his horse-drawn buggy and walking across the farmyard to deliver letters to his father, and hearing the news that President McKinley had been shot. One warm summer night, in advance of the predicted arrival every seventy-five years of Halley's comet, Les and I stood on his back porch and mused at the possibility of where the comet would appear in the immense night sky. As we looked out into the blackness of a clear Kansas night, he pointed a wavering finger toward the southwest horizon and said, "Well, the last time it was over there just above Graham's barn."

Events in his life provided him with engaging stories to embellish and charm anyone within earshot. Nearly trampled to death by a team of horses in his thirties and run over by a disc harrow in his forties, he survived falls from windmill towers, direct mule kicks to his chest, and being pitched off of hay wagons speeding down dirt roads. He drove fast, far too fast, all his adult life. As a teenager, I remember fixing fence by the road and looking up to see a 1965 Chevrolet Bel Air blasting down the road at eighty miles an hour, a slightly lower number than his age at the time. Leslie's wave and squinting grin was detectable through a windshield covered with a film of dust and pigeon droppings, and the tiny frame of Bertha was pressed backwards against the vinyl seat, sunken down so far that only the top of her thin gray hair was visible through the side window. My grinning Uncle Alvin watched the blue sedan roar past and shook his head vigorously as he yelled to me. "You know, he's no kid anymore! He shouldn't be driving that fast!"

In typical Leslie Cossaart style, he built an enormous barn in the 1930s, larger than any other in the area. Several years later, a tornado picked up the whole building; walls, roof, hay, and cows were sucked into the air by the large-scale spring twister, and not a trace of any of the items could ever be found anywhere.

When Leslie was in his fifties, his children were close to adulthood, and he and Bertha took care of Bertha's mother in her final years. A half mile across the section, my grandparents had the same live-in arrangement with Grandpa's father, Charles. Both remaining parents were in relatively good physical shape but slipping into expected mild dementia, both in their early nineties. They called it senility then. On more than one occasion, each parent had wandered off during a busy farm day while the working adults were consumed in their tasks. Uncle Leslie related the story with his usual tickled-to-death manner. "I was cultivatin' corn one afternoon and I looked off a quarter mile south, and there Dad and Bertha's mother were walkin' down the road, together. I drove the tractor back to the house, got in the car, and drove down the road to meet 'em." As Leslie slowed his car beside the two old people strolling down the gravel road, he casually called out the window, "You folks need a ride?" The couple smiled at each other, grateful for the relief from walking in the hot sun. "Sure!" they answered. So Leslie took each of them to their respective homes, escorting them one at a time out of the car with, "Well now, this looks like a nice place to stop!" And both escapees were safely returned.

Sometime shortly after his seventy-fifth birthday, Les was broadsided at an intersection of two county roads a mile north of his house. A larger grain truck plowed into his battered 1952 Chevy pickup, with both trucks traveling at high speed on the dirt roads. In that era pickups had a large running board along the bottom of the driver- and passenger-side doors with a mirror mounted on a tube metal frame. When his skidding truck came to a rest fifty yards out into the alfalfa field, an unbelted Les had been knocked clear out of the cab and was still clinging to the mirror frame. He insistently waved off an offer to have himself driven back to his home by the two occupants of the other truck, and in a rage and with two broken vertebrae, he stomped half a mile down a muddy road in his chore boots to reach home and be taken to the hospital. He wore a back brace for years after that, and from that point on was one bent old Cossaart.

Bertha and Leslie had a boy and then twin girls. His eyes danced when he told me of the two baby girls and how Mother would take one and Dad would take the other to rock them to sleep. Each girl was in a routine with her particular parent, and on more than one occasion, sudden wailing from one of the babies would be the only apparent evidence that someone had the wrong baby. Vera and Vesta were so identical, their senior portraits in the tiny rural high school yearbook looked to be photocopies placed next to each other on the page. Les and Bertha's son grew up to farm in the area, and he was roughly the same age as my dad. I heard a few tales from my father how Olin had evidently inherited Leslie's vigor for life and disregard for caution. All three children grew to be fine adults, and I liked them very much. I was proud to be associated with them.

Upland game pheasants were common on our section of land, and they would nest and seek shelter in the fencerows, choked with dried waist-high tumbleweeds. Republic County pheasant hunting at that time was some of the best in the world, and to walk out along a fencerow in the late fall could nearly guarantee at least one episode of a brilliantly colored game bird exploding from cover, its loud and startling squawk serving as its best defense. One blustery fall day Leslie's grown grandson was convinced by Les to walk along with him to hunt for pheasant. Leslie had retrieved an old double-barreled shotgun out of his closet for the afternoon, and it was naturally a large ten-gauge model. As Les and his grandson walked along, guns loaded and senses alert, a pheasant burst out of the weeds with wings flying in a low trajectory away from the hunters. Both shotguns fired in rapid succession, with both of Leslie's barrels discharging at once. The recoil from the heavy gun blew Les backwards, and for a brief panicky instant his grandson looked in all directions laterally and could not find his grandfather anywhere. A glance downward found Les lying flat on his back, his normally squinted eyes wide open, chuckling with delight, and both barrels aimed straight toward heaven. The pheasant flew away unharmed.

One of my friends talked me into taking a butterscotch-colored kitten home, and since I had more than enough cats at my place, I thought Les could use a pet. He had no animals around at the time and was absolutely tickled to receive the little companion. His grown children remembered the rule as they grew up: People stay indoors; animals stay outside. Les guarded his precious companion by keeping the cat indoors most of the time. To solve the need to say the cat was outside, he went to town, bought a small collar and leash, and walked the kitten around the side yard of the house a few times each day. Cats do not take well to such arrangements, but Uncle Leslie made it work. He laughed and talked to his pet while it strained on the end of the tether, his little neck pinched tight and his eyes bulging in desperation. Uncomfortable perhaps, but he never got away. Les also pounded a small iron stake into the front yard and fastened the leash to it. The cat could enjoy the outdoors while Les kept an eye on him through the kitchen window. One afternoon Les went outside just in time to see a hungry coyote about fifty feet from the cat, eying a potential dinner as the cat grew increasingly desperate in his containment. Leslie grabbed a spade shovel on the way to his rescue. The coyote understood perfectly and high-tailed it away.

I farmed about two thousand acres of land in 1987, about average for a viable grain farming operation in the region. My individual fields were large, and to perform a tillage task on any particular forty- or fifty-acre field amounted to at least an eight-hour stretch of driving the tractor and pulling an implement to work the soil, fertilize, plant the seed, or any combination of those operations. One or more support vehicles, providing supplies of seed, fuel, or fertilizer was required to accompany the tractor from field to field. Transporting these vehicles and tractors from one parcel to another a few miles away became a logistical pain in the rear after I found myself single again. This became Leslie's perfect opportunity to be useful, and his eyes widened when I finally asked for his help. Chuckling and peering through the windshield space underneath the top of the steering wheel, he loved to drive the old blue Bel Air down the dirt roads at unwise speeds and repeatedly shuttle me to my destinations. I always put on my seatbelt. Sometimes my heart would rise to my throat as I hung onto the door handle with one hand with Leslie chatting and laughing and taking his eyes off the road for perhaps a moment too long. He never crashed, but as he drove away I could occasionally watch a puff of dust billow up as the car would fishtail toward the roadside ditch. I could empathize with his departed wife in her days as a passenger. He provided me with an occasional thrill now and then and great taxi service for a couple of summers.

Harry and May

Through the winter months in following years I learned to weld iron with modest proficiency. Carl had installed a very nice heavy-duty wire welder in the shop. I forced myself to learn how to use it, intimidated though I was, and Carl was usually absent from the shop at the time. This MIG—Metal Inert Gas — welder was light years ahead of the old stick welder that Harry used. Once I had mastered it, Harry gave small nudges of approval to the work I was doing. I encouraged him to try it, but he quietly refused and stuck to his old antique buzz box. I spent a fair amount of time welding together cattle panels and pasture gates; my favorite project was to manufacture a frame out of used oilfield pipe as a stout structure to fasten boards and corrugated tin for use as small hog houses.

One evening Harry and I had both put in a full afternoon of welding. We were the only ones in the blacksmith shop; son Carl was out on a truck run and Martin, the other employee, was home with the flu. Harry motioned for me to follow him as he waddled wearily into the shop's office, about a five-foot-square area with a small, battered schoolteacher's desk rescued from the dump. A fine dust hung in the air from our end-of-the-day sweeping and was illuminated by a sixty-watt bulb hanging from the ceiling by a single black-and-white strand. Harry sat down with a grunt into an oversized wooden chair and opened the bottom drawer of the desk. He pulled out a bottle of cheap whiskey. When people would ask Harry what he owed his long life and good health of eighty-two years to, he always answered the same: "Always drink *good* whiskey," as he raised his chin in exaggerated pride. I could see by his choice of whiskey that his frugality trumped his philosophy.

He struggled with wavering fingers to unscrew the cap, raised it to his mouth, and leaned back slightly in the creaking chair. "Ahh, good medicine," he uttered and cast a challenging eye as he offered the bottle to me. Brown specks of chewing tobacco floated in the amber liquid and saliva dripped off the rim. The drinking code of honor prevented me from wiping it off, at least while he was looking. I took a generous swig as I felt his eyes focus on my chest, waiting to see me wince or choke. It went down hard and burned in a falling wave down my esophagus. My eyes squinted tightly as I handed the bottle back. We passed it back and forth several more rounds.

"You know, my first wife, she would take a drink now and then," Harry began without preface. "Frances and her folks," referring to his current spouse, "they're kinda churchy and don't believe in that sort of thing." His stare into space reflected his disappointment. His foggy eyes, sunken deeply in the folds of his eyelids, suddenly grew sad. Yet he smiled warmly as he spoke. "May, that was her name you know, would go to dances and have just a-good a-time as me, and then get up the next morning and put in a good day's work like myself."

But May got sick. Apparently she developed some form of head and neck cancer that ate a hole in her face and ended her life at thirty-five. "We was farmin' then, but I also ran the shop." Harry's blacksmithing supplemented the young couple's small farm in Kansas during the Depression. In desperately hard times of drought when farm prices were reduced to pennies per pound or bushel, he and his wife worked and began their family; first their son, Leo, was born, and then Virginia came a few years later. Harry's smile reflected a love that some fortunate men carry for a woman once in a lifetime. As the children were eight and twelve years old, their mother became increasingly debilitated. The cancer began to sap her strength, and she spent more and more time in bed. "I hired a good man to do the farmin', and I nursed May, round the clock, for 'bout a year." He paused, and the ever-present palsied movement of his head increased noticeably. His facial expression turned to anguish, and he choked, "She... just ... wouldn't..." Water suddenly filled his eyes. "Get ... no ... *better.*" His large torso became a statue in the big chair. Then he looked up and searched my face with a fifty-year-old question. We both stared silently at the concrete floor for several seconds. "And you know what?" he interrupted. He looked up at me with disbelief. "On the day she died, I went out in the yard to burn the trash. And when I walked back to the house, I caught myself *whistling!*"

My Cow Herd

I somehow scraped up enough money to buy five bred cows from Rita, my former employer with the beautiful herd of Shorthorns. She and I handpicked those out of a large pen full of young pregnant animals that would be the genetic basis for my future herd. In March of 1983 the first calf was born on the sunny side of my barn, and I was off and running as a stockman with my own cow herd. I steadily utilized more parcels of the pasture surrounding the house as I bought a few more cows here and there, and within several years the entire pasture was filled with my animals.

A friend of mine had some visitors come from Los Angeles, and they were eager to see a bona fide cowboy at work. With me in mind, my friend drove his guests out past my farmstead, where I was in the pasture next to the road, checking on my cows in the morning light. It was a hot summer morning and I had hurriedly dressed, so instead of a tall Marlboro man in cowboy hat and chaps, the visitors gazed curiously upon me: short in stature, hair nearly to my shoulders, green Adidas sneakers,

blue-jean cut-off shorts, and a Def Leppard T-shirt. No horse.
No hat.

Tyler

———————

My Doberman, Tyler, amused himself chasing rabbits around the farm with focused ferocity. In all his years of effort, he never caught one, but that didn't discourage him. I watched in amazement as one time, he was hot on the heels of a terrified rabbit, who skillfully dove through a hole in an old woven-wire fence that remained on the edge of the yard. Tyler slammed into the fence full speed and cartwheeled over it, landing on his back, and it disoriented him briefly. Without hesitation or evidence of pain, the dog leaped to his feet and resumed the fruitless chase. He plunged under barbed-wire fences and ripped open bloody wounds down his back in his pursuit of the elusive rabbit, but he never seemed to even notice the gashes that were several inches long.

He also loved to play a game with my first wife's horse. The big buckskin gelding was penned in an area that led out into a small pasture with a barbed-wire fence separating the horse from the driveway. The dog barked and tormented the horse, keeping a safe distance on the other side of the fence as horse and dog raced all the way down the driveway to the barren pen adjacent to the barn. While the horse was turning around in the small pen, the dog daringly dove into the lot, snapped at the horses' heels, and got the hell out of harm's way before eight hundred pounds of healthy horse could get in position with his potentially lethal kick. Tyler was quite adept at the game, and it went on for weeks. Finally his luck ran out as the horse wised up. I didn't see the blow, but I looked up upon hearing a shriek and saw Tyler dragging his own injured body out of the pen and into the safety of the driveway. A muddied hoof print was clearly emblazoned on the black hair of Tyler's rib cage. It probably took the dog a good half hour to struggle back to the front porch of the house, where he spent a lot of time over the next day or so. The game did not resume.

When Tyler was slightly past puppy stage, he got into the unfortunate habit of chasing the cattle out in the main pasture. Worse yet, they were the neighbor's cows; a stockman just up the road was renting the pasture at the time before I could fill up the main pasture with my own bovines. I heard gleeful barking out north of the house one morning and walked out to investigate. To my horror, Tyler had the entire herd, thirty or more cows, on a full run. This was a capital offense in cattle country, and I would not have blamed my neighbor for shooting the dog on sight. I was furious. I stomped out to the dog, screaming obscenities and waving my arms, and the dog finally heard me, thankfully before running the animals into the fence. He then realized he had screwed up royally. He slinked toward me to accept his fate. Without thinking, I grabbed the dog by the throat with my left hand, drew back with my right, and smashed my

Tyler in retirement.

fist directly into his big nose. That was the only time I could lay claim to punching a dog in the nose, or for that matter, the only time I ever hit him with anything. It was the last time he ever chased cattle.

When Missy and I split, Tyler remained with me. He was my sole and dedicated companion, easing the loneliness as the neighbors grew accustomed to seeing the big Doberman riding in the passenger seat of my pickup wherever I went. He was strong and silent, never vicious with anyone familiar, and remarkably tolerant with children, who could go as far as riding him like a small horse and pulling on his ears. But he was an effective watchdog and always seemed to sense if I was uncomfortable with anyone who drove into the yard. He hardly woke from his nap on the front porch as my friends drove in; Tyler let them walk in the front door nearly unnoticed. But when a rather shady young man in the area with a reputation for thievery once strode up my sidewalk, Tyler awoke from his nap, and the poor fellow backpedaled to the safety of his car as the dog snapped menacingly close to his genitals and forced him back into his vehicle. Tyler bared his teeth and barked with authority at visiting Jehovah's Witnesses, too, keeping them confined to the interiors of their cars.

In my single days I would sometimes visit the local bars, and one night I was in a tavern in Fairbury, Nebraska. I was not a local in that particular town and soon found myself reluctantly entangled in an argument over a young woman who was jealously supervised by a large and drunk young man. He suggested it would be proper to beat the hell out of me, and I could see no way out of it. Somehow I convinced him to step outside so as not to break any furniture. I didn't stand a chance; I wasn't much of a fighter, especially against someone as mean and large as he was. In fact, I had never been in a fight, outside of punching my dog in the nose. "Could you let me put my glasses in my pickup?" I humbly appealed to any sense of honor he might have had as an audience gathered, and I pointed to my little yellow pickup parked directly in front of the bar. I patted my shirt pocket where my glasses were supposed to be, at a time in my life *before* I needed glasses. "Hurry up, asshole," he growled as I opened my truck door and out jumped a seventy-pound Doberman. Tyler positioned himself in between me and the other guy, dutifully sat down, and stared up coldly at the man. My potential opponent instantly had a change of heart and muttered something about the no-good bitch in the bar who was suddenly not worth the effort.

One evening Tyler came up out of the creek next to the house reeking of skunk. Ordinarily he slept at the foot of my bed, but he stayed outside that night. The next night, the same thing happened. The third night, he finally got his revenge and appeared on the front porch with a dead skunk as a trophy. Several days later, he became very sick, and I took him to the vet. For a week the vet treated him intensively for hepatitis and pancreatitis, and Tyler finally pulled through, but with severe damage. From that point on, it was necessary to supplement his diet with daily feedings of cottage cheese and cooked macaroni to compensate for a nonfunctioning pancreas, and as time went on he required weekly steroid injections to bolster his arthritic frame. As I was eating my supper one night at Hubbell, a man remarked what good care I took of my dog. "I have to be good to him," I responded. "That dog has outlasted two wives."

A Special Calf

One of the goals of every stockman is to have a herd of cows that give birth without assistance, and for the most part, mine did just that. Regardless, a good cow-calf man is ever vigilant during the season that calves are born. The cows are exposed to the bull for an eight-week period, so I hoped all my cows would have their calves during a similar stretch of time nine months later. My calf crop was timed to begin dropping in February and go through March. "Dropping" is a pretty apt term because the cow usually stands up during birthing. The idea is to have the little calves up and running around, taking full advantage of the growing season that provides the lush grass to feed mama cow, who feeds the calf, and maximizes the weight gain. Containing the birthing period to eight weeks also allowed me to devote more attention to the herd before the all-consuming fieldwork ensued in April and May. A minimum of surprises is desired during calving time.

Cows have one calf per year, and that's it. If the calf is lost to a difficult birth, or later, to disease or accident, there goes the entire income for that one cow. The economics of raising cattle are tight, and a cow without a calf is an expensive situation. Instead of making money, she is costing money. So besides the heartfelt concern—and it takes plenty of that to be a decent stockman—there is a definite economic incentive to save the calf's life.

On a cold and rainy St. Patrick's Day morning, I was procrastinating in the early hours, thinking of excuses not to go outside and check the cows. From the kitchen window, I looked out to the lot adjacent to the barn and saw a black cow acting as if she had recently given birth, but I could see no calf on the ground. My dread increased at the thought of trudging through a muddy cow lot in thirty-some-degree temperatures and a driving rain. The cows approaching parturition were fenced out of the small lot next to the north side of the barn, where I worked and separated the cattle during drier times. It was deeply rutted, and with the saturating rains of the previous three days the thirty-foot-square area was a sloppy, soupy quagmire and instant death for a freshly born calf.

Great Plains range cattle have been bred to live on the open range. They do not do well if contained inside a barn during the cold and often rainy weather of February and March. The Central Plains of the United States experiences some of the most extreme and intense weather anywhere on earth; subzero temperatures and sudden blizzards characterize the winters that contrast to the triple-digit readings in mid- and late summer. Cattle prefer open spaces and have the healthiest calves on a well-drained area with plenty of elbow room. If there is a nice, dry barn nearby, they will not voluntarily go into it. To "shelter" them indoors in early spring is very unhealthy, and the surest way to make a range cow sick is to force her into an enclosed space. Their immune systems are not designed to exist in that sort of environment, no matter how clean the barn is. This basic health concept also holds true for newborn calves.

The fence separating the birthing area from the working lots next to the barn was far from cow-proof, and I had lived long enough to know the determination of a cow to searching out a bit of privacy while delivering a calf. Sometimes the first-calf cows, or heifers, make a lousy choice and put too much priority on seclusion and not enough on delivery conditions. But as I looked out the window, I remembered that all my heifers had theirs in February. I confirmed the sight of steam rising off the body of a newborn calf, lying in the muck, directly behind the barn. It had to be an older cow, and it made no sense that she would be so stupid. My heart sank.

When calves are born, the placenta breaks and a seemingly lifeless eighty- to one-hundred-pound blob of protoplasm is expelled from the birth canal and lands with a splash on the ground. For the most part, cows are remarkably good mothers, considering they do not attend Lamaze classes or even seem to pay attention to other cows during the birth process. It is all pretty much instinct. A few minutes after the calf enters the world, the mother meticulously licks clean every square inch of his fur, stimulating the circulation of the calf and providing critical warmth. If the calf can't get up out of the mud, momma can't warm him up, and he will quickly slip into hypothermia.

I stepped into my high-top mud boots, put on my hat, and hurried through the cold rain, zipping up my hooded sweatshirt and outer raincoat as I ran down the narrow concrete sidewalk toward the lot. The calf was motionless, and my adrenaline surged as I clambered over the steel gate and splashed through the manure and mud toward the shiny black object lying in the muck. I bogged down after several steps, and the muddy soup swallowed up my boots; I kept moving, and first one boot, then the next one, stayed glued down. Now I was in my socked feet. The goop was incredibly cold, and my long white tube socks turned to instant brown, and both came off in my last few labored steps toward the newborn. I leaned down and shook the calf violently, and the cow gave me a protective nudge with her giant nose on the back of my head. I threw my gloves over the gate and reached down to place my bare hands on the calf, covered with the thin and clear membrane of the spent placental sac. The mud, the worried and menacing thousand-pound mama looking down at me, the newborn body of the calf, and the cowboy soaked to the bone all had the same shiny wet reflection in the dull shadows of the late morning. The calf was so cold he felt like an inanimate object, and his breath was barely detectable. There was no way to warm him up out in the lot.

I placed my arms around the calf and was astounded at how heavy he was. I could only manage to raise half his body up before dropping him back down. He was moderately large as newborn calves go, at around a hundred pounds, but every ounce was helpless and dead weight, covered with slimy afterbirth. I heaved him up over my shoulder with all the strength I

could muster. It took a tremendous effort to stand, and I slogged through the muddy lot with one hundred pounds of dead weight over my right shoulder, my feet bare and legs numb. I kicked the gate open, tripped, and the calf and I landed back down into the manure. Mama displayed her disapproval more forcefully, and I felt her huge head rubbing across my bare back while my raincoat and saturated sweatshirt gathered up around my neck and shoulders. I expected to feel the ramming of her head squarely into my back at any moment, and my body to be decisively trampled into the shit by a confused and angry thousand-pound mother. Gasping for breath and exhausted, the calf and I lay in a heap of wet bodies until I could regain my breath, and at the first opportunity I managed to kick the gate shut between the cow and my slimy cargo. I had no time to reason with the cow that I had the best interests of her baby in mind. After what seemed like eternity kneeling in the pelting rain, I regained enough strength to hoist the calf to my shoulder again, and I trudged toward the house.

The calf and I fell again as I climbed the three stair steps at the front door. Mud, manure, and afterbirth splattered on the walls and over the floor as calf and cowboy tumbled onto the oak landing. I stood and grasped the calf by the front feet and dragged him down the hall and into the bathroom. Opening the shower door, I turned on the water to a temperature nearly too hot to tolerate. I heaved up the calf one final time, all my energy spent, and the calf and I fell into the shower into a collective, sloppy heap. The fiberglass shower stall boomed with an echo. The half-full plastic bottles of shampoo and conditioner were jarred off the shower shelf and landed on my temple and shoulder. The only muscle I could move at that instant was being used to gather air into my lungs. I lay prostrate over the body of the calf, a cartilaginous pile with his two hind hooves splayed out the open shower door. My body felt every bit as boneless. Bloody afterbirth and cow manure covered us and every surface of the shower stall. Our two faces lay pushed together on the floor, eyeball to eyeball, my ear submerged in an inch of brown water that refused to go down the drain. The door remained open as the hot water sprayed on the calf and me, water bouncing off us and covering the tile floor. I stood partway up and fell backwards onto the wet floor. I lay on my back to stare up at the splatters on the ceiling and gasp for breath. Most of my days as a farmer and stockman had routinely consisted of hard work, but this was beyond anything before. If there was ever a time when I could truly say I pushed my endurance to the limit, there it was.

I stripped my clothes and piled them in a brown wad on the floor. With the hot water warming up the calf, I vigorously rubbed and slapped to try and revive the precious little fellow. I quit rubbing for a moment and looked hard for some movement. An ear wiggled. His front legs twitched. The huge eyelashes blinked. The calf shook his head and let out a violent cough. His floppy ears slapped against his face, and he let out a bawl that echoed across the tile floor. He was alive! I screamed out a celebratory whoop, "YEEEE HAWW!!!" and it made my eardrums hurt. I washed the calf clean with the half bottle of shampoo, lathering up every inch of his black hair coat and rinsing him thoroughly. I even put a generous amount of conditioner on him, rubbed it all through his fur, and rinsed him again.

I stood up to wash the manure and blood off myself. The calf began to struggle instinctively, but I knew he would not be able to even begin to stand up just a few minutes into his new life. I let the hot water run on him as I hurriedly dried myself off and ran upstairs to put on clean clothing with newfound energy.

I came back down, shut off the water, and dragged the calf out of the shower onto the bathroom floor by his front legs. It took every towel I had in the cabinet, and his strength increased by the minute as I dried him off with pure glee. I laughed out loud as the concept came to me: This creature's first wide-eyed view of the world and life would not be the same as his fellow calf-cousins, to say the least. Those huge, black, beautiful, bulging eyes were fixed on my motions. He really didn't know enough to be afraid of anything. To complete the job, I got out a hair dryer and brush and blow-dried his entire coat. At that moment, as I watched his steady rhythmic breathing and looked at his clear and alert eyes, he was the most gorgeous thing I had ever seen. His pristine black hair coat shined in the bathroom light and felt more fuzzy and comforting than the sweetest stuffed animal of my childhood. He would be the envy of all his little companions out in the pasture.

Now the problem was to get him back to Mama. As I carried him down the hall, I was astounded at the mess we had made in the hallway and staircase. This was one time I felt lucky to be single and could picture an imaginary spouse's face as she surveyed the condition of the wallpaper. I proudly carried him outside, and since he had muscle tone, he seemed to feel twenty pounds lighter. I could hear the cow calling to her calf in desperate tones. She was telling me in no uncertain terms that she, not I, was the mom. There are few sounds that carry through the air with such trumpeting as a cow separated from her calf. She pushed and jostled the heavy steel tubing gate with all her weight; it would not be long before she completely flattened it.

There is a cardinal rule of common cowboy sense when dealing with cows and calves: Keep the calf in between yourself and the cow. The cow will certainly never harm the calf, but once the baby is out of the way, she will not hesitate to knock you senseless and stomp you into the ground. Cautiously, I placed the calf's feet down on the ground in front of her, and she seemed satisfied. Keeping my eyes on her, I quickly exited the lot by vaulting over the same gate. To my delight, the cow led the calf away from the muddy lot and into the open calving area where he was supposed to be in the first place. I stood by the gate and watched the bonding process begin. The calf soon figured out where the udders were and started on his first meal, a critical milestone. The first drink of milk contains colostrum that supplies concentrated nourishment and initiates the immune system.

I leaned against the steel tubular gate with aching muscles and happily watched the calf drink. His head jerked upward in spasms as he suckled his sedate mother, devouring his first warm meal. Satisfied enough to let them be, I returned to the house to clean up the mess. An hour of deliberate mopping and scrubbing, interrupted repeatedly for rest, returned the hallway and bathroom to a cleaner state. I fixed myself a small meal, sat down in my rocking chair in the living room, and dozed off while watching the television for a while. It felt wonderful to do nothing for a few hours, and reflect on my hard-fought little victory over the cruelties of nature.

With the waning hours of the afternoon the rain reduced itself to a drizzle and then halted. A cold front advanced through the skies and swept the moisture clean, and a brisk north breeze blew away the cloud cover to reveal the sun now and then. I ventured back outside, drove into town to retrieve my mail, and shared a cup of coffee with a few of the neighbor farmers who had gathered in the small grocery store. On rainy days it was customary for a handful of locals to migrate to this place, an old mom-and-pop store with creaky floors and the smell of cigarettes and coffee. A spirited card game went uninterrupted as I poured myself a cup of bitter brew from the urn. I told the tale of the muddy calf to a few of my contemporaries, though tempering the emotions and leaving out many details, realizing that my adventure was not altogether that uncommon for any other cowboy. To posture oneself as being unmoved and stoic while performing such ordinary heroics was consistent with the stockman's persona, which, like most of the other men, I wore like a suit of armor. The story provided some amusement for my audience, accompanied by quiet nods and chuckles from guys who had likely been in, or out of, my boots several times in their careers.

After a few side conversations I returned to my pickup and drove down the road at a slow and deliberate pace. Arriving home, I drove out to where I could check up on the new calf and read my mail in the comfort of a warm pickup truck. The precious little miracle was lying on the ground next to the cow, and I again reflected for a while on how pretty he looked. His sheen of black hair glistened in the sun and was a stark contrast to his muddy surroundings and the other calves covered with dried mud and manure. He was seemingly alert, although not on his feet like some of his companions. I attributed this to the ordeal he and I had shared many hours previous, and before returning to the house, I again congratulated myself on such a supreme effort. Every now and then, with enough effort, a man could swing the odds of nature in his favor.

It felt so good to lay my tired frame down on my bed that night. I fell asleep quickly, had a peaceful slumber, and awoke relatively late. Although the rain was long gone, the lots and fields were going to be muddy for a week, so there was no big hurry to get on with the day. I ate a light breakfast, watched a morning news show for a half hour, and put on my boots that had finally dried out next to the woodstove. My first order of the day was to go check on that little black bull calf. I walked out to the open calving lot with the soreness in my leg muscles still lingering with each step.

I stopped by the gate and surveyed the cows and calves scattered on the hillside. My eyes locked onto an unbelievable sight: a motionless black calf lying flat on the ground. I vaulted the gate and sprinted toward the still animal, and there was no mistaking it. My last few steps of running tapered off to a slow and resigned walk. He was dead.

The wind blew through his shiny black hair coat on his stiff body. I dropped to my knees, suddenly feeling as exhausted as I had felt twenty-four hours earlier. All my efforts, all the anguish and alarm, had added up to the sum total of the dead calf that lay in front of me.

Autopsies can be performed with reasonable reliability by any large animal veterinarian, but in most cases the cause of a farm animal's death is academic and the procedure is an unnecessary expense. In this case, however, I just could not let it go. The vet opened up the calf's body cavity and pronounced his findings: The calf had a septal heart defect, a congenital hole in the wall of his ticker that ensured nonsurvival. He never had a chance.

Hindsight had revealed the wisdom of the cow that I initially thought was glaring stupidity. Did her instinct tell her that the calf was doomed, so she chose to give birth in the muck? And the cow was silent. When calves are struck by lightning or have fallen off a cliff, most cows will bawl loudly for days while refusing to move from the sight of the dead calf. She seemed to have already moved on.

After I took a few hours to accept reality, a lesson I had learned long before came into my mind. When I was in my late teens, I began to clear some brush and a fallen tree near the barn. I was eager to use the chain saw and do work that I felt was very important. There was a lone cow in the immediate area, and I wanted her to move out of the way. She wanted to stay put. My shouting and even the roaring chain saw had little effect. No matter how much I chased her and yelled at her, she would run in a large circle, back to the vicinity of the downed tree, and resume her grazing. Frustrated, I stomped back to the house in a foul mood and angrily asked my grandfather why the stupid cow would not get out of the way. He answered with a chuckle and a puff of his pipe. "That cow knows her business much better than you do." So here was another cow, going about the business of her existence, as I ran in circles.

Connection

———————————

Through the years my old friend Mike and I kept in touch. We exchanged phone calls every month or so, and quite often he or I would have a premonition. For me, a simple image of Mike would enter my mind and vanish without much thought given to it, and then later in the day he would call just to say hello. On a February day in 1985, he came out to Kansas, and we were driving westward on I-70 in Colorado, crossing over the western Kansas border and heading to the Rockies for a weekend of skiing. He and I had never traveled together in the area before; when we were roommates at Purdue ten years prior he knew only vague details of my car accident. I had never revealed to him the exact location and had not been thinking of the accident as we traveled down the highway. Without warning, he suddenly told me he felt very sick and thought "something terrible is about to happen up here," as he pointed through the front windshield toward the approaching horizon, exactly where I had been flung into the median ten years prior. I looked at his face, and for the first time in our association, tears ran down his cheeks. He was more agitated than I had ever seen him. Alarmed, I asked if he wanted to stop, and I slowed the car momentarily. He said nothing but continued to wear a perplexed expression. Then, suddenly, his face relaxed and he said, "It's okay now. I feel better. Keep going." He faced me directly and grinned. I resumed normal highway speed and drove for the next hour marveling at a connection between the two of us that could not be explained rationally.

The Last Load

Uncle Leslie's grandson farmed his grandpa's land. Dave's tractor and mine sometimes passed beside each other during the growing seasons. If he wasn't his grandpa's favorite grandchild, he was certainly the one he saw the most. Dave would stop and check in on Leslie while he was doing fieldwork or tending his cattle. He was a bright, likable man. Dave was talented, hard working, and one of the best farmers I had ever seen. I admired his abilities. We worked on small farm projects together on occasion, but it was tough to keep up with his pace. We were friendly to each other, and now and then he would show up at my place and provide some help sorting cattle. When he was injured in an auto accident one winter, I spent every morning at his father Olin's farm, where Dave kept his own cows. It was easy to see the relationship between the father and son was full of conflict; it was not a comfortable place to be. Olin was in very poor health himself and nearing the end of his own life, debilitated from heart disease and emphysema.

Dave was introverted, but when he filled up on whiskey, the rage emerged. At the time I was having my own battles with marriage troubles and depression and felt safer if I avoided associating with Dave, even though I felt drawn to him due to our shared heritage. Now and then I caught a whiff of the area gossip regarding the Cossaart boys and their inability to keep it together. Dave had two young boys, and he and his wife had gone through a painful and protracted divorce a year before he decided to cash it all in.

Dave drove his pickup truck into a tree at about one hundred miles an hour; I'm pretty sure it was intentional. The two older generations of men and I watched them put Dave back into the prairie soil on a miserably cold and rainy autumn day in the cemetery where the other Cossaarts were buried. The rows of flat gray granite stones were set out in a fenced-off parcel surrounded by the ocean of ripening fall crops. I stood and reflected somberly on Dave's struggle with depression and thought long and hard about my own future. I pondered the genetic link. I bent down to address Uncle Leslie as he sat shivering on a metal folding chair under the small tent that sheltered the casket. In the usual candor of our shared words, I asked him, "How are you doing with all this?" Les shook his head slowly and uttered softly, "I've seen it all now. And I've run out of tears."

Harvest is harvest and cannot be postponed for long, even if someone dies. Dave's father, Olin, saw no option but to go ahead and harvest his son's standing crops, and he stubbornly fired up the combine. He thrashed through the next week with his oxygen tank clanking under the combine seat, driven on by raw grief and diverting himself with a work ethic he had hammered into himself for his entire life. Uncle Leslie's face bore the evidence of losing his closest grandson, but he was denied the same outlet for his own safety. He couldn't drive the larger grain trucks or tractors, and the family handed him small tasks like fetching water, mostly to keep him out of the way.

Olin finished harvesting the last soybean field on Uncle Leslie's farm and had a fraction of a load of beans that would not fit into the large truck, so he hooked up Leslie's seldom-used 1948 Farmall tractor and pulled an old wagon out of the shed. Fifty bushels of beans, about enough to fill the back of a pickup truck, were dumped into the wagon, rather than waiting for the next day and risk being left out in the rain. With the exhausting task finished, Olin drove the combine home to his own farm several miles away and collapsed into his bed, where he remained for a month. Leslie was forbidden by his children from operating his old tractor, which had no cab or even a fender to hang on to while getting on and off. A tumble off of the thing would have certainly killed him, and he was sad, weak, and ninety-two at the time.

The grain elevator in Mahaska did not have the capacity to handle the huge inflow of soybeans in such a short time frame, an expected and yearly condition. The lines of trucks grew long, and people had to sit and wait up to a half hour to dump their loads. A line of about twenty grain trucks and large tractors were standing stationary as a most remarkable sight slowed to a stop at the end of the line. It was Leslie, perched upon the steel seat of his old tractor. He had driven the small tractor two miles to town to dump his little load of soybeans.

The earflaps of his old hat were down, and the only facial feature detectable was his fierce determination. His big, tattered jacket obscured his shriveled little body as he bounced helplessly on the spring steel seat. The engine putt-putted, and Les struggled with all of his strength to push in the clutch pedal to stop. Leslie's cargo of soybeans was dwarfed by the huge trucks that each held more than ten times the amount of his load. The line of farmers stared in amazement, and the ones remaining in their cabs soon climbed out to get a closer look. The workers at the scale house and dump pit dropped their paperwork and scoop shovels to witness the sight.

I got out of my truck and felt moved to share my admiration for my great uncle with someone else. Without hesitation I struck up a conversation with, of all people, the middle-aged blonde woman standing beside a large and shining new truck carrying a load of soybeans from one of Russ Long's fields. "God bless him, he is just precious..." she said, as I suddenly realized she actually had a soul. The sight of my great uncle made my chest puff up with pride.

Several men and women began applauding as Leslie's grin reluctantly appeared and tightened on his face. As he sat on the idling and obsolete tractor, the elevator manager walked up to Les and shouted at him to go ahead of everyone else waiting in line, but Les repeatedly refused. He waited for his turn and dumped his load, and it seemed to take forever. Nobody minded. He stuffed the scale ticket into his pocket and drove his tractor and empty wagon back to his home.

Tobe

"This here dog is on social security." Harry nodded to the ancient coon dog snoring on the cool concrete shop floor. Tobe was about fifteen years of age but looked even older and walked with an arthritic gate. The old coon dog had lived a hard life. Harry and Carl had been avid coon hunters for years, and the main ingredient for chasing raccoons through the woods after midnight is a tenacious, scrappy dog that will sniff out a coon and chase him up a tree. Raccoons are smart and put up a stiff defense when cornered. Tobe's shredded ears and dozens of claw scars on his face and back bore that out. He had grotesque and odd growths on various areas of his skin, and his eyes, when open, were bloodshot and glazed over with cataracts. He had a hoarse, ridiculous bark, and in the winter would walk over to the door with an arthritic limp, stare blankly at the doorknob with his foggy vision, and persistently make his request to go outside to pee.

"BWORF!" he insisted, over and over, at ten-second intervals. There could be several men each working diligently at his own particular task in the shop while Tobe repeated his demand.

After he was ignored for a few minutes, usually it was the person hardest of hearing, Harry, who relented. "Damn it! Will somebody let Tobe out?!" he would yell forcefully over the noise of grinding wheels and hammers. Whoever had the softest conscience dropped what they were doing and obliged. Predictably in another five minutes, Tobe persistently stated his muffled and rhythmic request on the other side of the door, and someone stopped their work again and let him back in. It often appeared that the dog owned the place, and we were all there at the command of his bladder.

In the winter Tobe's sleeping place was a wadded-up old blanket, tossed onto the hard concrete shop floor near the woodstove. The short black fur on his bony back bristled with dandruff, and his wrinkled skin was dried out from constant exposure to the intense wood heat all winter. It was his place, and all shop activity sidestepped his little area. It was violated once by an unsuspecting salesman.

A representative from a regional hardware supplier showed up one day, and he looked quite out of place dressed in a suit and tie. He walked boldly into the noisy shop and asked for Mr. Stradley, and Harry looked up from tinkering at his workbench, which was also wisely placed near the stove. Tobe was awake but lying directly in the path of the approaching salesman. While anxiously introducing himself to Harry, the salesman gave the dog a gentle kick and muttered, "Out of the way, doggy." Tobe arose stiffly in silent annoyance, shuffled a few steps sideways, and circled in a limp around behind the newcomer as he passed by. The man got a few words out of his mouth and then abruptly yelled, "Yowww!" and leaped into the air. Tobe had taken a very firm and deliberate bite out of the man's left butt cheek. Neither the salesman's startled movements nor his rising anger had any effect upon Tobe. After delivering his vengeance, the old hound circled back to his original spot and lay down heavily again to continue his nap.

❊   ❊   ❊

Harry and I returned from lunch one day to find Tobe lying motionless on the shop floor. "Tobe...TOBE! Goddam' it, dog, WAKE UP!" Harry shouted. No response. Harry turned to me, frowned, and announced his assessment. "Dead." We both looked at each other, and he gave the dog a nudge in the tummy with his boot. Tobe's outer eyelids peeled open, followed by the inner membranes. He stared up at us, annoyed. Harry looked at me again and asked, "Do you think they make hearing aids for dogs?"

Harry and Doc

Harry and Doc were sitting on stools in the shop, keeping their distance from the woodstove that warmed them on a late winter afternoon. Both men showed the weariness that sets into the bones of old men. Neither could hear very well, so their conversation was sparse of words and loud in volume.

Doc Mannschreck ran the small lumberyard in Hubbell. He had been doing it for decades. I never heard why he was called "Doc." Well liked in the community, he was brusque in his manner, but his heart was as large as he was. He huffed and puffed when speaking from carrying his barrel chest and smoking too many cigars. He was shrewd but would never screw you for too much, and even when we could travel to a town where the prices were much better, we tried to support him. Besides that, it was fun dealing with the old man as his rotund frame would shift back and forth on the creaking floor. It was a real adventure poking around the dusty and creaky old shed where Doc kept his varied stock of finished and dimension lumber of every imaginable type. The hopelessly leaning low shed hulked toward the ground like someone desperately needing a nap in the tall grass surrounding it. Customers speculated how much longer it would remain standing.

Doc was jovial and warm, even though he tended to frighten little kids with his loud voice. He looked to be every bit as German as his immigrant parents, with a big, gray paintbrush mustache giving him the appearance of a walrus. I thought he looked like a huge Captain Kangaroo. Through the years Doc let it be known that he had a standing offer with any prospective parents in the community: If the couple named their child after him, they would get a free washer and dryer. I never recalled anyone naming their kid Walter Oscar.

Doc came into Harry's shop about once a week, and he was one of the select individuals for whom Harry actually stopped work and sat down to socialize with. As I quietly worked on a chain saw across the shop from the two old men, there was no problem overhearing them yell at each other's faces.

After a few sentences regarding the weather and various aches and pains, Doc changed the subject. "Well, I oughta go home and chase Lois around the kitchen, but I wouldn't know what to do with her if I caught her." He cast a question to Harry. "How's *your* sex life, Harry?"

Harry pondered a few moments, leaned back in his chair, and cast a glance to the bare chimney pipe rising from the woodstove. "Well, you know, Doc, it's like this." He paused and turned to address his friend directly. "Have you ever tried to poke a rabbit out of a culvert with a rope?" Both men shook with laughter. "When you get to our age, Doc," Harry continued, "sometimes I think my wife should stand on her head and I could just drop it in." They chuckled and traded comments back and forth for a few more minutes until Doc declared his statement of resignation to the aging human condition. "Aw hell, Harry, anymore I would just as soon take a good healthy shit." Harry's face instantly wore an expression of exaggerated astonishment. His eyes widened and he turned his body to directly face his friend again. "Doc," Harry carefully stated, "either you don't know how to fuck or else I don't know how to shit."

Tractors

I learned how to drive a tractor, *really* drive a tractor, at age four-teen. It was a big, long, bright orange and tan thing built in the early seventies, a Case 830, and the ride was bouncy as hell. It had no protective cab, and a great black vinyl seat with armrests contained my jean-clad bottom and occasionally the entire mechanism slammed to the frame when I happened to hit a large rut. A large six-cylinder diesel engine roared loud enough that I quickly adopted a good set of earmuffs. My uncle, well aware of a teenage boy's love for music, wisely bolted an outdoor radio on the broad steel fender within easy reach of my right hand. I was entertained by the AM rock-and-roll stations out of Omaha, Lincoln, and Kansas City, and I spent many a summer day singing at the top of my lungs to the popular songs of the day. Driving a tractor was my first real job, and I felt like a really important guy as I guided it back and forth across the fields in the blazing sun. My uncle rode with me a few rounds and then drove away in the pickup, leaving me to pilot my schooner out in the sea of soil. Now, when I hear Elton John's "Rocket Man,"

I recall the seat-in-my-pants feeling of pulling a thirteen-foot disk harrow across the black Kansas soil.

As a novice, I wasn't permitted to cultivate the weeds out of the growing grain sorghum crop, at the risk of wiping out any rows of tender plants. My job was cultivating the weeds out of the fallowed ground, that is, fields that were left unplanted for a summer. Keeping the fields free of weeds allowed the spring and summer rainfall to be stored up and provide the next season's wheat crop with a better shot at success. I considered it artwork; for the finishing touch, I soon learned how to finish off each field by making a pass on each end and erasing the tire marks where I had been turning all day. I would pull up on the hydraulic lever while exiting out onto the road, and the entire field would be smooth and uniform.

The first time I drove a tractor with an enclosed, air-conditioned cab on it, it made me glad that ours was broke down for the day. My uncle borrowed Russ Long's tractor, and it was newer, larger, and the comfortable cab shut out the noise and the hot sun. Russ came out to see how it was working for us, looming large as always. I was nervous as I pulled to a stop next to him. His suntanned forearm leaned out of the pickup window as he asked how things were going. "This feels like a Cadillac!" I shouted down to him. He just snorted with a puff of smoke spewing out beside his clenched pipe stem and drove off with an amused expression.

Tractor driving is an art as well as an acquired skill. By the time I was in my late teens I could judge the distance from an approaching telephone pole on the edge of the field while pulling a twenty-four-foot-wide implement and barely slow down as the end piece of iron on the implement missed the creosote pole by a few inches as I would pass.

After I began working for Russ, I drove his medium-powered John Deere model 3020, a masterpiece of 1960s American engineering. That model never wore out completely, and as long as you kept overhauling the engine and doing other minor repairs on a continual basis, it just kept on going. They were phenomenally fuel-efficient and surprisingly powerful, and the 3020, with its slightly more powerful brother the 4020, were tractors built from 1964 to 1972. There are many, many of these simple green tractors in the world that are still doing productive work today, fifty-plus years after their introduction.

Russ's 3020, as with most anything in his life, had a colorful history. Russ was hard on equipment, and the guys he hired to drive the tractors were often worse. Everyone in the area regarded the faded green tractor as some kind of ghost that could not be killed. In the seventies Russ had a hired man by the name of Webb, and Webb was a steady worker despite the fact he was an alcoholic and one time got so drunk on whiskey he passed out while digging for an ice cream bar and fell into an opened chest-type freezer at the Narka grocery store. Russ was kind in his description of the man. "I don't know what I would have done without the drunken bastard; he was good help." Once, as Russ was preparing to leave for a few days, he said, "Now, Webb, I don't want you drinkin' and drivin' the truck while I'm gone this weekend," knowing Webb's pattern of driving seven miles west to Hubbell and getting tanked on a fifth of cheap whiskey whenever he could find an unattended vehicle. Just to be sure, Russ drove his own car to the airport and hid the keys to the pickup truck and even the two old oversized grain trucks. His boss figured Webb would just have to spend the weekend being productive, and there was plenty of fieldwork to be done while Russ was off visiting his kids in Kansas City.

Some fieldwork did get done that weekend. But then Webb got thirsty on Saturday afternoon, and he drove the 3020 tractor to Hubbell. With a pocket full of cash from his weekly wages, he sat at the bar until he was sufficiently drunk. He staggered out the door into the hot summer afternoon and began driving the tractor home, weaving down the gravel road until he smashed head-on into the steel bridge railing over Rose Creek. The driver suffered only minor injuries, but the John Deere was banged up pretty bad. Several of the cosmetic sheet-metal panels got pitched into the creek. From that point on, an otherwise fairly aesthetically designed John Deere had a stripped-down look to it. But it still ran on, reliably and without complaint.

The 3020 had a wide front end, which meant the front wheels were set on an axle with a footprint of about five feet wide. This gave the tractor more stability than many of the ones built a few years earlier, which were often narrow front end models and built before rising power requirements were needed to pull the larger tillage implements. A narrow front type offered tighter turning ability at the end of the rows. However, the narrow fronts, like big tricycles, could tip over if you turned too quickly. One late May afternoon when I was still a teenager, my uncle was in a hurry to finish planting a field so he could jump on a plane that evening and fly out to watch the Indy 500 with us. He was, like many in our family, enthused about the race and enjoyed it nearly every year. Alvin had the throttle up as the tractor carried a rear-mounted planter that was lifted at the end of each pass by the hydraulic arms behind the seat, which makes the tractor unstable as it turns. Add to that the sloshing of half-full tanks of fertilizer being carried on a steel saddle bolted to the undercarriage. As he turned, his tractor pitched over forward; my uncle bailed out and leaped for clear ground out of the path of the tipping machine. Several days later, after coming back from town and obviously weary of answering questions and deflecting ridicule, he said, "I'm tellin' ya, if you want to get a lot of attention around here, just tip over a tractor."

Herbicides began being used in the early seventies, and at that time they were fairly simple compounds and needed to be applied with a lot of water; twenty gallons per acre of water/herbicide mixture would be sprayed out behind the seed-placing mechanisms on the planter. When I started working for Russ, we overloaded the 3020 with four hundred gallons of water (3,200 pounds of pendulum weight) with tanks so large I had to crawl over the back of the seat because the four-foot diameter plastic tanks blocked each side step. With a fresh load every twenty acres, the John Deere, a year past the need for an overhaul, roared and smoked with painful disapproval as it dutifully planted for fifteen days straight each spring.

One early June afternoon I was driving down the dirt road to return for seed. I had the tractor throttled up in road gear and was driving about twenty miles an hour as I headed back to the machinery yard on Russ's homestead. A two-inch-diameter plastic hose, plumbed directly from the circulating pump, burst and drenched me in a mixture of pre-emergent weed killer with the trade name Dual/Atrazine. I idled into the barnyard and parked the machine in front of the water hydrant. Stripping naked, I turned on the faucet, held the hose end above my head, and took an impromptu shower with fifty-degree well water.

The tired 3020 survived the last two years of Russ's farming career, and when I purchased all his machinery I had it overhauled again and demoted it to smaller tasks. I bought an even larger tractor for tillage and demoted the tillage tractor (with the climate-control cab, hydraulic seat, and stereo) to the planting work. It was a well-deserved retirement for the 3020, relieved to be given an easier role and shed of its twin two-hundred-gallon tanks.

The relatively modern John Deere 4240 then became my planting tractor. It had enough finesse to do the more precise work of planting but was strong enough to do it well. I installed an electronic seed monitor and replumbed the herbicide spray unit and tanks completely outside of the cab. The quiet and cool cab was a huge leap forward in tractor comfort, and the hydraulic-cushioned and upholstered seat was the best in the business at that time. It felt like I was sitting in my living room while I drove. I installed some very nice speakers and absorbed myself in music as I drove the endless hours planting crops. After my first marriage and when I was living alone, there wasn't much else to do in the evenings, so putting in extra-long days performing fieldwork was a good way to pass the time. I installed

Case and John Deere tractors.

high-powered lights on the top of the cab that illuminated the black soil far ahead of my path. Long-distance radio stations would boost their power deep in the night and broadcast a strong signal across the Plains, enabling me to listen to good rock-and-roll before CDs were invented. The tractor seemed to like working better at night; the cooler night air was easier on the machine, lowering the operating temperatures and increasing efficiency.

Some long hours were not by choice, especially during wet years with few windows of opportunity to work the soil. Overly wet spring seasons would drive farmers crazy and test my physical limits. At times planting season felt like an athletic marathon as I tried to squeeze in as many hours as possible between rainstorms. By the time the ground would dry up enough to till and prepare it for planting, a new storm system would be forecast a few days hence, and the race against time would resume once again.

Deep in the night on one particularly long day of fieldwork, I was pulling a field cultivator with my larger tillage tractor through a flat and uniformly smooth field of about fifty acres in size. I was very sleepy but determined to finish the field before going home to rest for a few hours. I stubbornly refused to yield to fatigue and gulped coffee, but my heavy eyelids closed for what seemed like a blink. It was longer than that. The last thing I recalled, my head shook violently from some internal alarm, and I awoke to find I was still moving. I looked behind my path and could only see a single tilled strip illuminated by my rear field lights. As I looked forward and to each side, it was also untilled. Somehow I had nodded off and the tractor had wandered into uncharted territory, yet still somewhere within the bounds of the huge field. I had no idea which direction I was headed, so I stopped, opened the cab door, and located the familiar lights of the small town a few miles in the distance as the thickening clouds approaching from the west obscured the stars. Having determined my approximate location and direction of travel, I gave up and drove for the nearest gate and home before I might fall asleep again and smash through some neighbor's fence. The next morning I returned and saw I had sleep-driven in a huge semicircle for nearly a quarter of a mile.

Tillage implements that are pulled by tractors are controlled by hydraulic systems powered by internal pressures generated in the transmission of the tractor itself. Steel-braided rubber hoses carry the hydraulic fluid, the consistency of motor oil, at 2,500 pounds per square inch, which raise and lower the implement into the ground. The implement is raised up onto the transport wheels to make turns while in the field, as well as when traveling down the roads from field to field. Safety stops are always recommended to be inserted onto the hydraulic cylinders to prevent accidental dropping during road trips. But that requires the farmer to get out of the cab and do just that, and sometimes we all get lazy. One time a neighbor was driving down the paved road with his eighteen-foot-wide disk, and a hose burst. Pressure was lost instantly, and an eight-thousand-pound collection of iron frame and sharpened metal blades dropped into the asphalt and plowed up ten feet of blacktop pavement before he could get it all stopped. "What's the matter, Fred?" the neighbors teased. "Roads not smooth enough for ya?"

A similar event happened to me a few weeks later while I was going down the road with a field cultivator. The word spread quickly. Walking into the small grocery store, Fred met my glance with a smile. "Tell ya what, Jimmy. I'll plow up the roads, then you can smooth 'em down."

After I took over the farm operation from Russ, he sometimes jumped into the tractor without my asking and did some field-work for me. Russ had a tendency to run into things, even more so as he got older, and with that in mind I reluctantly accepted his kind gesture to finish up a field for me after a very long day. I went home to shower and go for a cheeseburger and beer at the restaurant. By the time I got cleaned up and was driving up my driveway, Russ had completed the field and came down the road, pulling a disk with my tractor. I could see him puffing on his pipe through the tractor cab glass, and he gave me a grin and a proud wave as he passed. The back of the disk clung to about thirty feet of three-stranded barbed-wire fence that was being drug down the highway, a wooden fencepost bouncing along, and the whole mess undetected by the tractor driver. I watched in amazement for a few seconds, pondered the situation, and decided he should fix the problem himself when he got home to his place where the tractor would be parked. I drove out my driveway in the opposite direction, so as not to pass by his farm.

I soon bought an even more powerful tractor to pull the implements with greater ease. The John Deere 4430 was an impressive workhorse. During the first few months after it was delivered, I noticed that it would pull whatever implement we had without breaking a sweat. Farm tillage implements are designed to be pulled at a modest four to five miles an hour, but the 4430 was so strong it was always tempting to pull it too fast, throwing the soil like liquid and creating unwanted ridges in the fields. I then put on deep-cleated radial tires, a radical approach at the time, to keep the wheels from spinning when I slammed the throttle forward. The 4430 was built in the early seventies with little attention paid to fuel economy. It sucked down the diesel fuel like a pig: twelve gallons per hour versus a more reasonable four for the old 3020. In order to stay out in the field all day, we had to mount an extra fifty-gallon fuel tank on the front of the tractor. I could run my small diesel pickup truck an entire week on what the big brute would blow through the smokestack in an hour.

During a rainy spell, we had the 4430 put on the dynamometer at the Deere dealership. It was rated at 140 horsepower, with slight latitude allowed for increasing the power by turning up the fuel pump. I could hear the exchange between the shop supervisor and the mechanic on the intercom. "This is Jim Cossaart's tractor?" squawked the speaker box. "Yes, it is," the supervisor replied. The mechanic's voice continued. "Is he there with you now?" The supervisor smiled at me. "He sure is." The speaker box paused. "Well, I hope he's sittin' down, because this monster is cranking out 210 horses." That's why it burnt so much fuel. I agreed to let them turn down the fuel pump before it threw a connecting rod through the engine block or destroyed the transmission.

From the time I graduated to planting the crops, I steadily developed the pride of workmanship of planting straight and uniform rows. Straight rows are the icing on the cake that will testify to a farmer's ability and finesse for an entire season. Some farmers could drive rows as straight as a bullet's path; others could not or didn't seem to care. I heard two views on the subject. One man I knew would just snort and justify, "Hell, there's more plants in a crooked row." Another one told me, "Crooked rows ... crooked farmer." Probably because I thought I had more to prove, being raised a city kid and following in the footsteps of a near-legend farmer such as Russ, I made it a priority to drive as straight as I could. When I began my first trip down the length of the field, I would steadfastly focus my sharp young eyeballs on a particular fencepost, stick, or even a large dirt clod sticking up at the opposite end, and I could start my rows straight. Thereafter, if I adjusted slightly with each pass, by the time I got to the end of my field the entire set of rows was uniform and perfect. It required a lot of concentration, all the while monitoring herbicide pump pressure and seed-drop mechanisms. One day I received a compliment that I would never forget: A neighbor admitted to me that his three grown sons would argue about who would plant their field that adjoined my fields; none of them wanted to take the blame for having rows that looked crooked in comparison to mine.

Good-bye

In the fall of 1990 I drove to Wichita to visit Grandma in the nursing home. She was a few days short of her ninety-fourth birthday, and she could not rise from her bed. She was confused about most things but still in good spirits, and she tried hard to engage in conversation. As I looked down upon her, I realized it would be the last time. In her confusion, she asked who I was, yet she had the look of recognition in her eyes. "I'm Jimmy," I answered softly. Her eyes brightened, and for a moment I saw the grandma I knew. "From the farm!" The smile on her face quickly turned to worry. "Well ... is there someone there to take care of you?" I gave her an affirmative nod, and she seemed satisfied, then drifted away into confusion once again. A week later she was gone.

Economics

Large-production grain farming in the American Midwest underwent an incredible transition in the eighties. Small family farms sold out at a small business failure rate unprecedented in the nation's history. That decade represented the largest transfer of agricultural-based wealth, both intergenerational as well as between economic classes, in the history of the United States. Through foreclosures and acquisitions of smaller rural banks, large financial institutions garnered a great deal of farmland. Land was discounted in value from wholesale loan failures of farm operating and land ownership notes. At one point in the eighties the largest single owner of farmland in Nebraska was the Prudential Insurance Company. The Farmer's Home Administration, the "lender of last resort," was a federal agency charged with the task of lending operating capital and farm ownership loans to low-income and beginning farmers. Through loans guaranteed by the FmHA, both to local agricultural banks or directly to farmers, a lot of capital was put out there for family farmers, and when the farm economy started spinning downward, a budget-pressured Congress squeezed out the funding for the program, and the ones unable to acquire capital elsewhere had to stop operating. No money, no seeds, no fertilizer. The only option left was to auction off all the machinery for whatever the surviving farmers in the region were willing to pay for used equipment, which in turn glutted the market and devalued used equipment even further. Many guys hoping for a good payout upon liquidation of big-ticket items like tractors and combines were rudely surprised by what they ended up with. Many went bankrupt.

The capital requirements to farm suddenly became enormous. When I began large-scale farming in 1981, a typical year would require sixty- to seventy-thousand dollars to finance my inputs. Operating capital, all of it borrowed, was required for seed, fertilizer, herbicides, fuels, repairs, and hired labor and services. For many years in the eighties I was annually borrowing more in operating capital than my entire net worth. Utter insanity from a business standpoint, the situation was routine for grain farmers.

For a young farmer starting out, this was reality. There was always the hope for some good years to get ahead, but more often than not, it was a hopeful dream. I just kept pushing on, worked like hell, and hoped for good weather. I and my farming peers imagined that one good year on the horizon, with a deluge of harvested grain that would set us up on our financial feet again. That actually did occur during the magic of my first year. But as the years ground on, the greatest measure of success became simply to survive another growing season.

The western regions of the American agriculture belt are more risky to farm because they do not have the predictable rainfall found farther east. The rainfall amounts per year as you travel west from Missouri and Iowa into Kansas and Nebraska drop off in a gradient. About halfway through all Plains states—the Dakotas, Nebraska, Kansas, Oklahoma, and Texas—the climate becomes quite dry, eventually requiring irrigation to make growing crops feasible. The lush and tall corn crops of Iowa step down to shorter, waist-high grain sorghum and wheat in mid-Kansas, which in turn drop to the sparse and stunted wheat crops grown in eastern Colorado. Those must be grown on alternate years, leaving a field idle and weed free for a year to store up precious little rainfall for the next years' attempt.

When looking at the breadbasket of the American heartland, my farm is pretty much on the western limit of what can be feasibly done. Ironically, the edge of the giant Ogallala Aquifer was located only about ten miles north of my farm, and this huge underground lake covers a large region of Nebraska and provides irrigation that enables farmers to grow corn and soybeans with dependably high yields year after year. My ancestors had no idea of the undiscovered water source. My cousin Lowell illuminated that fact during the annual Cossaart family reunion one year. "Madam Chairman, I make a motion," he said, in the midst of the requisite boring business meeting to come after the huge potluck dinner, "to go out to the cemetery, dig up Great-Grandpa, and kick his ass for not moving another fifteen miles farther north."

The Great Plains, once labeled "the Great American Desert," is a land of extremes in terms of temperature, wind, and precipitation. The summers can be brutally hot, with blast-furnace heat of over one hundred degrees Fahrenheit for weeks on end. Hail, wind, and the more exciting tornadoes are constant byproducts of the continual clash of hot and cold air in spring and early summer. Crop disasters like complete hail-outs and flattening by extreme wind and brief, heavy rains are common. Expressing the prospects of an apparently impending income boon from a promising wheat field approaching harvest time one early July, my uncle looked over the top of his eyeglasses at me and expressed caution. "It all looks good now, but it ain't in the bin yet."

Farmers, wheat farmers in particular, survive on hope. That is essential, because at times there wasn't much else to hang on to. As the 1980s progressed, the net profits for American farmers diminished year by year. Frank's dad stated an example of comical hope in the face of the difficult conditions. "Yeah, I figure I lost about ten dollars an acre last year on my wheat." He continued. "But I'm gonna plant twenty percent more acreage next year to try and make up the difference."

Town Constable

In the late 1940s and 1950s Harry was the town constable for the Saturday night dances in Hubbell. These were quite the social events, drawing three hundred or so people to listen to polka bands and dance on the wooden floor in a space about half the size of a school gymnasium. Law enforcement in all of Thayer County, Nebraska, consisted of one sheriff and a few deputies, so Harry was asked to serve, as needed, walking among the crowd as the man with the badge. He was respected for his obvious strength, but, more importantly, he was good with people and knew how to handle drunks and conflict. "You're better to have the *good*will of the people than the *ill* will," Harry said while describing his constable days. With tin star pinned to his shirt, he wandered through the crowd with an easy smile on his face and a large metal flashlight in his hand; his massive frame and reputation for toughness was a wise embodiment of the local law. And yet he was one of *them*. "Sometimes folks would come up to me outside the tavern and offer me a snort of their whiskey," he recalled, "so I would put my mouth over the bottle and

tip it up away from the light, so it looked like I was drinkin' it."
He always remained sober.

He enjoyed the revelry among the crowd beyond the view
of his wife, who disapproved of drinking and dancing. Frances
stayed at home as Harry performed his duties. One time a big-
mouthed acquaintance created some domestic grief for Harry
when the man met Frances in a nearby town and she introduced
herself by name. "Oh, yeah, I know Harry," he volunteered. "He
takes a nip off my bottle now and then at the dances."

Sometimes Harry was needed to break up a fight. "A couple of
young bucks would be yellin' and puffin' their chests up when a
crowd was around. But ya know, when I would take them boys
out back in the alley by themselves, suddenly they really didn't
want to fight after all."

One night a man in a drunken rage drove his Model A on
the sidewalk while terrified pedestrians scattered for their
lives. Harry leaped on the running board of the car as it passed,
reached through the window, and seized the man by the throat
with his crushing grip. With calm determination he stated his
demand: "Now, you're gonna stop this car right now." He pulled
the fellow out of the vehicle and hit him across the forehead
with his long steel-case flashlight. The crowd parted before him
like the Red Sea as Harry dragged the unconscious man across
the street, opened his shop door, and lashed him to the anvil
with a log chain, where he slept it off into Sunday morning.
He smiled as he recalled the event. "After I finished my chores
that morning, I realized I forgot all about him," he laughed and
slapped his thigh. "So 'bout ten in the morning I came down to

the shop and let him go. It ain't just the preacher who can make a Christian out of a guy."

He had a great sense of fairness. If he encountered a developing fight, he watched from a distance to see if the conflict would resolve itself. If the odds looked poor for a man who was hopelessly drunk, outnumbered, or markedly smaller, instead of letting the disadvantaged get the tar beat out of him, Harry would step in between and get in the larger man's face. "How 'bout you finish this with me?" No one ever tried to finish anything with Harry.

*   *   *

By the time I knew him, he was long past his law enforcement role. But his legendary toughness hardened with age, and I witnessed it firsthand as I worked with him. Harry had two John Deere Model B tractors, 1940s-era two-cylinder antiques that would puff and sputter, and, to my ears, always sounded like they were on the verge of stalling. I was used to the smooth hum of a six- and even eight-cylinder engine, so I would rev up Harry's old two-lungers until they sounded right to my ear. They certainly did not sound proper to Harry. He would shout at me with great irritation, "Idle that goddam' thing down!"

One spring morning Harry and I were in the shop, and he ordered me to jump up on his Model B John Deere and move it forward a few feet. We were in close quarters in the confines of the steel building as Harry stood off to the side of the tractor; he impatiently motioned me forward as he was standing next to the left front tire of the tractor. The old machine had a hand-operated clutch and was made long before my time. I awkwardly engaged the hand clutch and the tractor lurched a few feet. "WHOA!" Harry shouted loudly, and my first instinct was to step in quickly on the clutch with my left foot. The problem was it was not the clutch but the left brake. Stabbing the left pedal on the Model B locked up the rear wheel and violently threw the front end to the left. The front of the tractor slammed into Harry and pinned his chest to the wall before I could get my feet straightened out. His face looked desperate, and he could only manage to wave his forearm. I panicked and quickly threw the gearshift to reverse and released Harry from his bondage. I was sure I had killed him.

To my surprise and relief, he staggered forward and looked at me severely. "WHAT THE HELL ARE YOU DOIN'?!!!" he screamed. "Get off that son of a bitch!" I shut the tractor off, expecting him to show signs of injury that would have crippled most men his age. "Where the hell did you learn how to drive?!" he demanded. I stuttered a sheepish answer as I remained frozen on the tractor seat. "I thought it was the clutch."

"The clutch! The clutch! You young guys don't know shit from a good grade of putty!" he roared, as the palsied shaking of his head built to a crescendo. His face was red and looked like it was going to pop. "Now get off of that thing and let's go have a cup of coffee before YOU have a nervous breakdown!" I followed the old man out of the building and across the street for our usual mid-morning coffee ritual at the tavern. I gathered enough courage and walking speed to catch up with him. He was limping noticeably as he put his arm around my shoulders and pulled me close with a crushing hug. Then he began to laugh and pushed me away forcibly. "You dumb bastard," he said in between chuckles. "From now on I'll stay clear when you're drivin'."

People rarely got one over on Harry, but one time my old Purdue roommate and Indiana farmer Mike stopped by the shop on one of his short summer visits. I introduced him to Harry, and as Mike shook hands, he gave Harry a direct and warm smile, previously warned by me, and remained unfazed by the bizarre grip. Harry gave Mike a mock quizzical look, pointed to him, and turned to me with a question. "Is this some of your wife's relation or your short-peckered friend?" I was single at the time. "Where are ya from?" Harry continued. "New York City," Mike answered with a straight face. I gave Mike a short tour of the shop, and we stood off to the side and watched Harry back his old tractor up to the hay baler. Balers are powered by a spinning shaft, and the splines of the baler shaft must be matched up to the counterpart on the rear of the tractor. As Harry lurched the tractor backwards, Mike walked over and deftly attached the mechanism as only a farm boy could. Harry looked down at Mike and frowned. "You're not from New York City, you smart-ass." With an annoyed glare, Harry watched Mike and me double over in laughter. He directed his voice to another man standing inside the shop. "Goddam' young guys," he spat as he pointed to us with his thumb. "They'll screw you if ya stand still and bite you in the ass if ya try to run."

In Harry's shop, one of my jobs was fixing chain saws. A simple small engine needs an electrical impulse at the right time to fire the gasoline mixture inside the cylinder. If there is no spark, the engine will not fire. To diagnose an electrical problem, I clamped the chain saw in a bench vise, pulled forcefully on the recoil starter rope, and measured the electrical impulse from the spark plug wire with a circuit tester. I was having trouble getting a good reading on the meter while Harry watched from a distance. After a few minutes he walked over to my workbench and grabbed the plug wire with his bare fingers. "Give it a pull," he said without expression. I thought of the times I had accidentally touched the plug wire, and each time the shock sent me into the air and bouncing on the concrete like I was doing a break dance. "Are you kidding?" I asked Harry. His face remained stony. "Pull it," he replied, while holding firm to the wire. I pulled it slowly, afraid to hurt him. "PULL THE DAMN THING!" he roared. Okay, he asked for it. I yanked on it forcefully, delivering the full impulse. Harry's face was unchanged as he absorbed the jolt. He let go of the wire and started to walk away. "Yup," he mumbled. "It has good spark. Must be a carburetor problem."

He also showed me his resistance to voltage when we were working on his 1951 Chevy pickup. With the hood up and the engine running, Harry rotated the distributor in an effort to time the six-cylinder engine by ear. He instructed me to tighten down the screw when it sounded right, and then gave me an odd look. He pulled off two of the spark plug wires with the engine still running. Looking me in the eyes, he stuck a thumb into the leads of each wire and fully absorbed twelve volts. His face and body remained relaxed as the engine sputtered and died. "Ever see a guy do that?" he asked. I was stunned. "Never," I replied. "Funny thing," he continued. "I can't wear a wristwatch either. I put 'em on my arm and they quit workin' after a day or two. I guess I just plum drive 'em nuts."

A customer needed some welding done on a hay feeder, a six-foot-diameter cage of tubular steel. He had placed it on the muddy ground behind the shop. It was a damp day as Harry threw the switch on his arc welder and hooked up the ground clamp to the feeder. With a steady and rhythmic palsy of his head, he nodded his head forward, which tilted his welding helmet over his face as a thousand times before. As he struck his arc to the metal, the farmer and I turned our faces away from the brilliant flash. "AAAAHHHHHH!!!" A bizarre groan came out of Harry's mouth as he struggled to let go of the handle that held the welding rod. It was locked to his gloved hand for several seconds as Harry's body served as an electrical conduit to the wet ground. He managed to release himself from its grip, jumped back a few feet, and dropped the holder to the mud. He staggered a few steps backward as he pulled off his welding helmet. As the customer and I stood with our mouths open, Harry smiled at our startled expressions. "You boys drag that feeder into the shop onto *dry* pavement. But first I have to go take a shit." He waddled away to the outhouse behind the shop.

Harry was generally patient with people but especially kind to children. No matter how busy he was, he would always stop to talk or play with kids. I watched him try to teach his grandson how to pound a nail with a hammer, and the child occasionally missed the target and landed a blow to Harry's battered fingers.

He steadied the block of wood again. "Try again," he laughed with each miss. His grandsons would sit on his lap and steer the wheel of his old pickup truck as they would chug slowly down the main street in town. He taught his grandsons how to ride and handle the few horses that he kept nearby.

Although always gentle with children, Harry could be downright brutal to misbehaving animals. He spent a good deal of loving time and effort building a two-wheeled cart for his grandsons, and I was helping him hook it up to a young and contrary horse. No sooner had we placed the harness and attached the hitch than the horse began bucking and backing up. Pieces of wood were splintering as the equine forced the cart backwards into the side of the garage. "Whoa, horse, whoa. WHOA, DAMMIT," he screamed, but the animal paid no mind and kept destroying his cart with each lurch backward. Harry pointed his finger and spoke to the horse as if it were a person. "You son of a bitch. I've had just about enough of you..." The words trailed out of Harry's mouth as he disappeared around the corner of the garage and returned with a worn baseball bat in his hands. He slowly raised the bat in a big-league stance as the offender continued its misbehavior, swung the bat full force, and connected with the left side of the horse's head. The animal snorted, shook his head, and staggered but continued breaking apart the wagon. Harry studied him for a second. With no change to his expression, the old blacksmith waddled slowly around the other side of the wobbling animal's face. He swung the bat again with all his might, delivered a solid blow to the opposite side of the horse's head, and we both watched a full-grown horse drop to the ground unconscious. I stood there scarcely believing what I had just witnessed. Harry looked upon the still animal lying on the ground and turned to me. "I had to even him up," he flatly stated. Harry unhitched the wagon, now standing on its side, and began gathering up broken boards with methodical nonchalance. I couldn't keep my eyes off the horse and studied the animal for a minute until it began to awaken. The horse slowly rose to its feet, and we led the groggy animal back to his pen and removed the halter. "He'll be a good 'un someday," Harry finally said, breaking the silence between us. "If he wasn't, I'd a shot him a long time ago."

Our Secret

———————

Very late one bitterly cold January night, I heard Leslie's weak voice at the other end of a phone call. "Ya better … come over," and I knew exactly who it was. I sprinted out to my pickup and sped over to his house in a full-blown blizzard to find a brightly illuminated kitchen door wide open while a gale-force wind roared and blew snow into the house. Huddled next to the propane heat stove and in an old wooden kitchen chair, his ninety-two-year-old bent little body fought hard to balance itself. He was covered with a tattered and oversize denim overcoat with years of wear and dirt and patches that he himself, as well as Bertha, had sewed on. His big fuzzy mittens were cast onto the floor, each in a pile of melting snow on the worn linoleum. His winter hat was still on his head, and he had it pulled down so far that only his mouth and nose were visible. His long white cotton socks were soaked, one of his high-top neoprene overboots lay by itself on the floor, and the other one was still out in the snow. His false teeth clattered violently as he slumped forward. His breathing was shallow and quick, and his cold little body was consumed in uncontrolled shaking. I carefully leaned him back in the chair and knelt down to feel his feet.

Apparently worried about the neighbor's cattle bawling out in the barnyard, Les ventured out into the snowstorm to turn on the hydrant and fill a water tank for a pen full of thirsty beef calves. Knocked to his knees by a strong gust, he could not stand up. He crawled on hands and knees about two hundred feet through a long snowdrift to reach the house, and the snow packed into the tops of his high rubber overboots as he labored along. He somehow managed to open the outside kitchen door, fall in, dial the telephone, and struggle into the chair while waiting for me to arrive.

Dashing into the bedroom and pulling a thick old quilt off his bed, I wrapped him up like a baby, enveloping his ragged coat and overalls, which were soaked from the knees down to the cuffs. I opened a kitchen cabinet and tossed pots and pans onto the floor until I found one large enough to fit both his feet into. After filling it with hot water, I carried it over to Les and pulled his one remaining long cotton sock off. I lifted his feet from the floor and placed them into the water. I was startled by a strong yell of pain, the first noise out of his mouth since I had entered the house, and it gave me encouragement that his will to live was still residing in his shivering frame. I gathered up more blankets and wrapped him up until his form was barely recognizable. In all my time with Leslie it was by far the longest he had been completely without words. Bare and bony size ten feet sat at the bottom of the black steel kettle full of steaming water as his shaking subsided and he leaned in silence against the old propane heat stove.

I warmed a can of Campbell's beef barley soup in a small saucepan on the propane cook stove and poured it into a stained coffee cup. He eagerly opened his mouth for a warm spoonful, his facial shivers abated, and he gave me the first brief eye contact I had seen. He pushed his two arms through the folds of his loosening bedspread and began slurping the brown mixture, hanging on to the cup with his own trembling hands. Fear and gratitude filled his eyes. Over the next hour he warmed up enough to remove the quilt and step out of his soaked overalls. I helped him to the bathroom, but even in his state he insisted on doing things himself behind a closed door. A few minutes later he emerged and I escorted him to his bed, neither of us saying a word. I helped him lie down and stretch out and covered him up with several more blankets. Satisfied with his prospects for a night of rest, I told him goodnight and flipped off the light as I turned to leave the room. Les raised a hand in the air and pointed a finger toward the ceiling. "Thanks," he said quietly. "Anytime," I replied with equal tone. Then, with a final thought, he added, "Don't tell the kids." Knowing that revealing his latest adventure would jeopardize his independence, I conspired. "I won't," I replied softly. And I didn't.

The spring and summer came and went, and our secret remained secure. The following autumn Uncle Leslie took it upon himself to move into a nursing home in Belleville, Kansas. Temporarily, he stressed, which was hard to believe for most everyone but him at the time. His children were having health issues of their own, and he wanted to ensure he would not be a burden. Articulate and mobile, he quickly found new acquaintances in all halls of the facility to tell his stories to and cultivated yet another new audience, in many instances a captive or nonverbal one.

But in early April he decided he'd had enough and wanted to go back home. About six months after walking in, he walked back out and returned to the house he was born in. On seeing him arrive back at the farm, I remarked in admiration, "Les, there aren't too many people who walk out of those places." "I know!" He beamed yet another grin, puffed up his chest, and tried to stand a little straighter. He had racked up yet another bragging point.

The following June one of his twin daughters called me on a Sunday morning. I drove over to Leslie's house and found both Vera and Vesta with Les in his living room. He was sitting in a large overstuffed chair, looking detached and disoriented as he stared into the space of the large room. They asked him questions that he could not answer, and he responded with uncharacteristic annoyance and impatience. I pulled up a wooden chair and looked into his cloudy eyes, wide open with wonder and confusion. As his two children retreated to the kitchen to call the doctor, I studied him intently. He looked into oblivion and said softly, "It's ... snowing in here." I tried to picture what he could possibly be seeing at the time, some vision conjured by a brain that was short-circuiting from a likely stroke and rapidly failing him as we sat alone together. His eyes searched the room for a few more seconds, and then his vision locked onto mine and he snapped to a brief moment of clarity. The light was dim, and his eyes were open wider than usual as he searched for an answer. In all our conversations, most had been light-hearted, but we had some fairly profound and deep talks as well. This time I really paid attention. He leaned forward slightly toward my face and in precise diction he uttered softly so only he and I could hear, "I'm in trouble, aren't I?" Our eyes locked, and I silently answered his question with an affirmative nod of my head as he looked far into me for his confirmation. His eyes retained their hold on mine as I slowed my nodding to a final standstill. It was an unspoken good-bye. He then returned to staring in amazement at something that only he could see and never looked at me again. I wordlessly helped him shuffle out to the waiting car, and his daughters drove him to the hospital. He walked in with only light assistance. With characteristic dignity and style he climbed into a bed of his own volition and silently slipped into a coma. The following morning he was gone.

My friendship with Les came at a critical point in my life. He was perhaps my truest, most uncomplicated friend at the time, and all he ever wanted was my company. As Bertha gave him the example and energy to wake up each new day, so he did with me. I remember thinking that if such a fragile old fellow could keep moving forward with such enthusiasm, then so could I.

Several months after his passing, I attended the estate auction of his few modest possessions. I bought a set of his little green coffee cups, and sometimes as I drink from them now, I can still recall the grounds settling to the bottom of the cup and remember his proud little grin.

His old house stood empty for several years, and the farm ground was eventually sold to a large farm interest that never knew Les. Knowing the purchaser's history of bulldozing old farmsteads, I walked into the empty house one fall day before the land sale was completed. With deft hands and a smile I unscrewed the tarnished Coca-Cola bottle opener from the kitchen wall. My great uncle or aunt used it to open the soft drink bottles for us kids. It proudly holds a similar position beside my own kitchen sink. It stands as a monument and a reminder to persevere with dignity and humor. Those are Cossaart family traits.

Molly

"Take this fan down to Molly." Harry gave me a slight smile, like he always did when he knew something I did not. "She lives right across the street from Carl, on the north side." Harry held out a small Emerson electric fan; it was one of those old-fashioned kind built in the fifties and similar to the one Grandma got her fingers into years before. His instructions surprised me in the middle of an afternoon full of heavy repair jobs waiting, so I figured Molly must be quite special. "You have to announce yourself at her door; she can't see much, but her hearin's pretty fair." Then another smile. "She's a hundred and two years old." I jumped into my pickup and coasted down Main Street to deliver it.

I located a small single-story frame house in the middle of the block, a modest white bungalow with a neatly mown lawn. The cracked concrete sidewalk was swept clean, and my boots clunked onto the front porch floor. I tapped hesitantly on the wooden screen door that rattled loosely in the frame. After a few moments, I knocked again with more insistence. The afternoon sun through a window illuminated a tidy and plain living room, clean and museum-like with sparse and simple furnishings. An overstuffed and dated red couch held down the worn but spotless carpet. The nap had been laid over in an array of stripes from recent vacuuming. Except for the subdued hum of a refrigerator, the inside of the house was silent, and I could soon detect the faint shuffle of light footsteps upon the linoleum floor of the kitchen. "Yes, yes, I'm here," a soft voice lilted in the air. I stopped my knocking and stood in reverent anticipation of the unknown. I had never seen anyone 102 years old.

She appeared in the middle of the living room, her careful little steps coming to a halt in the center of the room and three paces from the door. I looked upon a slight figure, bent to about five feet tall with a full head of curly salt-and-pepper hair. Her eyeglasses had heavy plastic frames, and they circled magnified eyeballs that gazed dimly in my direction. Their foggy focus searched earnestly for information. I spoke in upright diction directly toward her, and she listened alertly. "Oh. You're the Cossaart boy. Mr. Stradley said you would be right over. You don't waste time, now, do you?" She smiled while her eyes kept searching, as if speaking to my shadow. "Come in, come in." She motioned with some enthusiasm, raising her head a bit and moving her withered arm in the air.

I carefully stepped inside, taking care to buffer the screen door from slamming as if something might break. Glancing backward at the few steps of my dusty work boots, I searched the carpet for any dirt tracks I might have made. "I brought your fan to you," I bashfully stated. I remembered her age and prepared to restate my words in greater volume, but she cut me short. "Oh, that's nice. It's getting to be plenty hot lately." She was 102. *A hundred and two.* The realization nearly buckled my knees.

"Put it on the table here and plug it in, please." She motioned in the direction of a small wooden stand. I dutifully placed the fan upon it and pushed the two-pronged plug into the chocolate-colored receptacle. I turned it on at low speed, and she held her hand out to feel the movement of air. Her thin curls danced lightly in the breeze. "Ah yes ... that's very welcome in this kind of weather." Her words trailed off, and she turned her wavering eyes to find my face. "I can see that you're dark." She contemplated my outline. "Whose boy are you?"

My father's name jumped out of my mouth. "Raleigh," I answered proudly.

"No..." She paused and thought carefully. "And who was his father?" she asked again.

"Reuben."

She looked down at the carpet, and I could see her brain was working just fine. She shook her head slowly and thought for a few seconds more. The wandering eyes stopped their movement, and she squinted slightly and asked again slowly. "And who was *his* father?"

"Charles David," I replied. I knew my family lineage well and was delighted to exercise my knowledge. I could see where she was going with this.

She studied the air for a moment and announced, "Charles... Charles... And his father was an undertaker. Also by name of Reuben..." Her smile broadened as she looked up toward my face, as if her vision had cleared slightly. She pointed with a wrinkled hand that was covered with age spots and nodded toward the closed screen door. "Mr. Cossaart lived in the house across the street. I remember him when I was just a little girl, no more than five or six years old at that time..." She cleared her throat slightly, and my head began to spin as her words sank in..

"Old Mister Cossaart... old Mister Cossaart..." she repeated. "I knew," she paused and pointed a slightly curled finger toward my chest. "I knew," she continued, "your *great ... great ... grandfather.*"

..day and go through, without
, to San Francisco and Los An-

tourist sleepers in which ex-
ists travel, are carpeted, up-
of in rattan and have spring
pring backs, mattresses, blank-
tains, pillows, towels, etc.
$5 for a double berth, wide
and big enough for two.
route lies through Denver. Colo-
prings, the wonderful canons
lks of the Rockies, Salt Lake
d Sacramento.
rates and also for illustrated
ziving full information, call on
rest agent of the Burlington
or write to J. Francis, G. P. &
Omaha, Neb.   10-27-5

e isn't a family in Nebraska that
ord to do without a good general
uring the year 1896. The semi-
State Journal, published at
t, is the paper that most thor-
mits the needs of Nebraskans,
it is edited especially for Ne-
os, and in addition to all the
nation and foreign events, it
nore state news than any other
nd gets it to its readers from
ive days earlier than the old-
ed weekly. The magnificent
igton bureau of the Journal will
specially important feature this
ews-making year of 1896. The
I's foreign service will come in-
play during the war scares and
l readers will get all the news.
you take a paper take the best
get for your money, and in
ka this means the Semi-Weekly
ournal. You get 104 papers a
r $1.00, which makes it almost
as a daily. Always recollect,
two papers a week, one on
y and one on Friday. The
l is offering $2.50 in cash prizus
ts, beside liberal cash commis-
It will pay you to get up a club.

TIMES and The New York
Tribune one year for only $1,
ce of either paper alone.

Take a Paper.
can subscribe for any paper
zine published in the United
at this office, and save from 25
nts on each subscription. Come
our figures before you send
bscription away.

R. G. COSSAART,
—DEALER IN—

Furniture,

UNDER   ALL
TAKING   ITS
IN   Branches.

Wall Paper, Window Shades, and Baby Carriages.

Ag't for the New Home Sewing Machine.

M. T. CLEARY,

DEALER IN

LUMBER
and
COAL.

Carry in stock CEMENT PLAS-
TER.

Good Grades.   Low Prices.

Estimatss Furnished on Application.

main himself w
lay on a sofa
to him

THE

HU

W.

CORRESPO

The

PRESID

NEW

Will, as always
BUSINESS FRI
THE NEW
of the country, b
All the news
Reports. Short S
elaborate descrip
FAMILY PAPE
We furnish
papers]

Or

Address all c

Write your name
New York C
will be maile

R. G. Cossaart, undertaker advertisement.

Rain

It was about mid-August 1988, and the future was looking bleak in the farm economy. Nevertheless, it was time to get the wheat ground ready to plant. Like most Augusts in Kansas, it was one of those one-hundred-plus-degree days that just seemed to suck the last breath out of every living thing. It had been just shy of two months since we had had any rain. I had eaten lunch at home and returned to the field. I parked my pickup in the entrance to the field and began walking toward the tractor, about two hundred yards away. Walking as slowly as I could, I consciously kept my respiration rate low. Move slow, breath slow, think slow, I commanded myself. Create no more body heat than necessary for locomotion. The black prairie dirt was baked into a billion fist-sized dirt clods that made my ankles turn painfully under my work boots. My work gloves protected me from the scorching hot steel of the tractor's handrails as I hoisted my body up on the steps and turned the cab door handle. One-hundred-fifty-degree air slammed against my face as I opened the door to the glass enclosure, which had become a solar oven. Leaving the door open, I started the tractor engine, turned on the air conditioner, and scurried backwards down the steps as the radiator fan blasted into my face. I backed up a few paces from the roaring engine to let the air conditioner catch up and cool the cab off for a few minutes before re-entering.

The John Deere 4240 was the more comfortable ride of my two large tillage tractors, and I was grateful for the cool environment on such a brutal day. I sat in the firm cushion chair as I dragged the twenty-four-foot-wide implement behind me, raking swaths of soil in quarter-mile long strips on the vast and tabletop-flat area of farmland. With decent moisture the productive soil in the field would pulverize to pancake-flour consistency, but the heat had baked the clay content in the dirt clods like forgotten cookies. It appeared all I was accomplishing was breaking each large clod into three or four smaller ones. "Arranging clods," I had once told my neighbor. But there was a huge schedule of fieldwork to be done over the next month, the ground needed to be tilled several more trips before planting in a few weeks, and to be a wheat farmer, one had to have blind faith that it would eventually rain.

Endless hours of boring fieldwork in the tractor cab required a good stereo system, and I had a station that broadcasted from Lincoln, Nebraska, about one hundred miles to the north. The rock-and-roll helped temper the monotony as the dust boiled up in my path beyond the back glass window and at times obscured my vision. The voice of worry in my head resurfaced as I stared into the cloudless sky, and I tried not to think of the financial disaster looming without any prospects of rain. The disc jockey's voice blew out of the speakers. "Sorry to tell you

John Deere 4240 cab.

this, folks, but it looks like we may have some rain to ruin our weekend..."

Sorry to tell me? I couldn't believe it. The sorghum and soybean crops were shriveling by the day. There wasn't enough moisture in the ground to germinate the wheat to be planted, and a fifty thousand dollar note was due in two months. I thought, *We don't want that little weekend barbecue to be postponed, now do we? My God, we might have to wash the spots off the new car.* Here I was, driving a tractor in a "farm state" in the "Heartland" of America, and the voice on the radio had no clue what I was doing, or for that matter, where *he* was. I was getting paid less than minimum wage while carrying close to a quarter million in debt and supposedly growing food for the nation. The message was clear to me as a farmer: My business, my heritage, and my future were all going to hell in a broken-down handcart, and no one gave a shit. Not many people even gave it any thought at all.

Political pundits still mentioned "the farm vote" once in a while, as if there were indeed a remnant of something that existed in 1950. A hollow term. Even in 1990 livestock and grain farmers comprised less than *one-tenth of 1 percent,* or a *statistically insignificant* portion of the American population. That sure didn't translate into many electoral votes. I heard some well-meaning talk about "saving the family farm" now and then, but for most of my contemporaries and me in the Great Plains, the muted voice of concern was too late. It was gone. There wasn't the political will in this nation to save us.

But in the moment the disk jockey made his statement, there was fieldwork to be done. I felt like slamming the tractor to a halt, jumping on top of the hood, and facing north to the distant city from which such a stupid weather wish was broadcast and yelling at the northern horizon. I just kept driving, glared at the radio, and screamed so loud it made my lungs hurt. "SCREW YOUR PRECIOUS DAMN WEEKEND!!! WE NEED THE RAIN, YOU IDIOT!!!"

Cordless Phone

———————

Kevin Rose was a good friend and a good man. He was a couple of years my junior, and he worked for me an entire season. A year after Russ died, I planted large acreages of winter wheat in the fall, and an industrious and likable Kevin came to the rescue, it seemed, for many, many hours of fieldwork were required. Rarely had two young men worked so hard and had so much fun doing it. We had to squeeze in all the hours that we could in order to get a large planting task completed in ten days. The newly purchased tillage tractor of Russ's was not big enough to accomplish it all in daylight hours. Kevin and I bolted some powerful lights on the roof of the tractor cab that would illuminate the vast seedbed in front of us the length of a football field. Between us we would often go several days in succession putting twenty hours straight on the John Deere's hour meter. He had entered into a marriage without much thought and soon discovered he could not stand his wife at all. One early morning he showed up and we talked about what we each had for breakfast. His wife, deep in a pregnancy she was too immature to handle, was in an especially foul mood. "Every morning I have a bowl of oatmeal," Kevin said without expression. "Denise has a bowl of rusty nails." To avoid her he would drive my tillage tractor through the night as he pulled an eighteen-foot-wide disk, a twenty-four-foot field cultivator, and finally a twelve-foot-wide grain drill as we sowed six hundred acres of wheat. We covered a hell of a lot of ground with a small tractor that fall.

Over the winter months I scraped up enough money to keep Kevin busy, and the two of us built a splendid little repair shop by remodeling the old corncrib. We installed a huge overhead door that we could pull shut and work on our equipment as the small woodstove in the corner lessened the chill. We beefed up the frame then insulated and put siding on my grandpa's old building. We didn't know much about construction, but our rudimentary carpentry skills got us by, and we retrofitted the building with a concrete floor and brightly illuminated walls with a workbench running the entire length of the thirty-foot building. On one of my trips to Wichita to see Grandma, she was so pleased when I described our winter project that she promptly wrote me a check for nearly all the materials.

In the early eighties, cordless phones had just hit the market, and I bought one for the shop. Talking on one felt like riding a bike without training wheels. I could pull out the long retract-able antenna and walk around the parked tractor and describe something for the John Deere parts man with total freedom. After that phone call, I walked back up to the house to grab my bills to be mailed and left Kevin busy at work finishing up his job of changing oil in the big tillage tractor. After filling the crankcase with seventeen quarts of motor oil, Kevin fired the tractor up, gave a quick scan under the roaring engine for leaks, rolled up the wide shop door, and guided the giant thing out into the daylight to fill the tanks with diesel fuel.

I came back from the house and walked into the open shop to see an obliterated cordless phone pulverized into the concrete floor. Kevin had run over it with a thirty-thousand-pound tractor. "Oh, for God's sake," I murmured. I walked back out of the shop and told Kevin what had happened. "Damn, Jim, I'm sorry about that," he shouted over the loud buzz of the motor on the fuel barrel. I shook my head vigorously. "Hell, I left the damn thing there. Just a case of cranial rectalis, I guess. Ah, well, I gotta run to town before the post office closes. Anything you need?" He shook his head, and I piled into the pickup and drove up to Mahaska.

When I returned, the big overhead door was closed down, and Kevin had the concrete floor of the shop swept up, with the dust still visible in the air illuminated with fluorescent light. No phone, or even the remnant of such, was in sight. "Where'd the phone carcass go?" I asked as he warmed himself next to the woodstove. "I swept it up and dumped it into the burn barrel. With all the rest of the trash." Kevin was always efficient and neat, and while I was uptown, he'd cleaned up all the burnable trash, stuffed it into the old fifty-gallon drum behind the shop, dumped a half gallon of number two diesel fuel on it, and lit it.

The earliest cordless phones were expensive—three hundred dollars—but there was a warranty with it, I recalled. The salesman waxed on about the great no-questions-asked guarantee on the new cordless invention. "No matter the reason," he said.

Kevin stood beside me as I called the 800 number and asked again about the guarantee. Yes, they insisted, simply send them the inoperative phone and write on a piece of paper exactly what the problem was. Enclose a check for fifty dollars, and they would send a new one, no questions asked. Great, I thought.

As the trash fire subsided we fished out the squashed hulk of plastic, warped and smoking, and rinsed it off with the garden hose to cool it down. The antenna was twisted into a small ball and the buttons on the facing were welded together in a puddle of black goo. We giggled like children as I wrote our specific service complaint with the phone, placed the note on top of the plastic pancake, and stuffed it into the cardboard box.

Two weeks later, the new phone arrived in the mail with the packing slip. Nothing unusual was printed, and Kevin and I could only imagine the look on the face of the repair technician as he opened our box with the mutilated phone and read the three words I had neatly printed on the half sheet of typing paper: *NO DIAL TONE.*

Reinspired

Several years after finishing his education, Frank and Donna boldly chased their dreams and moved to Colorado. They found good jobs and established a new home where they could enjoy the outdoors with their new and deserved leisure time. As I always knew them, they appeared to me to be the ideal married couple, and I viewed their relationship as something to aspire to, even after I divorced again and settled grudgingly into a single farmer's lifestyle. Individually and as partners, they became, and still remain to this day, my own personal heroes.

During a particularly low point in my existence, I drove ten hours west to visit them in Fort Collins to escape the triple-digit Kansas heat and the weariness accumulated from farming and living alone. Frank and Donna took me to clear streams in the high mountains and refreshed my soul with their enthusiasm and love. I returned home reinspired. Six hours after I left their driveway and began my trip back to the farm, my friends ushered into the world their first and only children, twins, a boy and a girl, on the afternoon of my thirty-third birthday.

Frank and Jim.

Bachelorhood

My friend Scott and I were sitting in the Hubbell tavern and eating supper together after a long day of work. A man in his sixties entered the bar and bought a six-pack of Coors and was fidgeting about as the bartender put it in the paper bag. The aging bachelor was considered odd and reclusive. He was treated with outward politeness by others, but otherwise his solitary manner invited mild suspicion and even jokes. He looked up at us and gave a brief acknowledgement, nervously scanned the environs of the bar, and promptly left.

"Now there's an example right there," I started.

"Of what?" Scott had no idea what I was talking about.

I continued. "Just look at that guy. He's been single all his life." The man who had just exited had lived by himself on a farmstead that had been steadily falling into disrepair since his parents passed away twenty years prior.

"There's a perfect example of what happens when a person's distortions run unchecked."

My companion gave me an annoyed expression. "Please translate," he asked.

I used simpler English. "That's what happens eventually if you remain single for long enough out here in the boonies. Ya get weirder by the year if there's no one living with you to tell you when you're full of shit." Scott nodded wholeheartedly. Like me, he was single as well. My thesis required no further elaboration.

Bachelorhood was something I had reached a gradual acceptance of over time, especially after two short marriages. But it was still always hard to deal with, day-to-day and long term. I had enough of my mother in me to keep a clean house and wash, fold, and even iron some of my clothes. My cooking was adequate, and I could dress myself and not look like a dork. The lawn was mowed, my pickup and car were neat and clean, and I tried to keep up with current events and an occasional good book. But life is meant to be shared. Harry once spoke of the need for a companion. "Half this world is meant to screw with the other half. When that runs out, holdin' hands is just about as good."

As the 1980s passed, waves of young people like Frank and Donna made an exodus. The age and gender profile of the Great Plains began to resemble how it was when the prairie was first settled: predominantly married couples and single males.

Alone in my house with my thoughts and neuroses, I had no close friends or even a counselor for reality checks. The loneliness that motivated me to jump in the pickup and drive seven miles west to Hubbell was nearly equaled by the strength of my innate introversion. On several occasions I pulled up to the bar, got out of the truck, and peered into a plate-glass window full of drinkers and diners, mostly families. The bashfulness then took control, and I promptly got back in the pickup and drove back home. All the while wondering just what in the hell was wrong with me.

✾　　✾　　✾

To be sure I wouldn't miss out on any human contact, I had a pretty cute message on my answering machine, a fairly new invention in 1989 and an essential item in the house of a bachelor who was rarely inside except to sleep. "Hi. This is Tyler, Jim's dog…" My goofy baritone impersonation of a gentle old Doberman's thoughts came over the recorder. "Now leave your name and number after the beep, and don't just hang up, or I'll come over and eat your cat." My sister Elaine who lived in Fort Wayne, Indiana, called one day to demonstrate my clever voice message to a younger acquaintance of hers. On the day she called, it was a rainy afternoon, and I was actually in the house and answered in person.

What met my ears that day was a delight. I had not had a decent conversation in months, and my social life was practically nonexistent. To suddenly be talking with a bright and bubbly young woman was totally unexpected. I discovered she was single. Our conversation turned more interesting and even became flirtatious. As the months went by, we exchanged long letters, pictures of ourselves, and many more phone calls. I remember seeing her picture for the first time, and I was instantly struck by the fact that besides being intelligent, she was cute as could be. Petite, long and straight blonde hair, confident and adventurous. For a guy in his thirties who had all but given up on ever having another shot at romance, what more could I ask for?

At last I had someone to write to. I composed long and descriptive accounts of my days on the farm, and I was delighted to see her letters that landed in my mailbox. It felt as if I were a bachelor sodbuster in the late 1800s, cautiously investigating a mail-order bride. After a half dozen car trips to Fort Wayne and back over several months, she bravely took a bold invitation from me to come and visit the farm. Instead of waiting at the train station and offering my hand as she stepped down from the passenger car behind the steam locomotive, I waited in the Omaha Airport as she got off the 737.

For me, the need for a partner trumped my gut and its uncomfortable concerns. Michelle had grown tired of city life, and her career had hit a dead end. Stress and fear reduced her weight to an alarming thinness. Undoubtedly she saw her move to the prairie as an opportunity to try a new lifestyle and reestablish her health. We both felt we were in love. I feared it to be my last chance, so, in the fall of 1990, immediately prior to wheat-planting time, I borrowed my cousin Lowell Cossaart's one-ton pickup truck and twenty-foot stock trailer and drove it out to Indiana. We loaded all her modest possessions, including her little Honda Civic hatchback car, into the trailer and moved her into my farmhouse.

Into the next year Michelle eagerly tried to adapt to the farm, and she enjoyed the peace. She was intimidated by the large machinery and found the arduous, sometimes punishing workload and farm work ethic a curious and foreign concept. "Let's take a break," she said an hour or so into a task we shared. In all honesty, I replied, "Break? What the hell is that?" She learned how to garden, and although she had never grown anything beside a houseplant, she did her homework and by the second season grew a pretty respectable vegetable patch. Michelle took a marginal interest in tending the cow herd. We gathered a new assortment of farm animals, and before the monetary fortunes of the farm began their final downward spiral, she enjoyed most aspects of the life.

❋   ❋   ❋

My dog, Tyler, my constant old companion of seventeen years, died while Michelle and I were returning from a hurried trip to Indiana for a funeral I didn't want to attend. Tyler lay in a frozen state in my shop for a week, an indignity that filled me with remorse. A week later, I chipped away at the frozen sod and buried him on a hillside in the pasture with a twelve-inch-square limestone rock on which I had inscribed his name using a shop grinder. His resting spot is next to the seventeenth fence post north of the pasture gate, on a point beneath a perfect view of both the rising and setting sun.

Leonardo

At the Annual Reynolds Community Consignment Sale, I had some extra cash and bought a brakeless 1951 four-door Chevy and a pygmy goat. "Pygmy goats never get very big. This little fella will grow to the size of a German shepherd," the young woman with the pretty brown eyes assured me as she handed me the end of the baler twine that was looped around the little goat's neck. I had always heard goats were useful for eating weeds around the yard that no other critter would touch, and besides, my wife thought he was so terribly cute. I carried him to my pickup truck, saw the absence of intellect in his eyes, and sarcastically named him after DaVinci. Leonardo started out about the size of a toy poodle, passed up the shepherd comparison, and just kept on growing. By summer's end we had a full-sized goat on our hands. The pygmy part must have been expressed in the recessive gene.

Goats have to be one of the strangest-acting, strangest-looking creatures on earth. The pupils, the dark center parts of eyes that are round in humans, are flattened and horizontal in goats. It gives their gaze a bizarre look; it is easy to see why the ancients often characterized evil spirits in goat form. Leonardo's blank and alien expression made me realize we certainly were on different brain wavelengths, if he had a brain. In goat interaction, the hard head is used as a weapon of defense and attack. Leo began the habit of butting into hard objects and the rear ends of visitors with his forehead. I always had the idea that if I hit Leo across the head with baseball bat, he would probably just blink and wonder what that noise was.

Leo's leaping ability soon went beyond any fence or pen constructed to hold him. He broke every rope or chain I would tie him to a tree with. I gave up and let him wander free around the yard.

Leo was a "kid" when my young Doberman puppy, DJ, was growing up. The young dog and the goat soon became fast friends and spent most of their time running around the barnyard together and napping in the sun. As I sat on the front step tying my bootlaces, I heard the sound of approaching hooves, only to see the goat and a half-grown Doberman pinscher galloping in unison at full speed. The dog would have one of the goat's ears firmly clamped in his teeth as they would tear by, caught up in their collective glee and running over whatever happened to be in their path. The dog took on goat-like mannerisms, while the goat acted a bit like a young dog. When approached, they both looked up at me in unison with identical and quizzical expressions.

Then they started exploring beyond the confines of the farmyard. Their trips became more daring and led them farther away, and their running abilities enabled them to get as far as six miles from the farm, according to the reports from neighbors. The two chums were gone for entire afternoons, and the community shared tales of goat and dog galloping happily through the countryside. I spent far too much time trying to track them down. When I stopped a neighbor to ask if they had seen my goat and dog, their amused response was predictable: "Are they traveling together?" Trying to smile past the ridicule, I answered wearily. "Yes, they do this a lot lately."

A deer hunter in the area had seen some movement across the field as he peered through the scope of his rifle. What he saw through the magnification astounded him. "I'll be damned," he said to his hunting partner, still in the pickup. "I believe that's Jimmy's goat. And dog." Both the dog and the goat were friendly enough, and they welcomed the company of the two men as they drove toward the odd couple frolicking through the cornfield. The men tried to pick up the goat and put him in the back of the pickup, but Leo would have nothing to do with that. He insisted on staying with the dog, who insisted on riding in the cab as he did with me. After several minutes of wrestling the animals in vain, they gave up and permitted both goat and dog into the front seat of the pickup. It was a roomy cab but still made for a crowded ride back to my farm. I was fueling up the tractor when the hunters' pickup pulled into the yard. The door opened and out jumped the long-absent passengers. I thanked the hunters for the safe return of my animals, and they drove away. I could see the driver and passenger vigorously shaking their heads through the back window glass.

A friend of mine parked his new Camaro in my drive, and we had a cup of coffee in the kitchen one morning. Rising to get some sugar, I glanced out the window in horror: Leonardo was on the hood of the new car, unable to get good footing, ice-skating with his hardened hooves on the black paint job insufficiently protected by the factory clear-coat finish. My friend went ballistic, sent me the bill from the body shop, and refused to come back to the farm until the goat was gone. Another friend stopped by on his way to the lake with his boat in tow. An irritated voice on the phone later that night angrily described a gnarled steering wheel and goat poop in the back of his nice boat. It became a daily amazement to find the next tool, shoe, or tire that was chewed up. Any object lower than five feet off the ground was doomed. If I bent over to pick something up, I ran the risk of being butted without warning or reason. His appetite and ability for destruction grew far out of proportion to even his enlarged stature.

Michelle was overly tolerant with the goat, making endless excuses for his daily campaign of destroying garden plants, tools, checkbooks, dangling wires on vehicles, and valve stems on tires. I expressed my growing rage with each incident of destruction and was past my limit and wanted him gone. Halfway through my wife's pregnancy, Leo made a fatal error in judgment. As Michelle strode up to him in the front yard and sweetly greeted her precious pet, he jumped up and landed a direct blow to her bulging belly with his two front hooves. Later that day I heard the answer to my prayers. "I think you're right, Jim," Michelle said. "That goat has to go." All of a sudden my spouse and I were in rare agreement about something, notably the damn goat. The next day, I delivered the goat to the local livestock auction barn and instructed the clerk to mail me the check. I couldn't contain my smile as I drove away. A group of young cowboys spotted him entering the loading chute. Barbecued goat meat is considered quite a treat in cowboy culture.

My New Friend

———————

As the years passed, Billy's path and mine crossed often. I kept my old acquaintance from the county fair at a distance, even as I began to associate loosely with him in social situations. He seemed a bit gentler than in the past, and we got along. In a rural setting with a limited cast of young people, one cannot afford to exclude anyone or soon there won't be anyone to talk to.

In 1980 he still had a little hell-raising left in him, and his adventures were well known. Billy was having relationship troubles with his girlfriend, and out of a small sense of guilt he stopped to call her at a phone booth that was on the paved highway running through Reynolds, Nebraska. He was driving a huge four-wheel-drive pickup with a souped-up engine and enormous mud tires that made the truck's undercarriage stand a good foot off the ground. Billy's contrary mood was fueled that day with the usual dose of alcohol. The running argument between them continued where it had left off the day before, and the fuse of Billy's frustration had been lit. "Yeah?" he shouted into the phone, "Well, listen to this..." He left the chirping receiver dangling and walked toward his truck while his girlfriend heard the engine rev to a fever pitch. She heard a loud crash and then silence on her end. Billy had run over the phone booth repeatedly until he flattened it into a pancake of broken glass and crushed aluminum. A week later I told my hired man to phone me from Reynolds where he was taking a flat tire to be fixed.

"Can't," he replied. "Billy ran over the goddam' thing."

During that time, I began to notice his face was constantly twisted with pain. At first I assumed a hangover, but he looked more miserable every time I saw him. He was living with a constant and excruciating headache, dizziness, and severe nausea. He could not work and began drinking whiskey nonstop and consuming every drug he could swallow to kill the pain. To get to sleep each night required the bizarre act of placing a blow dryer to his forehead and turning it on high. Only this seemed to numb the dagger that was splitting his skull. One night the hair dryer set his mattress on fire.

Over the course of a year, Billy was bounced from medical doctors to assorted specialists before being shoved off to a psychiatrist for pain management and counseling. No one could explain his pain, ballooning girth, or a dozen other maladies that turned his existence into a nightmare. Overalls became the only clothing he could get on. His feet and hands swelled, and his face took on a monster-like look with a protruding brow and an enlarged lower jaw. His teeth no longer fit together, and his vision began narrowing from the periphery. Suicide was beginning to look like a rational option.

Out of desperation Billy staggered into the University of Nebraska dental school to ask why his teeth were so far off. A sophomore dental student who was assigned to him did a routine exam and alertly notified the Growth and Development Department. X-rays were taken of his skull, and within one hour he was diagnosed accurately. Billy had a benign growth at the base of his skull causing his pituitary gland to hyper-secrete human growth hormone to his full-grown body. Housed in a small cavern, separate and just beneath the brain, it was normally the size of a pea. Billy's growth had expanded his to walnut-size, impinging on his optic nerve and crushing the critical pituitary gland, the "master gland" of the body's complex system of chemical regulators. He was immediately referred to an endocrinologist who prescribed proper pain medication and pursued life-saving treatment: chemotherapy, surgery to remove the bulk of the tumor, and limited radiation to finish off the invasion. Billy's recovery took months, but his pain was extinguished and he slowly resumed a somewhat normal life, with serious limitations. From then on, his bodily hormones needed to be artificially regulated, and he began carrying an assortment of pills and injections wherever he went.

Billy's diagnosis was acromegaly, which caused his already-mature body to grow in the only places it could: face and jaw, hands, feet, and much of his soft tissue, including his internal organs. An operation was performed to open his airway. The organs in his chest and upper torso were slung and supported with a fibrous mesh inside his visceral cavity, or as he put it, "like that plastic netting they put over the frozen turkeys."

Without a functioning adrenal system, Billy needs lots of naps but also requires lots of caffeine to function. In an "adrenal crisis" brought on by fright, overheating, or chilling, he needs a quick injection of adrenalin to prevent his body from shutting down. A case of moderate dehydration or heat exhaustion to a normal person would prove deadly for him. He was always tall to begin with, but his condition and increased bulk made him appear as a relative giant, yet paradoxically he became brittle and vulnerable. He became ever mindful of his precarious hold on life. The realization of his fragility led to some remarkable enlightenment that I began to hear in our talks. In my days that were often starved for good conversations, I then found myself preferring his company to most others.

Several weeks before my son was to be born, Billy stopped to chat with me as I was doing some fieldwork. "You know, Jim, when that kid comes out and you feel a love like you have never felt, you realize that this is what life is all about." When he had something to say, I listened intently. He soon became one of my better friends.

In spite of the untold daily difficulties, he walks through his days with a smile. He is kind to all others and has raised a fine son. He looked after his aging parents well. Billy is a good mechanic and farmer. If I ever get down, I think of his answer when I asked if he ever felt sorry for himself. "Yeah, it's rough some days. But there's lot of folks have it lots worse, and every day I see the sun come up, it's a damn beautiful day."

Jim and Billy.

My Baby Boy

Several weeks before David was born, I stopped at the home of cousin Dave's parents, Olin and Lorene Cossaart. Olin sat motionless in his recliner as his oxygen unit purred behind him. They both broke into sad, sweet smiles when I let them know our baby's name was to be David. On the sixth of October 1992, Michelle and I walked into a hospital in Lincoln, Nebraska, clad in T-shirts and shorts, comfortably dressed for an eighty-degree day. Michelle's contractions came with increasing, predictable regularity, until about midnight. Then progress came to a halt, and a decision was made with frightening conclusion: The baby was quickly slipping into anoxia and must be rescued by caesarian section. Fifteen minutes later he emerged from Michelle's abdomen, and the nurse burst through the swinging stainless-steel doors. He was quickly bathed and wrapped in a blanket, wailing and glowing under the orange glare of a heat lamp. He quieted as he was dried and swaddled. Without hesitation, I picked him up and held him close to me, and he became serenely alert. With his mother unconscious, his first impressions of the world were formed in my arms; it was just him and me. I paced the halls hour upon hour and stared out the small windows to see snowflakes swirling in the air. At all times, a continual hypnotic lock tied my newborn's eyes and mine together until exhaustion overtook me and I fell asleep in a hallway recliner, and David slept in my arms.

Tornadoes

Kansas? You lived in Kansas? Weren't you afraid of tornadoes? I hear that a lot. Such looks of incredulity from people who ask that question sometimes make me feel like a brave man. To live in the Plains is to be aware of the incredible power of nature, and this awareness keeps people humble. After living through storm seasons year after year, a callous grows over the fear and a person becomes strangely used to the annual spring excitement.

To study their characteristics is an exercise in the incredible: Tornadoes can pack up to three hundred mph winds at their cores and can cut a path anywhere from a hundred feet wide to a full mile. They can blow every window and door out of a sturdy house like mine, yet be capricious enough to leave a stack of mail undisturbed on the kitchen counter. In the path of a tornado, objects such as lumber, sheet metal, and motor vehicles become missiles. Nothing can survive them; no building, outside of a nuclear reactor core containment unit or some military installations, can stand up to a tornado. I have seen the aftereffects only a few miles from my house: Blue Harvestore silos crushed like empty beer cans, crumpled cars perched in tree branches, and the entire side of my barn lying on the ground like a giant pancake in the mud.

One time I asked Grandpa if there were ever any tornadoes that hit the farm. "Ruth was mopping the floor of the upstairs bedroom," he began. "And she wasn't quite keeping up with the rain that was being driven right through the edges of the windows. We both heard the roar outside, and the next thing we saw, the windmill was gone and the hen house was split into two pieces." Grandpa respected them, but when the warning was issued, it never seemed to rattle him one bit.

They sound like a freight train approaching in the distance. I once heard one chugging and churning about twenty miles off, and it was eerie as hell. In my life I have never actually seen an on-the-ground tornado in real time. But I did watch a funnel cloud, a still-skyward-developing tornado, dip and dive and disappear again up into the dark clouds from whence it came. It was a balmy, strange late afternoon, and the energy in the atmosphere was palpable. Dark, low clouds were swirling and passing across the sky as I heard the pickup truck radio declare we were in a tornado watch area. As I walked toward the house and was standing on my sidewalk, I gazed upward. A very tight, smooth hole in the dark cloud was about five hundred feet above my house, and slowly swirling as it approached. I watched it intently as it seemed to make no progress toward the ground but continued to move to the east at about twenty miles an hour. As it approached, wildly varying gusts tore a few live leaves and twigs off the trees in the yard, and the wind howled through the power lines. As the funnel moved directly over the house, the wind suddenly died. It was instantly quiet. I could hear the coins as I nervously fumbled with them in my front jeans pocket. The birds stopped chirping. After ten seconds of incredible silence, the circling hole in the heavens moved on, the wind resumed roaring, and the branches swayed as before.

When my father was in high school in 1937, the basketball team was to play a game in Washington, Kansas, about thirty miles from our farm. It was a terribly stormy night, the power lines blew down, and the game was cancelled at the last minute. At scheduled game time, a tornado picked up a full train car load of coal and pitched the hopper car and its contents through the roof of the empty gymnasium. No one was there, so no one was hurt.

Executioner

Whenever I heard Reg's high-pitched cackle entering the blacksmith shop, I had the urge to puke. Instead, I spit on the concrete floor. Every few weeks this human annoyance, a wiry sixty-something farmer, would drive into town from his small acreage on the edge of Hubbell. He was Harry's nephew-in-law. His piercing, chirpy exclamations outside the shop door signaled the arrival of the biggest smart-ass in town. Nearly every word out of his mouth was cruel or insulting, yet he found great entertainment in it all. Reg and Harry seemed to work together quite harmoniously, usually fixing some piece of farm machinery that Reg had broken. Harry let the shrill chatter blow past his face like smoke and turned a deaf ear to the incessant banter. I held a mild admiration for the old blacksmith's patience, armor, or whatever enabled him to work in such a relaxed state around Reg. Turning off his hearing aid probably helped.

Harry's niece lost her mother when she was a child and was essentially raised by her father as the Great Depression was loosening its grip on rural Nebraska. She married young and disappeared into adulthood in the same town where Harry had his shop. In ten years of working in the tiny town, I rarely saw her. In the shop, Reg yelled crude comments about women that turned my head in shame and made me thankful there weren't any women around. Reg and his wife were childless; whether that was their tragedy or the good fortune of the unborn, it wasn't up to me to say.

In my first few years of having to deal with him, I attempted to cut him down with sarcasm and dirty-mouthed insults, but it seemed to roll off him like water. His only response to my retorts was even more cackling and a ratcheting up of my rage. So I began the habit of taking an unannounced break. Whenever Reg entered, I walked off the job to have a cup of coffee across the street. Harry understood why.

I tried for years to view the man with tolerance and forgiveness, I really tried. But in my last year of working for Harry, I threw in the towel. Harry's ancient coon dog, Tobe, was on his dying legs, and the pitiful old hound began moaning and crying out in pain with increasing frequency. Finally Harry decided to end Tobe's misery, and in Harry's world of values, a quick bullet through the forehead was the dignified thing to do for his old companion. But Harry couldn't do it. His palsied shaking couldn't hold a steady aim, and his crooked finger could not grip the trigger. He asked Reg to do it with a .22 caliber rifle. I was gone that afternoon, and when I returned the next day and asked about the dried blood on the shop floor, the details were made known to me by a sad-eyed Harry.

Reg missed the first time, and shot the dog through the nose and one eye. Howling and circling and blind, Tobe had to be restrained by the neck, and by then was moving too much for a gun to be safely used. Harry shouted at the executioner to do something.

So Reg picked up a three-pound forge hammer. He swung at the dog repeatedly, aiming for the head but only hitting his target now and then, beating the dog about the face until he and the dog finally got lucky, and old Tobe slowly went down in the most agonizing and undignified of deaths. Reg was laughing and cursing the animal the whole time, accusing the dog of not sitting still and taking his bludgeoning. When Tobe finally gave his last spasmodic kick, Reg shouted with gleeful triumph. When I heard about the episode, I had to walk out behind the shop, lean up against the sawmill shed, and have a good cry. I vowed never again to even acknowledge the man as long as he lived. The thought of Reg would elicit vivid fantasies of smashing the smirk from his face with the back of a coal shovel. He confirmed the darkest of my assessments and brought the beast out of my soul.

A few years later Billy called me. He relayed the story of how Reg was cleaning the underside of his tractor-mounted mower and had propped it up on two stacks of concrete blocks as he lay on his back to clean the muck from under the housing. The blocks toppled over, and the mower pinned him to the ground. The sharp edge of the mower blade severed the artery in his neck, and he bled to death in his driveway. His screams for help went unheard while his wife was inside washing his dirty overalls.

When I hung up the phone, I pondered about the brevity of life and the dangers of farm equipment. As I passed the hallway mirror, I felt mild shame for the smile on my face.

Good-bye to Harry

I had been working on and off with Harry for ten years. In 1992 he was eighty-six years old and still opening his shop every morning by himself. By this time his son had long established his own small trucking firm and spent most of his days on the road doing short and medium hauls throughout the Midwest. Carl once revealed through a sad expression: "It's a decent job; the hours are awfully long, and the pay ain't so hot, but I can be my own boss, and I don't have to be around Dad." Indeed, Harry had become such a pain that he drove Carl away for good. Years before, Carl really had a burgeoning business in his own right, but that required daily interaction with his father and a sharing of the shop. Harry's comments and criticisms that were directed at me I could take, most of the time, but sharp words cut his grown son much deeper and finally wore Carl down.

Frances met me one day on the sidewalk and said, "I sure appreciate you helping him out. Lord help us the day he can't get down there anymore." The *us* meant her. I had always admired Harry for staying active in his old age and even possessing the will to learn a few new things. But I painfully watched the increasing burden he placed upon his wife, who would have preferred to weave rag rugs on her loom and spend less time washing sooty overalls.

Harry held on tightly to his frugality into his old age, and he felt a woodstove in the house was good enough. One day Frances rebelled, and when Harry returned home that evening, there was a new propane heat stove installed in the kitchen. He objected vehemently, but Frances shouted loudly enough for him to hear, in case his hearing aid was turned off. "I'm getting too old to be packing in wood anymore," she declared, "and that's that!"

Harry kept a soup can full of an old gasoline and oil mixture on the shelf about ten feet from the woodstove. The massive cast-iron stove that provided heat for the poorly insulated shop was actually an old coal furnace that had been pulled out of a demolished house in town. On cold mornings he filled the stove with sawmill scraps and kindling and tossed in a can full of gas mixture. With the stove door open, he leaned his body back after he struck a safety match and flipped it inside. A second passed before the explosion occurred. A boom reverberated through the tin building and flame spat a foot or so out of the opening of the iron stove. This was his usual method of lighting the daily fire, and after one explosion that visibly rattled my nerves, Harry just chuckled at my expression and answered with "I never have to clean the chimney, you know." Of course he didn't. Any buildup of creosote was blown into the sky.

When the shop caught on fire, I was surprised only that it had not happened earlier. Harry was using the acetylene torch one day when I was not there. Stumbling around on the concrete floor in his mud-covered overboots, his palsied grip on the torch waved the flame in the air as he moved and ignited the cup. The fire began to spread up the tarpaper coating on the wall, and Harry scrambled for a five-gallon pail of water that was next to the forge,. Water is not very effective on a solvent fire, and Harry quickly began losing the battle. A farmer coming out of the tavern across the street saw the old man staggering out of the shop's front door, frantically waving for help. The fire alarm sounded, and the volunteer fire department extinguished the flames that had consumed a third of the building.

I arrived about an hour after the fire. Thick black soot dripped from the ceiling, and a thin film covered everything in the shop. Several men were sorting out the burnt items and cleaning up the water-soaked mess while a visibly exhausted Harry sat on a folding metal chair being comforted by another older man. "One more bucket of water and I'd a had it whipped," I heard him tell the man. Suddenly recognizing me as I approached, he angrily snarled at me. "Where the hell were you?" I let it pass and joined in the cleanup. Over the next few weeks and with a lot of help from local farmers with more time to spare in the winter, the shop was eventually put back into working order.

※　　※　　※

Harry had been seeing less of me since the previous October, when I experienced the greatest moment in my life: the birth of my son, David. From the moment I saw my baby boy, I was never to be the same. It was exhilaration beyond any experience in my life. The buzz was a hundred times more intense than any drug ever taken. From that moment on, little David was more important than anything. Overnight I had changed from a workaholic farmer into a dedicated, fully present daddy. Suddenly all I wanted to do was be around my baby boy and keep the fires going in the woodstove in my farmhouse.

I began spending less and less time near Harry. Out of a sense of obligation I checked in on him every few days, and I tried in vain to describe the feelings of a new father to a man who came from a world where working men and babies rarely mixed. He was jealous of my new affections and angrily predicted my financial ruin from "just laying around the house." Every other comment that came out of his mouth was coated with bitterness. One day he faced me, forcefully grabbed both of my shoulders and barked into my face, "That little woman and her baby are gonna be your downfall. You need to straighten out right now. You're spending too much time with that *kid*."

That did it. I had waited until my thirty-sixth year of life to become a father. Many times I had given up hope of ever having a child, suffering through horrible relationships and fearing that I was somehow predestined to follow in the footsteps of my dead bachelor uncle. I had become a successful farmer and learned many rare skills around the old blacksmith through the years. But the simple presence of this son of mine eclipsed everything I had ever done in my life. Not much else mattered. Not even this old friend who had given me so much. Yet my core recognized some validity in Harry's statements. He wasn't begrudging me fatherhood, even though his words said so. He

Daddy and David sleeping.

was feeling abandoned and feared for my future. But I acknowledged none of that. I shook my head and removed his arms from my shoulders. I placed my left hand on his. "Harry," I enunciated slowly. "Good-bye." And I walked out the shop door. That was the last time I saw him outside of his casket.

Windmilling

The need to put food on the table drove me to do some creative things. By 1991, the farm was barely breaking even. After trying to work a regular job for wages, I decided to try to make some money by presenting myself as a regional windmill technician. The old water-pumping types so often seen in farm scenes, especially in the Plains states, became my intimate friends to supplement my steadily dwindling farm income. "If you can't find a job," I told a friend, "make one up."

The mechanics of a water-pumping windmill are not that complicated. They are a simple design that has remained essentially unchanged from the 1940s: A machine that is well engineered, reliable, and durable requires only the most rudimentary maintenance.

Three different brands that I usually worked on were Aermotor, Deshler, and Fairbury. Aermotor was, and still is, sold throughout the nation. The Fairbury Windmill Company had been out of business since 1960, yet their mill was still my sentimental favorite, as it was the one on my farmstead and a model that could be effectively rebuilt by cannibalizing parts from battered and unused Fairbury models scattered throughout the countryside near my farm.

After a few jobs, I became a regional celebrity of sorts. The Salina *Journal*, a paper with respectable circulation, did a front-page article featuring me working on a windmill, complete with color pictures. The Rodale Press's national alternative farm magazine, called *New Farm*, also did a very nice article with a front-cover picture of me perched atop a thirty-foot windmill tower, complete with straw hat and my jean pockets stuffed with tools. I received many nice letters after those were published, and it gave my little firm good exposure. Business picked up, and fixing windmills kept me busy and groceries on the table for about two years as I drove to countless jobs in my little red Ford Ranger, proudly displaying a simple magnetic sign on each door that read *Windmill Service and Repair, Narka, Kansas*.

To be a windmiller required a bit of showmanship, and when working on a windmill I put on my straw hat, complete with chinstrap to keep it from blowing off in the high wind, exaggerated my Kansas drawl a little more, and told a few corny jokes. While working on the mill, the farm family invariably gathered around the base of the tower and tried to converse with me as I worked up high. Out of kindness I always cautioned them to step back out of harm's way from tools or bolts raining from the sky and also to avoid looking up whenever possible to prevent sore necks the next morning. I occasionally pulled practical jokes when I had an audience. My favorite trick was to ask the young man of the family to toss me up his pliers. No one ever throws an object straight up in everyday life, and most clumsy

Fairbury Model 7AA windmill.

attempts ended up with pliers thrown into the feedlot or the pond, far off target of my outstretched hand thirty feet up.

Most people I worked for were grateful for a young man that would show up and lovingly rejuvenate their old family farm windmill. I enjoyed lots of home-cooked meals and an occasional beer in appreciation, thank-you notes, and even pictures drawn by little kids. I also had a few delightful brushes with fame; I became pen pals with Roger Welsch, Nebraska author and television celebrity, and even gave advice over the phone to one of the Beach Boys about his wind-damaged Aermotor windmill in California.

❊   ❊   ❊

Windmilling was interesting work, although brutally physical from hoisting things into the air and beating on iron with hammers. At the time my physical condition became extraordinary for a farmer approaching middle age; it was like doing a heavy weightlifting workout daily. I enjoyed the feeling of my renewed muscles but felt exhausted at the end of most days.

With our new son in our lives, we needed the money. It is amazing what I did when we desperately needed that next one hundred bucks for groceries or the electricity bill. Working in the summer heat was especially difficult; I recall several instances of heat exhaustion. One vivid memory is when I vomited a shower of red Gatorade all over a rancher's new white pickup truck parked at the base of his windmill before I passed out, still strapped by my tether line to the top of the tower.

One incident scared me terribly. On a windy day, when I should not have been atop a tower, I needed the cash so badly I violated my better judgment and climbed another tower. Assembling an eight-foot-diameter wheel, I clamped the brake mechanism with a vice grip to prevent the partially constructed wheel from rotating as I bolted together six large sections of metal bands and dished sheet-metal blades. A blast of wind broke the hold on the wheel, the vise grips tumbled to the ground, and a half-assembled windmill wheel began violently spinning, striking my chest on the first revolution. I tumbled

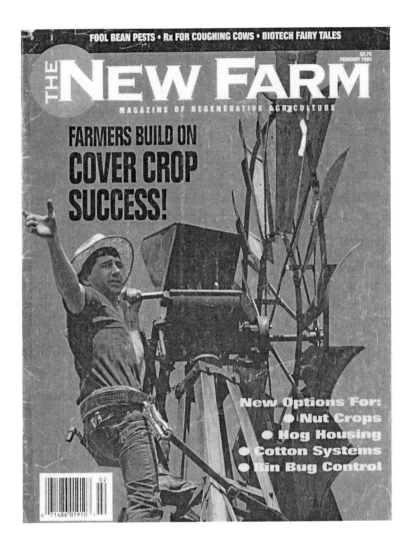

The New Farm
MAGAZINE OF REGENERATIVE AGRICULTURE

FEBRUARY 1994

FOOL BEAN PESTS • Rx FOR COUGHING COWS • BIOTECH FAIRY TALES

FARMERS BUILD ON
COVER CROP
SUCCESS!

New Options For:
● Nut Crops
● Hog Housing
● Cotton Systems
● Bin Bug Control

Magazine cover with Jim on a windmill.

over backwards and hung upside down by my safety belt and tether. The off-balance wheel picked up speed, shaking the thirty-foot-tall steel tower so hard I was convinced the entire structure would collapse with me affixed to it. All I could do was hang inverted and shield my head while bolts and pieces of jagged sheet metal were sent flying, bouncing off the tower frame and the soles of my upturned boots. I cursed and screamed and by the time the wheel was bare of metal and the violence had subsided, I was in tears. I had forsaken my rule of never working alone, so no one was even around to witness it.

The only other time I violated the don't-work-alone rule I was again punished harshly. As usual, I needed the money quickly, and I was standing on a horizontal strut on a tower about twenty-five feet off the ground. A fellow windmill enthusiast once cautioned me, "Never trust your entire body weight to a single bolt." I placed my full weight on the end of an angle iron held with one bolt—and it broke. Down I went, tethered to the vertical main frame by my safety belt. The weight of my falling body broke succeeding horizontal pieces as I went down, shearing off bolts and frame pieces every ten feet. I landed on the concrete platform, feet first. The impact rattled my brain to a state where I didn't know where I was, or who I was, for perhaps a half hour. I then crawled, literally, back to the pickup truck, managed to hoist my body into the seat, and slowly drove home in a daze. Initial X-rays revealed no fractures to my legs, but with no health insurance, I could not afford to investigate further. From that point on, my right ankle hurt like hell, and I went through my days strapped into high-top laced work boots

Climbing a thirty-foot tower.

so I could walk. Years later I would finally be free of the limp and the pain with major reconstructive surgery.

I knew all the while I could not sustain such a dangerously physical job for very long. One windy and subzero night became my watershed moment. I received a call at about ten o'clock a few days before Christmas from a local rancher who was in desperate straits. His windmill had broken, and it was the only source of water for his herd of cattle that were in a distant pasture. Hauling water was not an option. The windmill was turning, he said, but something up high had broken because the pump rod for the well was not doing its usual up-and-down motion. I knew the likely cause was a broken pin up in the top of the gearbox. And as always, I really needed the cash. So I put on all the clothes I could find and drove thirty miles into Nebraska to his place.

I climbed the tower with so many clothes, it was a major effort to raise my leg for each rung of the ladder. About seventy-five thirsty cattle were crowding the dry tank, screaming at the top of their collective lungs for water that wasn't there. The volume was deafening; any communication with the rancher was impossible. The wind was a steady thirty miles an hour and the temperature far below zero, making for a wind chill that was beyond belief. I strapped myself to the top of the tower, took off my gloves, and fumbled to hammer out a broken, greasy metal pin while holding a tiny flashlight in my teeth. My fingers went numb, and the water streaming from my eyes froze on my face. The ten-minute ordeal seemed like an eternity, and as I crept down the ladder, water began pumping into the tank.

Warming my stinging hands over the defroster vent in his pick-up, I turned to the rancher and said, "This is bullshit. I'm going to find an easier way to make a living." The next day I phoned the University of Nebraska dental school in Lincoln and began inquiring about what it would take to become a dentist.

❖　　❖　　❖

When I finally became eligible for student loans, I climbed no more towers and became a full-time graduate student. Still limping noticeably as I walked through the halls of dental school, I violated the established dress code and wore high-top lace-up boots to bolster my fragile ankles for an entire year. When confronted about my choice of shoes by one of the more detail-oriented and protocol-stiff professors, I simply asked that he give the oldest member of the class a break, and part of the rationale of entering dental school was so I could stop climbing windmill towers for a living. He relented and let me wear the boots, as long as they were polished.

Monte

Monte lived on a small acreage near Hubbell and would occasionally wander into Harry's shop. I asked him to work for me as I repaired water-pumping windmills throughout north-central Kansas and south-central Nebraska. I tethered my safety belt to the top of the tower and went about the business of repairing the mill. Monte stayed below, hoisting up the necessary parts and tools to me and providing the muscle power to operate the block and tackle that would be fixed to the tower's main frame. There was a lot of time for the ground man to sit and wait, so he entertained me with his one-sided conversations he was so adept at. It was like having a history or political science lecture delivered to you for the price of a workingman's wage. I learned a lot of western American history while tightening windmill bolts.

Monte drove most people absolutely nuts due to his nearly incessant talking. A voracious reader, his brain was overflowing with facts and figures, mostly historical or political. He was a thoughtful liberal, often expounding his concern for social causes and current political events. Any mention of history in a conversation, if one could get a word in edgewise, would send him into a near dissertation of whatever topic had arisen. Monte gleefully shared his tremendous store of knowledge with a rapid and seemingly endless stream of words. In a rural Kansas environment comprised of marginally educated people, his message was rarely appreciated, let alone comprehended. If I had the time to spare, I could listen to the guy for hours. I understood the aversion many had to him, and at times I watched with amusement the baffled and annoyed expressions he could generate among ordinary working folks.

"You know, looking at that empty Coke can reminds me of the Pure Food and Drug Act of 1910, which addressed the practice of the Coca-Cola company to include a cocaine extract in their product. Due to the unfortunate death of a small girl from consuming too much of the soft drink..." On and on he would ramble in precise diction and a raspy low voice, always with a specific point to his lesson. A few interjections of "oh?" and "how come?" or "no kidding" from me were all that were needed to keep the lecture on track. His humorous anecdotes, love of his subject, and gentle persuasive skills often made me picture him as a loveable and quirky museum curator somewhere.

One terribly hot and humid day Monte and I were working on a windmill near Syracuse, Nebraska. The model of mill was a rare one of 1940s vintage, and it was missing a brake component. All we needed was that one critical part, and making the seventy-five-mile trip home to obtain it from my stockpile looked to be really unpalatable to both of us. We were tired and pushed to our limit from the oppressive heat, and we badly needed the money that a finished job would provide. The next day required us to be on a job nearly 150 miles from where we were standing.

Frustrated, dehydrated, and exhausted, Monte and I resigned to our rotten luck and climbed into the pickup truck. Curses and spit were cast out of both of the windows, and we had gone about two miles before we both spotted a battered and rusty windmill tower. It held exactly the part we needed up at the top of the mill, on exactly the same rare old model windmill gearbox we needed. I slammed on the brakes, and we lurched backward and turned forward into the drive of a long-abandoned farmstead. Monte's eyes met mine, and we broke into a perfect shared grin. There was our little cast-iron piece, thirty feet up on a shaky tower, beckoning us to come up and retrieve it.

So here arose a moral quandary. We were both honest men, and we discussed the issue of stealing. Were we really stealing? Surely no one would miss such an insignificant little piece of junk. The wreck of a mill had obviously been sitting unloved for thirty years or more and was doomed to be swallowed by the earth in another thirty. The farmstead was long abandoned. We could have researched land maps at the county courthouse, but that would have taken up the entire next day.

Our shiny code of ethics would have to suffer a slight tarnish for the benefit of practicality. On went my safety belt and tether strap, and up the tower I went, my weary body renewed with the excitement of our sudden, unexpected fortune. I removed the casting and placed it my shirt pocket before unbuckling my tether. I looked upon the setting sun, broad and low on the horizon, with satisfaction and hope. I remained for a few seconds atop of the tower and heard the whine of truck tires approaching from half a mile down the highway. My joyful mood collapsed from the sudden slowing of a very menacing-looking man in a pickup truck, and he ground to a halt, pickup sideways to our smaller truck in the seldom-used driveway entrance, obviously to block our escape. He was not happy.

"What in the *hell* do you think you're *doing*?" he roared up to me with a frightening vehemence. Monte was silent as he stood sheepishly next to the base of the tower. "Well," I stammered, "we're fixing a mill down the road, and this is just the part we needed. We meant no harm, sir. We will be glad to pay you what it is worth. We just didn't figure anyone would mind." I felt like a five-year-old caught stealing candy.

"You didn't figure!" he screamed out the cab window.

"Well, we were in a hurry, and..." He cut off my plea. "Everyone's in a goddam' hurry nowadays! What the hell is wrong with people anymore! I'm gonna go get the sheriff!"

With that threat, he revved the engine and began to take off. Monte suddenly waved his arms above his head to stop the angry man. "Wait!" Monte shouted, as if he had some rational and conciliatory thing to say. He smiled gently and stepped toward the truck. *Great*, I thought. *Monte is going to pacify this guy with some wisdom and smooth out this whole awkward situation.* Monte rarely spoke to clients, so his taking the initiative gave me a little hope. Monte's easy smile remained for a few seconds as he stepped forward. Five feet from the man, his face relaxed and turned serious. "Aw, ya cranky son of a bitch. We didn't want to do business with you anyway."

The driver's face, momentarily relaxed, reddened and tightened grotesquely. He fixed his scowl forward and accelerated with a loud screech of the rear tires. The exhaust from his tailpipes sprayed forcefully as his red pickup truck blasted down the highway, presumably to find a sheriff that was likely a good twenty miles up the road.

My weariness returned like a wave to my body as I leaned up against my truck and unsnapped my safety belt. Monte and I downloaded our encounter and discussed ethics and honor, peppered with snickers and guffaws. I scrawled a note on a piece of spiral notebook paper with one word. "Sorry." I placed the apology under the coveted iron casting and laid it within plain sight on an overturned cattle water tank. We drove home with clear consciences, no word from any sheriff, and a messed-up schedule for the next week. As with all dashing of ambitious plans, that eventually faded in importance.

Monte and I repaired windmills together for another year after that until I retired from my brutal and unique profession.

Sold the Cows

Beginning dental school meant leaving the farm and moving to Lincoln. I still had fifty beef cows, and Billy, recovered well from his adenoma surgery, expressed an interest in buying them. I loved my cows like a bunch of old friends, and parting brought tears. But I could think of no one else better to entrust their care to.

Cattle are sold by the pound, officially weighed and bid upon in a public market. The closest livestock auction barn was thirty miles away in Belleville. So Billy and I decided to make the sale fair by getting an accurate weight on all fifty or so cows and opening their sale to the factors of the open marketplace.

One September morning all the cows were coaxed from the far end of the pasture, rounded up, and corralled into the holding pen, then loaded up into three twenty-foot stock trailers mounted to three-quarter-ton pickups. The girls were all packed like terrified subway commuters, jostled and shaken down gravel roads, then unloaded into the auction pens amid harsh shouts of strange men. Billy and his brother took their seats in the grandstands at the sales pavilion and called out the winning bid on every cow. The cows were all reloaded back into the same trailers and driven back to the farm. They walked gingerly out of the trailer and commenced their contented grazing in the tall grass once again with little residual effect. But there had to be some aspect of them that wondered, "What the hell was *that* all about?"

Dentist

"You're going to be a *what?*" If I had a dollar for every time I heard that one, well, I'd have a lot of cash. I had mused about it for years as my farming fortunes steadily declined, and suddenly it didn't seem like such a kooky idea. My reasoning: I was good with my hands, and I have always had a nonthreatening manner. I knew I could be a good dentist. Since childhood, I had considered the idea of becoming a medical doctor, and in adulthood the idea of being a doc still held its appeal; however, I didn't like the direction that traditional American medicine had taken. The medical doctors I had met seemed distracted and hurried and at the mercy of the drug companies and insurance corporations. It looked like the whole industry had sold their souls to the devil.

The dentist I knew appeared to be more like a craftsman than his medical counterparts. He had a more prevention-oriented philosophy. In regards to treating human maladies, the dentist was more inclined to nailing the barn door shut instead of letting the animal get out and then work at chasing it around the barnyard. And here was the clincher: After being un- and misdiagnosed for nearly two years, Billy's mystery was figured out by a dental student at the University of Nebraska College of Dentistry. I wanted to be a part of that.

"You can't get into dental school. It takes a lot of brains and connections to get into those places." I heard statements like that over and over. My rural contemporaries shook their heads in disbelief. But it just fueled my determination.

I got a haircut, shaved, put on a tie, and drove up to Lincoln for a fact-finding appointment with the admissions people at the College of Dentistry. They were encouraging and friendly, and they spelled out what it would take to get in. The numbers were daunting. Almost to the person, the applicants were straight A students with strong biology and other life-science backgrounds with supporting experiences in places like dental labs. Often they were previously hygiene students or dental assistants, and a good number were the offspring of practicing dentists. Not too many ex-farmers. My agricultural degree from 1978 suddenly looked puny.

I had become the only person I knew that grew up in the city and became a serious farmer. Now the prospect of achieving something even more unlikely sparked a fire in me. I didn't yet quite know how I would do it, but David's daddy would become a dentist.

I plunged into summer school. For eight weeks I drove my junky old pickup a hundred miles north to Lincoln and attended my first academic classes in seventeen years. To obtain one of forty-three slots out of 750 applicants, I needed to get straight As in some heavy classes like Physics and Organic

Chemistry. My undergrad average from Kansas State ended up at 3.4, and I realized most of the other applicants carried averages close to 4.0. I had to sell myself as a reliable older student that would offset a dulling of intellectual brilliance with my personality. I made regular visits to the dental college campus across town during breaks in my regular classes at the main city campus. "I hope I get into this place someday," I once confided to a dental professor who had befriended me after a few months. "Me too," he replied with a flat smile. "You're here more than some of the dental students."

After several weeks of copying down organic chemistry equations, I feared that my brain had atrophied from the long academic absence. I watched the young men file into the lecture hall; individualism of the 1970s had apparently gone out of style. All of them nearly to the person wore a T-shirt with some logo or unintelligible slogan regarding their last frat party, and they sported identical crew cuts. They seemed to grasp the lecture material with a bored nonchalance, while I furiously scrawled notes, squinted with confusion at the chalkboard, and felt waves of nearly incomprehensible material drown me. *That's it,* I thought during a discouraging day. *The learning mind turns off and never returns.*

To my surprise it came back on after about a month. I hired a tutor for Physics and entered into an "old guys' club" with two other determined fellows in my Organic Chem lecture. Every spare moment I wrote flash cards with reaction formulas and walked around with a book outstretched in front of me as I pushed my toddler on the swing set in the park.

The admissions interview was the pivotal moment. A panel of six middle-aged-to-old men sat comfortably on a narrow carpeted platform a step above me as I sat in a single chair. They questioned my background and intent to be a dental student. The boldest member of the group cast out a final challenge to shake me. "What are you going to do when we *don't* accept you?" My eyebrows rose as I thought for an answer. "Well," I said, not hiding any drawl in my speech, "ya might as well accept me. Else I'll be back here year after year until ya do." They roared with laughter as I respectfully dismissed myself.

In the autumn of 1994, and largely due to my mother's initiative in renewing communication, my parents came out to see us in Lincoln. Two weeks prior, I received my acceptance letter to the UNMC College of Dentistry. Mom was pleased. She was always in admiration of physicians and dentists as I grew up, and I suppose she had all but given up hoping that I would ever leave the farm. I drove her and Dad past the dental school building where I would spend the next four years. Mom took three-year-old David by the hand and led him to the park, where she played with him on the slide. She went down once by herself, much to his delight.

As they drove away, my mother's wave good-bye was her last one to me. On their way back to Indiana, Mom fell to the floor from a massive heart attack in a motel room in Jacksonville, Illinois. I have few regrets in my life, but in regard to my mother, it's a huge one: I wish I had not taken her for granted. I wish that in the push-and-pull struggle of growing up that I had dropped the wall and held her closer. I wish I had not pushed her away as I was trying to keep my son in my life. Perhaps somehow she now understands.

Dental school was brutally hard. As the oldest member of the class I enjoyed more of a colleague status among my instructors, which offset the frustration of the academics. It took a little longer for me to absorb the massive amount of didactic material. I piled up enormous student loans, as working outside of school was impossible because of the rigorous academic and clinical loads. My relationship with Michelle, though we never touched one another in abusive anger, had degenerated into daily, sustained, hand-to-hand emotional combat. But I could not abandon my little buddy or even leave his mother on her own. By this point I was taking Prozac and a moderate dose of Lithium to keep from spiraling further downward, plus a blood pressure med to keep my hands from shaking. My chest pains convinced the doctor to perform a heart catheterization on me, and the negative results confirmed the weekly occurrence of panic attacks.

At the graduation ceremony, David, Michelle, all three of my sisters, and my father were in the audience. As I walked across the stage, I carried three items in my pocket: a single cuff link inscribed with an "A" that belonged to Alvin, a square windmill nut from a Fairbury windmill, and a small decorative pin from my mother's sewing box. As my name was called out, I heard my usually muted father give a war whoop from the back of the auditorium. James K. Cossaart, DDS. "First doctor in the family!" Dad boomed with delight as he hustled toward me at the reception afterwards. "Isn't that *something!*"

Returning

Harry was lucid and present until the end and did not linger more than a few days on his deathbed. As I sat in the pew of the Methodist Church in Hubbell, I leaned over to a woman that I knew from sipping coffee with Harry at the restaurant. "He always told me this was the only way we'd get him in here," I whispered over the organ music. We shook with subdued laughter.

After the funeral, I saw Carl's huge frame standing on the concrete steps, bathed in the afternoon sun. He was dressed in an out-of-style suit that no longer fit him and bent over a little more than usual. He dutifully greeted well-wishers, and I waited my turn. He shook my hand with his crushing grip and stood up stiffly. "You know, Harry was a great man and all that stuff," I said to him. "But I've always thought you were twice the man he ever was." Carl's face lost the self-conscious grimace, and his lower lip began to quiver. I thought his legs were going to buckle beneath his large trunk. He began to beam, tried to spit out a few words, and finally let go with, "Th-thanks, Jim."

After several moments of a speechless grip on my forearm, I withdrew, placed my hand to my heart momentarily, and waved good-bye.

Where I Am From

As I look at the environment I have lived in for most of my life, I can see changes in Section 1-1-1. Invasive species like eastern redcedar and mulberry trees, unheard of thirty-five years ago, proliferate if special efforts are not made to control their spread. It seems to be hotter in the summer than it used to be, and the effects of global climate change have come home to our little patch of prairie in ways I am not able to quantify or predict. In the black void of night I see more flashing red lights, single points from cell towers and multiple sources of blinking indicators from a group of wind-power generators, which I can see if I drive one mile north and reach a slightly higher elevation.

A moonless night reveals a trillion stars in the crystal-clear atmosphere of the Great Plains, hundreds of miles from any significant source of light pollution. If I look twenty miles to the distant northwest, I can see the buildings of a confined animal feeding operation, a CAFO containing twenty thousand sows in one unit. Another gargantuan CAFO containing upwards of thirty-six thousand sows has established itself three miles to the north-northeast, thankfully downwind of the prevailing northwest and southwest wind flow. These CAFOs violate every value that I hold, and they are disturbing invaders to what was once, without exception, perfectly clean air. Every single crop acre in all directions from my place is planted to GMO corn and soybeans, complete with periodic dosages of sprayed-on herbicides, fungicides, and insecticides applied with airplanes and giant ground rigs controlled by satellites.

*　　*　　*

Now that I live off the farm, I miss the silence. During any given day on the farm, I can stand anywhere, listen closely, and not hear a trace of human-made noise. Now as an adult, it is still easy to briefly pretend the rest of the world doesn't exist. Rural Kansas sunsets are glorious with the sparse clouds in the western sky all awash in shades of pink, orange, and indigo. As it is on the ocean, the horizon is as low as the earth's curvature permits. The greatest thickness of the earth's atmosphere that can be observed by humans makes the round orange ball appear to flatten slightly just before it slips over the edge.

I do not miss the grinding poverty or conversations that go no deeper than the weather. I don't miss the hard physical labor and the anxiety that accompanies an economic venture where all the odds are stacked against you. I do not miss worrying about the weather and commodity prices and the whims of the government and banking systems. I do not miss the prevailing conservatism that is in place out of tradition and habit and the exasperation of living in a state of the Union that keeps voting into office the same corrupt and selfish people that are screwing the voters the most.

I sometimes identify with my great-uncle Leslie and my grandfather when I remember each of their battered little bodies, weather-beaten from the harsh prairie environment and worn out from physical work. The skin on my body bears witness to the effects of the Kansas sun and wind over the course of twenty-some years. My neck and forearms are permanently pockmarked with UV damage. The whites of my eyes reveal a history, particularly when I grow weary. Every day, because of long-ago car crashes or cow kicks, in various locations of my body, things hurt.

By watching my grandfather, I learned how to work and can turn the drudgery inflicted upon Adam in the Garden into my own meditative worship of the creative force that made me. From Alvin, Dad, Grandpa, Russ, and Harry I have a thousand practical skills at my disposal. My family heritage is fully alive inside of me.

And in the glimpses of my son I see an inherited spirit and a potential greater than mine. David is a sensitive and brilliant young man, and an academic superstar at the University of Nebraska. I do not pray but instead thank the universe, or whatever, for blessings received, and occasionally curse it for injustices perceived. But I pray now and then for my only child's eyes to open and remember just who his father is.

I am always cognizant of the weather and still constantly assess how much rain we have had and how much we need. I look at people that don't know which direction a summer storm comes from, and they seem strangely out of touch. When I work indoors, the human-made cocoon feels illusory, and after three or four hours I have to get out and make sure the sky is still there. When I walk out the door and into the air, *that's* what's real. And after a while, just any-old sky won't suffice; I need to be in the center of an immense Great Plains sky.

Everything grows: bluestem prairie grass, wheat, baby calves, and baby boys. While I learned how to deftly handle barbed wire and heartbreak, Uncle Leslie figured out how to unwrap the Little Debbies. If you are alive, you are learning. I once saw a quote scotch-taped to a grad student's office door in the biology building at Purdue University that quite possibly sums up my beliefs: *Growth is the only evidence of life.*

From all my years of bowing to the forces of nature, I know full well how little I can control. Yet I also know how hard I can work to influence those things that I actually can. Depression, that old dancing partner of mine, is a distant memory and, in retrospect, looks like a colossal waste of time. Hard work and ambition are great diversions but no more effective at achieving a truce with the hard facts of living than antidepressant drugs. Human relationships, be they friends or spouses, are essential for happiness, but if they aren't right, are no better a solution to loneliness than a six-pack of beer. It is tough to find someone who can lovingly share a life like my parents and grandparents could. But by witnessing their love, I never completely gave up my belief in that natural state of living, or its possibility for me.

The only thing certain about a human existence is loss: of friends, family, farm, and finally, self. To this day, I still miss my uncle Alvin. I have come to realize that the long unresolved grief surrounding him and Russ was the driving force that caused me to make so many bad decisions, in regards to finding a companion. Through teenage eyes I saw my grandparents deal with their loss. As I watched those two very elderly beings rejoin the dance of life, I realized the principal difference between a happy life and a miserable one is one's relationship to the stark and unavoidable reality of loss. Harry the blacksmith told me with authoritative wisdom after I bemoaned the death of a cow from a lightning bolt. "Now, listen here. Them that *have* must lose. Them that *don't... can't. Dammit, enjoy it all while it's here."*

❊   ❊   ❊

We moved to Vermont, and with Dad's help, I bought a small dental practice in the town of Middlebury. I soon hit my stride as a relaxed and empathetic dentist and built a loyal following of patients. But at the same time, my marriage with Michelle finally collapsed, and she returned to Nebraska with son David. The details are not important to this story, but my precious little boy grew to become a stranger to me, unable to be a friend to his mother and father at the same time. My body's wisdom—the debilitation I felt as I lay in the hammock ten years prior when learning of his conception—was confirmed in the reality that finally came to pass. David's birth was the high point of my life. His removal was the most profound tragedy.

Paradoxically, coupled with the loss of my son, my life returned to me. I ditched all the medications. I lost twenty pounds. Alone, I regained my health. I began to sing spontaneously. I began to smile.

✻   ✻   ✻

Six months later, the miracle of my life occurred. I met a wonderful woman, down-to-earth with an understated and deep beauty, a quick and practical mind, and a deeply caring soul. She turned out to be the love I had been rehearsing for all my life. Life became, well, the way I always thought it should be.

When we met in 2002, Deb had two teenage girls, and I quickly grew to love them. After they both graduated from high school and moved away to college, Deb and I decided to move back to the farm. We sold the Vermont dental practice, packed up all our belongings in a single Penske rental truck, and landed on the farm five days later.

In March of 2008 the farm was a pitiful, neglected wreck. Zero upgrades and the bare minimum of care had been performed in fifteen years. Careless renters, and at the root of it my own neglect, took its toll on the place, and my grandparents' lovely old farm was at the tipping point of complete degradation of all fences, cattle lots, and buildings, most alarmingly the house. Junk vehicles littered the barnyard, and eight-foot weeds choked everything in sight. The pastures were overgrazed and full of invasive trees. The cropland had been reduced to a sterile medium to grow chemical-dependent GMO corn and soybeans. As I stood in the front yard and surveyed the place in panoramic view, it was one of the saddest feelings I have ever experienced.

Jim and Deb.

By that time Dad avoided even stopping by the farm for a period of several years. "It just depresses me," he said.

Once we had a day to absorb the initial shock, our energy level exploded in a furious ten-day, dawn-to-dusk heavy cleaning and removal of the previous renter's junk. The basics like water and sewer were quickly hooked up. With money earned from the sale of the Vermont dental practice, we took it upon ourselves to rehabilitate the house from the septic tank on up: new heating and air, twenty-three windows replaced, wiring and plumbing, and lots of plaster and paint. We bought a few cows.

We embarked on an ambitious plan to heal the entire farm: cutting the invasive tree species and replacing all the barbed-wire fences in the native grass pastures, as well as rebalancing the native grass with prescribed burning and planned, sustainable grazing methods. We built driveways, ponds, terraces, and other conservation measures into the topography of the soils. We rehabilitated the tool shed, the shop, and most dauntingly, the barn, which was close to the point of collapse. The water well was refurbished, and all the power and phone lines were replaced. We had decades of accumulated junk buried. We landscaped around the house. We began returning long-abused farmland to native grasses and alfalfa.

I received my license to practice dentistry in Nebraska. After a year of sporadic fill-in dental positions in Lincoln and Fairbury, we got lucky and found two dental practices in Geneva and Hebron that needed us. After a year of being a subcontractor dentist for the corporate entity that owned them, we defied yet another prevailing trend and bought the two offices and cultivated their success. It sometimes struck me as ironic that the same rural Kansas/Nebraska area was both the site of my most spectacular failures and then my greatest successes.

❋   ❋   ❋

In 2011 Dad came out to the farm to see us. He made the trip from Indiana with my sister, Elaine, and they made for great traveling companions. He was relaxed and pleased to be staying in the farmhouse once again.

Pasture post-rehab.

Farm buildings post-rehab.

Dad had emerged again in my perception to become my hero. At ninety years he was in amazing physical and mental shape. His weekly routine consisted of twice-a-week visits to the YMCA, where he did a light workout on the weight machines and a good, vigorous walk around the indoor track for thirty minutes. He told me he was disappointed that he had to give up his beloved racquetball games. His calcified aortic valve, leftover damage from a bout of scarlet fever as a child, would no longer pump the blood enough for such strenuous activity. After passing out on the court twice, the doctor advised him to find an easier game. So he switched to tennis for a year, but then that became too much as well.

But he continued a modified and disciplined physical routine. He also stayed current and relevant. He dressed well. He was the only ninety-year-old I knew of that used his laptop computer daily, read voraciously from a Kindle, and talked to me on his iPhone. I watched him age with class and thought often how he was serving, once again, as an example for me to follow. Now he was teaching me how to be an old man, and how to do it well. He strode through his extreme old age with his head held high and full of clear-minded optimism. Like the lessons he tried to impart when I was a boy, he seemed to be saying, without words this time, "Now pay attention. I'm only going to show you this once."

A few months prior to his visit, I drove down to Wichita, and my cousin Ruth Ann and husband, Rick, loaded my grandparents' old bedroom set into the back of my pickup. Deb and I placed them in the second-floor room that had been my father's

Dad and Jim in 2009.

and Uncle Alvin's former bedroom. The same one where, twenty years earlier, I watched Dad cast a watery-eyed gaze out the north window after being told the next occupant of his childhood bedroom would be his unborn grandson, and we would be naming him David Raleigh. Now my father would be spending the night in his childhood room, and I was very, very pleased to be able to offer him that opportunity.

I took Dad for a grand tour around the farm in the old pickup truck. It was the most satisfying of rides for me. After four years of hard work, the Cossaart farm was neat as a pin, and the house was completely restored. All the fences had been replaced, and the barn was standing straight and had been freshly painted. The large shop and machine shed were attractive matches to the house and barn, and new cattle-handling facilities graced the old lot north of the barn. All the rouge cedar trees had been cut. The whole place was back in balance and reflected the love that Deb and I had put into it. The entire Cossaart homestead looked like a showpiece.

As I slowed the pickup to a halt at the highest point of elevation out in the pasture, Dad and I sat in silence and surveyed the grand panorama of the entire 384 acres. He turned to me, and his head was shaking slightly. I saw water in his eyes, which he was fighting hard to contain. "Son," he whispered, "this place has *never, ever* looked this good." And I think those were the nicest words he had ever said to me.

I reflected back on the history between my father and me. This old man, still sharp and clear, sat beside me and beamed with pride. I idolized and yet feared him as a child. I tried to hate him and push him away when I was failing as a farmer and as a man in my thirties, when the disappointment in his eyes were merely a mirror of my own self-assessments. I had pushed him away and hurt him after David was born, yet he welcomed me back into his life as soon as I got honest with him. And now my dad and I were truly together again, surveying the landscape that contained so much history for both of us. A thought hit me. It caught me quite by surprise. What if, what if ... all the struggles on the farm, all of my misguided attempts at marriage, all the effort it took to get through dental school,

Dad and Jim, 1958.

all the risk of a career change, and the work and sweat it took to repair and rejuvenate this old farm ... what if *it had all been done for my dad?*

Well, what if it had been?

I guess that would be okay. Nothing wrong with it. Little boys grow up and in some way never stop trying to please our fathers. I am no exception. And, based on the character of the man that is my father, that fact is just fine.

*   *   *

With the farm, and myself, fully healed, I felt the need to keep growing. The ranch will be fine. We found a good man to care for it. He raises organic grass-fed beef and has become a dear friend. I'm leaving the soil this time with a smile on my face. The rejuvenated old place can be loved from a distance. It will provide a good outlet for my restless energy and the need to see a good sunset. The land will always be here, waiting for me.

Epilogue, 2015

After six years of sustained effort, the Cossaart Ranch is now a
healthy, sustainable unit. Deb and I took a long overdue vacation by car and went as far eastward as we could without dropping into the Atlantic Ocean. We had both always wanted to see
Cape Breton Island off the eastern reach of Nova Scotia. While
passing through Vermont, we stopped at our favorite restaurant in a small mountain town. It was an area close to where
I used to practice dentistry years ago. After dinner, we took a
walk through the charming little town, and there stood a building for sale that used to be a dental office. Six months later, we
opened for business. It is yet one more adventure that we have
shared over the past twelve years of our marriage: We created
a dental practice from scratch. We make a good team. We like
working together.

After the first week of business, I decided to place a large
map of the United States on the ceiling of my operatory to give
my patients something to look at. "Now where did you live
before coming here, doctor?" a patient asked me. I took a laser

pointer out of my drawer and focused the red dot on the Kansas-Nebraska border.

Reuben and Ruth Cossaart's eight grandchildren and spouses.
Photo taken in the pasture by Deb Cossaart.

Acknowledgments

Thank you—to all those who helped, and all those who hindered. Both guided me along a path that led to where I am now, and that is a place full of contentment and optimism. Most of all, I am grateful for my amazing spouse, Deb, whose love and support have enabled me to fulfill my dreams.

CPSIA information can be obtained
at www.ICGtesting.com
Printed in the USA
FFOW01n0621171215
19435FF